Markets & Democracy
in Latin America

Markets & Democracy in Latin America

Conflict or Convergence?

edited by
Philip Oxhorn & Pamela K. Starr

LYNNE
RIENNER
PUBLISHERS

BOULDER
LONDON

Published in the United States of America in 1999 by
Lynne Rienner Publishers, Inc.
1800 30th Street, Boulder, Colorado 80301

and in the United Kingdom by
Lynne Rienner Publishers, Inc.
3 Henrietta Street, Covent Garden, London WC2E 8LU

Library of Congress Cataloging-in-Publication Data
Markets and democracy in Latin America :   conflict or convergence? /
   edited by Philip Oxhorn and Pamela K. Starr.
   Includes bibliographical references and index.
   ISBN 1-55587-716-8 (alk. paper)
   1. Latin America—Politics and government—1980– 2. Democracy—
Economic aspects—Latin America. 3. Latin America—Economic
policy. 4. Economic policy—Political aspects. I. Oxhorn, Philip.
II. Starr, Pamela K., 1958–
JL960.M357   1998
320.98'09'049—dc21   98-7421
                                                                                         CIP

British Cataloguing in Publication Data
A Cataloguing in Publication record for this book
is available from the British Library.

Printed and bound in the United States of America

    The paper used in this publication meets the requirements
∞ of the American National Standard for Permanence of
    Paper for Printed Library Materials Z39.48-1984.

    5 4 3 2 1

Contents

v

Introduction:
The Ambiguous Link Between
Economic and Political Reform

Pamela K. Starr & Philip Oxhorn

The recent history of Latin America has been dominated by a regional journey toward a liberal political and economic order. Throughout the hemisphere, countries have shed their extended experiences with statist economic policies and authoritarian political systems in favor of market-based economic strategies and more democratic means of governance. In the mid-1970s Latin America was characterized by closed economies and authoritarian governments; today the region is dominated by open economies and democracies. Most observers would agree that this new political-economic landscape is a vast improvement over what it replaced, but there is less certainty about what its final character might be and even whether it will endure.

The end point of these striking reforms will depend largely on the nature of the relationship between them. For decades, commonly accepted wisdom held that democracy would naturally arise from a foundation of free markets (Lipset, 1959 and 1994; Rueschemeyer, Stephens, and Stephens, 1992; Diamond, 1992; Rostow, 1960). Once developing countries managed to get their economic policies "right," this situation would produce growth and encourage liberal individualism that, over time, would generate an environment conducive to the development of democracy. Even today, this wisdom continues to permeate much of the literature on democracy and political development and remains dogma in the foreign policy of the United States and other advanced industrial countries. Although some within this school of thought have narrowed the determinism of the original argument by accepting that free market economies may be only a necessary precondition for democracy rather than both a necessary and a sufficient condition, the essence of the proposed causality remains unchanged—free

1

market economies promote democratization. The implicit, if not explicit, assumption remains that the two processes are inherently so compatible that the success (or failure) of one will ultimately lead to the success (or failure) of the other. Although short-term trade-offs have generally been recognized (Haggard and Kaufman, 1995), the long-term view is that democracy will be associated with economic growth and improved standards of living. Economic failure is often seen as the death knell for democratic regimes, and economic success (at least in the long run) will condemn authoritarian regimes to the dustbin of history. A large body of empirical evidence indicating a long-term relationship between higher levels of economic development and democracy seems to prove this inherent compatibility between economic and political reform. But does this theoretical argument correctly identify the relationship between economic and political liberalization?

A second frequently accepted wisdom in the literature on political and economic liberalization argues the opposite. This body of literature insists that rather than being inherently complementary, market-based economic reform and democratization are inherently contradictory phenomena (Waisman, 1992 and Chapter 2 and in this volume; Acuña and Smith, 1994; O'Donnell, 1994). The reform of a bankrupt, statist economy tends to undermine living conditions for a large segment of the population in the short and even the medium term. In a democratic setting, these casualties of economic reform will at some point tend to use their electoral voice to express their discontent with such policies. Since in the early phase of reform the beneficiaries of economic reform tend to be more diffuse and less numerous than those hurt by the process, economic liberalization tends to produce negative electoral results for a government whose mandate to govern is determined democratically.[1] By raising the political costs to governments of adhering to democratic practices, economic reform hinders both the consolidation of democracy where it already exists and the extension of democracy in countries where it is limited or does not exist at all. Equally, democracy is seen to undermine economic reform because of the constraints elections impose on governments' ability to implement reforms that could be electorally costly. Political and economic reforms thus tend to undermine one another.

Which of these two lines of reasoning is correct? Do market-based economic reforms promote or hinder democracy, and does democracy inhibit the economic reform process? These questions go to the heart of Latin America's current dilemma. How can the region consolidate and extend democracy while also implementing essential but costly economic reforms? In other words, can Latin America aspire to both democracy and open, competitive markets?

To answer this last question, it is essential first to understand how political and economic reform processes interact in Latin America. Yet in general the literature on Latin America's transformation has not directly addressed this interaction. Authors have most often considered either the forces that shape democratization in the region or the forces that shape economic reform; few have considered the dynamic interaction between political and economic reform.[2] The possibilities that democratic regimes might survive in spite of a lack of economic reform or that democracy might even be the *reason* for the lack of such reform, for example, are rarely discussed. Researchers have focused instead on the ability of democratic regimes to survive economic crises because of their unique sources of legitimacy and on their ability to change the policy course when failure becomes apparent. Remmer (1996) found that democracies demonstrate considerable capacity to survive economic crises compared with authoritarian regimes, in part because democratic institutions provide mechanisms that allow for, if not encourage, the adoption of economic policies that can resolve crises through leadership competition and rotation.[3] Conversely, the possibility that successful economic reform might reinforce authoritarian political structures tends to be discarded out of hand—at least for the longer term.[4]

The conundrum suggested by these contradictory and ambiguous tendencies within the literature on economic and political reform is only deepened by another increasingly robust empirical finding: successful economic reform is largely independent of regime type.[5] Moreover, whereas certain sequences in economic and political reform are arguably more likely ultimately to prove successful (Armijo, Biersteker, and Lowenthal, 1994; Haggard and Kaufman, 1995), no path has proven necessarily fatal (or assured of success) for either continued economic liberalization or nascent democratization. Even the "worst" case of simultaneous economic and political liberalization in Eastern Europe has proven less fragile than might have been predicted. Such findings are surprising because they suggest that any hypothesized relationship between economic and political liberalization must at best be very weak, at least for specific national cases and historical periods. This possibility has produced a significant body of literature arguing that research should focus on factors other than political regime type in understanding economic reform, factors such as the nature and number of actors influencing policymaking and how such influence is mediated by party systems (Geddes, 1995; Przeworski and Limongi, 1993; Remmer, 1990). In other words, the institutional and political context in which economic reform policies are adopted is seen as mediating the relationship between economic and political liberalization. Paradoxically, however, this context seems at best to be affected only indirectly by whether a particular country is ruled by an authoritarian or a democratic government per se. Among the relevant factors mediating this relationship, perhaps the most important concern the nature of participation and contestation in a given country—the two variables Dahl (1971) uses to define *polyarchy* (Remmer, 1996).

This volume takes as its point of departure the need to look beyond the categories of regime type to understand the contingent nature of the relationship between economic and political liberalization. It does so, however, not because the categories of "authoritarian" and "democratic" regime are seen as flawed in some sense or as too general to be of analytic use. Rather, research designs that focus on the authoritarianism-democracy dichotomy are weak because they have implicitly assumed that economic and political liberalizations are related to one another in a theoretically predetermined way. In other words, previous studies have tended to assume a fully complementary or fully negative relationship between economic and political liberalization when, in fact, the relationship is contingent on a variety of other factors, including the nature of the regime initiating the reforms, as well as the specific reforms themselves.

More generally, this book is premised on the idea that political and economic liberalizations are characterized by *autonomous* logics that in any given context can be complementary, contradictory, or even directly unrelated. The dynamics of contestation and participation in a particular national context influence the logics of economic and political liberalization so as to make them mutually reinforcing, contradictory, and sometimes largely independent of one another. This reality is not limited to democratic regimes; authoritarian regimes are also characterized by pluralism, albeit limited pluralism (Linz, 1975). Thus, the specific nature of the relations between the state and different actors within society is central to the relative success of any economic strategy (Evans, 1995). Institutional and social structures mediate the dynamics of participation and contestation (however limited) by determining which actors are relevant, influencing each actor's objectives, and creating incentives for the adoption of particular types of policies.

Political liberalization may flow from economic liberalization, as arguably happened in Chile (as well as in South Korea and Taiwan). But successful economic liberalization can also create a political dynamic that stymies further political reform, which may have been the case in Mexico during the Salinas *sexenio* and may eventually prove to be the case in Cuba (and China as well). Conversely, a successful transition to democracy may set the stage for subsequent economic liberalization, as it appears to have done in Argentina, Ecuador, and Bolivia. But democratic regimes can also give opponents of economic liberalization the ability to block successful reforms, which appears to be the case in Brazil, Uruguay, Venezuela, and, to a certain extent, Colombia. Moreover, crucial decisions regarding democratic or economic liberalization may be made completely independent of each other, as the chapters by Armijo and Starr in this volume suggest. Nor is this ambiguity unique to the current period in Latin America. The historical record for the past one hundred years provides an almost dizzying array of contradictory tendencies concerning political and economic liberalization (both within and among countries). This book thus focuses on the factors that determine the ultimate relationship between political and economic liberalization in any given Latin American country.

The book begins with a look at the logics of liberalizing. The three chapters in that section address the interplay between political and economic liberalization from a broadly theoretical perspective. In Chapter 1, Philip Oxhorn and Graciela Ducatenzeiler consider how the character of civil society in Latin America mediates the relationship between political and economic liberalization. They argue that the historically high level of poverty in Latin America has weakened civil society and thereby undermined its capacity to mitigate the potentially negative impact of economic liberalization on democratic consolidation. Without an effective voice in policy circles, the majority of Latin Americans are unable to protect themselves from the costs of economic reform. As reform undermines their living standards, they will likely lose confidence in the political system, which has failed to respond to their needs. The authors conclude that in the Latin American context, economic reform will thus tend to undermine democratic stability until and unless a more egalitarian distribution of wealth allows a significant strengthening of civil society.

In Chapter 2, Carlos H. Waisman concurs with Oxhorn and Ducatenzeiler's conclusion that the logics of political and economic liberalization tend to conflict. For Waisman, the ability of Latin American countries to mitigate this conflict—and thus the future of democracy in the region—depends on both a strong civil society and a state with the capacity to regulate an emerging market economy. Further, the liberalization process itself will influence the capabilities of the state and society. Although a series of inhibiting factors has minimized the conflict between political and economic liberalization during the early phases of Latin America's transition, those factors will inevitably fade. Waisman thus concludes that the ultimate extent and character of democracy will reflect the relative strength of the state and civil society.

The final chapter in Part 1, by Manuel Antonio Garretón, argues that Latin America's tentative movement toward greater economic and political liberalization must be understood within the broader context of the still ambiguous processes of socioeconomic and cultural change that characterize the region. These macro-level changes have produced what Garretón refers to as the disarticulation and recomposition of the Latin American *sociopolitical matrix*—the relationship among the state, the system of representation, and the socioeconomic basis of social actors that is mediated institutionally by the political regime. Latin America's "classical" matrix was state centered and reflected the effective fusion of the state with both representational and socioeconomic spheres. This matrix seems to have been irrevocably undermined by the consequences of economic reform, and Garretón argues that it is unclear what will replace it. The new matrix may be some combination of elements from the classical matrix with newly emerging patterns of social relations, or it may be a genuinely new matrix characterized by the simultaneous strengthening, autonomy, and complementarity of its component parts mediated by a democratic political regime. The ultimate outcome will depend on progress made in strengthening the state and systems of representation, achieving greater autonomy and reinforcement of civil society, and, more generally, strengthening democratic politics.

Part 2 is the first of two sections that shift attention away from broad theoretic considerations in favor of case studies. The two chapters in Part 2 take up the cases of Chile and Brazil to demonstrate empirically how economic liberalization restructures the institutions that govern the relative capacity of civil society and the state to shape policy outcomes and how this situation influences the consolidation of democracy.

Chapter 4 demonstrates how the process of economic liberalization in Chile has weakened the political voice of a large segment of civil society and thereby reduced the reach of democracy. Manuel Barrera argues that economic reform undermined the institutions that had given the Chilean popular sectors political access during the years of autonomous economic development. Without replacement institutions, an important segment of civil society has been effectively excluded from the daily operation of Chilean democracy. Barrera believes the liberalization process has created opportunities for new mediating institutions to replace those that have disappeared, but it remains unclear whether, when, and in what capacity such institutions might develop. In the meantime, the popular sectors will be unable to participate fully in Chilean democracy, meaning democracy will be restricted rather than broad-based.

In Chapter 5, Philippe Faucher considers the mediating role of state institutions on the consolidation of democracy in Brazil. Faucher argues that Brazil's inability to implement an effective anti-inflationary strategy throughout the 1980s was caused by the weaknesses of key state institutions (or ungovernability in Faucher's terminology). The resulting powerlessness of a succession of governments in the battle against inflation threatened to undermine the legitimacy of democratic governance in Brazil but also unexpectedly opened a window of opportunity for the reform of state institutions needed to enhance governability in a democratic context. The hyperinflationary crisis of the early 1990s, born of repeated failures to stabilize the Brazilian economy, weakened societal opposition to the costs of stabilization, which enabled even weak state institutions to implement an effective assault against inflation. The success of the Real Plan translated into substantial societal support that enabled the government to take on the entrenched interests within the state opposed to reform. Faucher is moderately optimistic that the government of Fernando Henrique Cardoso will be able to take advantage of this opportunity to reform state institutions. If successful, institutional reform promises to strengthen the Brazilian state, enhance the effectiveness of democratic governance in Brazil, increase the legitimacy of democracy within Brazilian society, and thereby further democratic consolidation.

Part 3 retains the focus on case studies initiated in the previous section, but it considers a different causal link in the relationship between political and economic liberalization. Rather than consider how economic reform impinges on democracy, the three chapters in this section examine the impact of politics on economic liberalization and what that implies for the consolidation of democracy. Taken together, the chapters in Part 3 look at the impact of political institutions, constituent pressures, and political coalitions on fiscal reform, privatization, and monetary stability in Brazil, Argentina, and Mexico.

Peter R. Kingstone begins this exploration of the politics of economic reform with an analysis of fiscal reform in Brazil. Kingstone agrees with Faucher that success in the battle against inflation has dramatically improved the potential for democratic consolidation in Brazil, but he is very pessimistic about the survivability of the happy complementarity between economic and political reform. He argues that the nature of political institutions in Brazil will militate against the fiscal reform that is essential to long-term economic stability. Through an extensive analysis of the Cardoso presidency, Kingstone concludes that the character of Brazilian electoral laws and of the broader political system is responsible for this problem. The peculiar nature of those political institutions makes it extremely difficult for the Brazilian executive to construct broad-based legislative coalitions that support policies of national importance. Instead, the Brazilian political system empowers narrow, distributional coalitions (particularly in the areas of tax, civil service, and pension reform) capable of blocking the fiscal policy reform that is essential for continued economic stability in Brazil and ultimately, according to Kingstone, to the consolidation of Brazilian democracy.

In Chapter 7, Leslie Elliott Armijo considers the forces that led governments to adopt a policy of privatization in three Latin American countries—Argentina, Mexico, and Brazil—and, for comparative breadth, one non–Latin American country—India. Armijo's analysis of nine administrations in these four countries leads to the conclusion that governments will undertake neoliberal reform, at least in the case of privatization, when doing so is either in the interest of key domestic political constituencies or, at a minimum, is not detrimental to those actors on whose support the government's survival relies. For Armijo, the constellation of cases she considers suggests that no direct link exists between political liberalization (or the lack thereof) and any ensuing economic reform. The decision to adopt neoliberal reform seems to depend less on regime type than on the peculiar mix of political constituents backing any government considering economic reform measures.

The final case study in this volume concentrates analytic attention directly on the mix of constituent pressures and how different mixes might influence the capacity of Latin American governments to sustain neoliberal reforms. Pamela K. Starr focuses on two countries, Mexico and Argentina, which adopted very similar monetary policies in the process of neoliberal reform yet experienced very different capacities to sustain that policy during the mid-1990s. Like Armijo, Starr accepts that economic forces had an important impact on the events under analysis but concludes that the most important factors shaping the outcome were variations in the coalitions of societal forces backing each government and the environment in which they operated. Returning to a theme broached by Faucher, Starr argues that hyperinflationary crises produce a tight political coalition supportive of exchange rate stability as part of a broader stabilization program. Once inflation is defeated, the domestic costs of monetary stability gradually undermine the strength of that anti-inflationary coalition and governmental capacity to sustain this element of the neoliberal policy package. Starr's conclusions thereby reinforce the argument put forth tentatively by Armijo that no clear relationship exists between regime type and governments' capacity to carry out neoliberal economic reform. To the contrary, the determining factors seem to be the composition and relative cohesion of a government's political coalition.

Part 4 contains some conclusions regarding the nature of the interplay between political and economic liberalization in Latin America. The eight previous chapters offer significant evidence for our contention that the relationship between market economics and political democracy is more complicated than is commonly admitted. Rather than pointing to a clear causal link between the two, the chapters in this volume demonstrate that the factors shaping the liberalization process can have a very different impact in the political and economic realms owing to the distinct *logics* underlying each. In this final chapter, we consider five forces shaping liberalization highlighted in the preceding chapters and illuminate how each tends to structure the reform process. We also address the circumstances under which neoliberal economic reform is likely to constrain democratic practices. The compendium of evidence presented in this volume also suggests to us that the evident affinity between political and economic liberalization in Latin America during the 1980s and 1990s appears to be more a coincidence than an inevitability. To increase the likelihood that this lucky coincidence will endure, we conclude with a few limited policy insights gleaned from our contributors' findings. The potentiality for complementarity between political and economic liberalization is real, but since it is not inevitable policymakers must understand the complex interplay between the two to achieve an effective dual transition.

Notes

1. One striking exception to this generalization has emerged in countries that have suffered hyperinflation. In that environment the losses produced by economic reform in specific sectors of the economy (most notably in the public sector and import-competing firms) appear to be a lesser threat to living standards than does high inflation, whereas a rapid reduction in price increases produces a large number of beneficiaries from reform in the short term. In hyperinflation, therefore, economic reform tends to be politically popular, at least in the near term. Evidence of this dynamic is offered in Nelson 1994b, 1994c; Rodrik, 1994; Starr, 1997; and Chapters 4 and 8 in this volume.

2. Three important exceptions are Bresser Pereira, Maravall, and Przeworski, 1993; Smith et al., 1994; and Nelson, 1994b.

3. It is important to note that this emphasis is largely a response to concerns that democratic regimes, especially new ones, will be incapable of implementing politically costly economic adjustment policies, the second accepted wisdom. This view was dominant until only relatively recently among both researchers and (not surprisingly) many Latin Americans as authoritarian regimes supplanted democratic ones in response to severe economic crises in the 1960s and early 1970s. See Oxhorn and Ducatenzeiler, 1998; and Maravall, 1994.

4. Chile is the most obvious example supporting the assumption that economic reform will not reinforce authoritarian political structures. Economic success eventually coincided with a transition to democracy, although the military regime remained in power for almost seventeen years and the economy had entered into sustained economic growth several years before the transition even began. South Korea and Taiwan also can be interpreted this way, even though it took more than a generation in both cases for democracy to emerge. The historical clock has still not run out on authoritarian regimes in China or Mexico, although economic *reversals* may be a factor in the latter's ultimate democratization. The literature on democratic transitions has suggested that economic success, although less common than economic failure, might be one factor causing authoritarian regimes to begin processes of democratic transition. This strategy allegedly would allow the regime to take advantage of the legitimacy that it would enjoy due to its economic success in order to constrain the extent to which the democratization process is allowed to go. See O'Donnell and Schmitter, 1986; Huntington, 1984.

5. For example, see Haggard and Kaufman, 1992 and 1995; Nelson, 1990 and 1994b; Bates and Krueger, 1993. Excellent reviews of much of this literature are found in Geddes, 1995; and Remmer, 1990. This is consistent with earlier findings that economic performance more generally is also largely independent of regime type. See Hartlyn and Morely, 1986; Przeworski and Limongi, 1993.

Part 1

The Logics of Liberalizing

1

The Problematic Relationship Between Economic and Political Liberalization: Some Theoretical Considerations

Philip Oxhorn & Graciela Ducatenzeiler

The optimism surrounding Latin America's unprecedented reencounter with both democracy and market-based development strategies has led many analysts to overlook one of the most enduring aspects of the region's political economy: extremely high levels of socioeconomic inequality and their political consequences. Instead, much of the current theoretical and policy-oriented work on economic restructuring in Latin America echoes modernization theories from the 1960s by assuming that "all good things come together"—that economic and political liberalizations are so intrinsically complementary that countries engaged in either will ultimately achieve both high levels of sustained economic growth and a relatively stable political democracy (Kohli, 1993; Leftwich, 1993). The now considerable evidence of a long-term correlation between economic development and political democracy is said to demonstrate that the current wave of market-oriented economic reforms in Latin America will ultimately allow countries in the region to overcome historical problems of economic backwardness and political instability for the simple reason that markets (as opposed to the state) are the best guarantee of sustained economic growth.[1]

This "neomodernization" perspective is fundamentally flawed.[2] It fails to take into account the ways in which extremes of socioeconomic inequality undermine the development of civil society. Almost facile correlations between development and political democracy are of very limited use for understanding Latin America's current political economy because such correlations ignore the role played by civil society in mediating that relationship. Whereas strong civil societies provide for inclusionary forms of liberalism, weak civil societies in Latin America have resulted in exclusionary forms of liberalism.

Our argument will be based on a *collectivist* model of civil society, which contrasts with a more liberal view equating the spread of the market with the growth of civil society (discussed later). Civil society is defined here as

> A rich social fabric formed by a multiplicity of territorially- and function-ally-based units. The strength of civil society is measured by the peaceful coexistence of these units and by their collective capacity to simultaneously *resist subordination* to the state and *demand inclusion* into national political structures. (Oxhorn, 1995a: 251–252)

The capacity of these self-constituted units to define and defend their collective interests helps to ensure the effective representation of all of the principal interests in any given society. Strong civil societies thus avoid or at least lessen the tendency in capitalist societies for the interests of dominant actors and social classes to completely subordinate those of other, less powerful actors and social classes. Conversely, weak civil societies tend to be characterized by extremes of social segmentation.

It is important to emphasize that we define "democratic regime" on the basis of Dahl's concept of *polyarchy* (1971), with the additional requirements that elected officials should not be removed from office arbitrarily, that the authority of elected officials should not be seriously constrained by nonelected ones (particularly the military), and that an uncontested national territory clearly defines the voting population (O'Donnell, 1996). We are concerned here only with *political democracy,* not with maximalist definitions of democracy (cf. Macpherson, 1977) or what is often referred to as *social democracy.* Although we will discuss problems of social equity at length, we do so only to demonstrate how they threaten the stability of democratic regimes. Social equity is not a defining characteristic of democratic regimes; nor should a minimal level of social equity be considered a prerequisite for such regimes to emerge. Democracies have emerged in a wide variety of contexts, but they have tended to prove viable over the longer term only in a very few. This focus on the societal context that best supports democratic regimes is hardly new. Dahl and even Schumpeter (1950) discussed it at length—albeit more in terms of a societal consensus than of the collective organization of society, which is our ultimate concern. Finally, policies enacted by democratic regimes can have significant effects on that societal context, thereby improving or worsening the prospects for their own future survivability.

What follows is a preliminary effort to retrieve a critical political economy tradition by applying it to one of the most important issues in Latin America today: Will the market-based development policies being implemented throughout the region strengthen or undermine existing democratic regimes? We argue that high levels of inequality throughout Latin America, the class structure determined by that inequality, and the weakness of civil society are key factors threatening democratic stability. In other words, historically high levels of income inequality have generated weak civil societies that are unable to mediate a positive relationship between economic and political liberalization.

The chapter is divided into four sections. In the first, we explore the ways in which, historically, economic and political liberalizations have rarely coincided in Latin America. The second section argues that the reason for such disjuncture has been the structural nature of inequality throughout the region. The implications of extreme levels of inequality are then explored in terms of the weakness of Latin American civil societies. Finally, the concluding section begins to develop a theory of civil society which suggests that the specific nature of a given country's civil society mediates more generally the relationship between economic liberalization and political democracy.

The Historical Disjuncture Between Economic and Political Liberalism in Latin America

As already noted, the neomodernization perspective is founded on the correlation between higher levels of economic development and political democracy. This is one of the most consistent findings in comparative politics, despite important regional variations (Przeworski and Limongi, 1993). A variety of theoretical explanations for this correlation have been developed, building largely on those first sketched by Lipset (Lipset, 1959 and 1994; Rueschemeyer, Stephens, and Stephens, 1992). In general, these explanations suggest that higher levels of wealth are likely to be associated with greater equality of distribution and that economic development is likely to lead to higher levels of communication infrastructure, including literacy, which is essential for democracy to function. High levels of industrialization are also seen as requiring complex, decentralized political systems that only democracy can accommodate. Moreover, development allegedly brings in its wake a variety of other positive forces that erode the traditional and atavist values that contribute to authoritarian political cultures throughout the developing world. As Lipset concludes: "Belief systems change; and the rise of capitalism, a large middle class, an organized working class, increased wealth, and education are associated with secularism and the institutions of civil society which help create autonomy for the state and facilitate other preconditions for democracy" (1994: 7).

What needs to be emphasized is that these processes are inextricably intertwined with the spread of the market, which is why the current market-oriented economic reforms are viewed so favorably from the perspective of promoting democracy. In this very liberal view, civil society is synonymous with a vibrant market economy in which rational individuals decide to live together to further their private, individual interests (Oxhorn, 1995a and 1995b). Groups and group identities lose any sense of intrinsic value; instead, individuals voluntarily join or leave groups based on the maximization of personal interests. In this process, they acquire values of trust and tolerance and learn how to cooperate and compromise. The ultimate result is a democratic civic culture (Almond and Verba, 1963).

Latin America has rarely conformed to predictions linking economic liberalization and democracy, even during periods of rapid economic development. Latin America's obvious exceptionalism in the mid-1960s served as the basis for the first major theoretical challenges to that kind of economic determinism (O'Donnell, 1973; Collier, 1979). Moreover, Latin America has had a long history of free trade experiments. Economic liberalization actually reached its peak in the 1920s, and in many countries current efforts at economic liberalization date back to the mid-1960s (Díaz Alejandro, 1983). Whereas the nature of Latin America's external economic relations has evolved to reflect growing levels of industrialization throughout the region, economic liberalization without political liberalization has been far more common than democracy with economic liberalism. Conversely, the region's most impressive period of popular-sector incorporation in terms of growing real per capita incomes, social mobility, and "social rights of citizenship"[3] coincided with extensive and growing state intervention in the economy, considerable economic protectionism, and the region's previous wave of democracy (Oxhorn, 1995a). This was the period during which much of Latin America followed a very illiberal development model based on import-substituting industrialization (ISI) first introduced during the 1930s and 1940s. The failures of that model (in terms of economic stagnation and crises), its successes (significantly higher levels of industrialization and a concomitant growth in the bourgeoisie, middle, and working classes), and the more ambiguous impact it had on the tremendous expansion of the state continue to determine the dynamics of Latin America's political economy to this day.

This obvious complexity belies any simple correlation between economic liberalism and political liberalization. A variety of other variables reflecting a general regional economy and specific national political economies affect this relationship. As Díaz Alejandro cautioned long before any consensus emerged on the need for restructuring and greater economic liberalism:

> It does appear possible to argue that the role of the foreign sector in Latin American development has been exaggerated and indeed mythologized. . . . Even in a small country the foreign sector will influence only indirect-

ly many key developmental variables, such as productivity in non-export agriculture, willingness to save and decisions to invest in human capital. Income distribution and political participation will be more influenced by these and other domestic variables than by whether effective rates of protection are 10 or 150 percent. (1983: 46)

We can begin to appreciate the importance and nature of these domestic variables by examining the dominant patterns of development in the region in greater detail.

Latin America experienced its first liberal wave toward the end of the nineteenth century, a period known as the golden age of oligarchic domination. Economic liberalization, however, did not coincide with political liberalization or the development of democratic patterns of government; economic liberalism and political liberalism were not parallel processes. Instead, economic liberalism coincided with political norms that, far from integrating subaltern groups, had their origins in autocratic and authoritarian practices. Those political practices were inspired by positivism and its bon mot "order and progress" that sought to legitimate the illustrious despot or the liberal dictator.

The first wave of economic liberalism was closely associated with the integration of Latin America into the world market through primary material exports and the importation of manufactured goods. By the second half of the nineteenth century, technological change had begun to open up unprecedented opportunities for trade. The advancing industrial revolution in Europe and the invention of the steamship, among other things, laid the foundation for sustaining economic growth (despite periodic, sometimes quite severe, downturns in the world economy) that lasted until the Great Depression of the 1930s. The long periods of political turbulence that had followed independence in most countries in the region subsided relatively quickly. National economies became integrated for the first time, and elite interests began to converge as the new economic opportunities depended on the maintenance of political stability (Oszlak, 1981).

To the extent that economic resources were generated in the external market, the creation of domestic markets was essentially superfluous. Incorporating the subaltern sectors was not an imperative of the economic model; on the contrary, the incorporation of new groups was seen as a major threat to continued oligarchic dominance and political stability. Indeed, much political instability from the 1870s on was the result of new groups demanding such incorporation. Yet, no Latin American country pursuing policies of economic liberalism during this period allowed the popular sectors to be integrated into the political system. At best, those governments gave the middle sectors a secondary position. Civil society remained subordinated to a project elaborated and directed by elites in the pursuit of their own narrow interests. Elitist modernization at the end of the nineteenth and the beginning of the twentieth centuries (just like the almost Stalinist industrialization policies begun in a number of countries in the 1930s) was a policy choice made by elite actors in control of the state with virtually no input from the rest of society. It is no coincidence that a Chilean intellectual of the period, Valentín Letelier, considered Bismarck the incarnation of the desired political direction.

In this context, political liberalism was antithetical to an economic model based on economic liberalism. To at least attempt to legitimate their continued rule, Latin American elites had to turn to illiberal ideologies, foremost of which was positivism.

Latin American positivism was considered an extension of economic liberalism. Those in power claimed to be civilizing the Americas and promoting progress through positivist despotism, tolerating political liberalization only to the extent that it did not threaten the status quo or undermine existing laws (Zea, 1980). Positivist intellectuals argued that order and progress could be achieved through the scientific management of public affairs and did not hide their sympathy for technocratic and authoritarian regimes. For example, the Mexican Porfiriato demonstrated an indisputable effort toward modernization under the direction of positivist intellectuals known as the *científicos*. But Mexico was not unique. The intellectuals' influence led to technocrats running a number of countries, including Mexico, Chile, Argentina, and Brazil.

Just as the dictatorship of Porfirio Díaz is the best example of positivism in practice, the most important positivist theorists were the Argentines Domingo Sarmiento and Juan Alberdi. The inherently authoritarian nature of positivism is perhaps clearest in the work of Alberdi. Even though he rejected dictatorship, Alberdi championed strong presidential governments that maintained monarchist and aristocratic elements. His authoritarianism was a more modern type capable of influencing elections, dominating public opinion, and imposing modernization from above (Halpérin Donghi, 1987; Lynch, 1992).

Positivism and liberalism did not always coexist peacefully.[4] Conflicts were rarely resolved in favor of political liberalism; instead, they ended in a type of compromise that, in the best of cases, resulted in a limited democracy that used electoral mechanisms to legitimate oligarchic domination or arbitrate rivalries among the oligarchy's different factions (Dabéne, 1994). Costa Rica and the countries of the Southern Cone (Argentina, Chile, and Uruguay) were relative exceptions. But even there, whether by limiting suffrage (as in Costa Rica and Chile) or violently repressing the labor movement (Argentina and Chile), oligarchies controlled access to the political system into the twentieth century.[5]

In sum, the economic liberalism that undergirded the development model in the region until the early twentieth century was fundamentally antidemocratic. Social and political exclusion was viewed as essential for Latin America's continued economic success. Greater levels of social integration would require not only greater political liberalization but radical changes in the region's development model as well.

The first opportunity for such a change in the development model came with the crisis of economic liberalism caused by the Great Depression. The international economic turmoil unleashed in 1929 led elites throughout the region to search for a new development model that was inward looking and much less dependent on unregulated market forces—import-substituting industrialization. By the early 1950s, this new model was firmly in place in the region's larger economies. Higher levels of popular-sector social integration were achieved as the region's economies again showed evidence of economic dynamism. But such integration was generally the result of extensive (and growing) levels of state intervention rather than of liberal orthodoxy.

The growth rate in Latin America during the years 1950–1980 was one of the highest in the region's history—as Garcia and Tockman (1985) note, even greater than that achieved by the United States during its take-off years. This growth created a significant capacity for economic integration in Latin America for roughly thirty years (Altimir, 1981). For example, calculations by the Comisión Económica para América Latina y el Caribe (CEPAL) of the general level of "structural mobility" of ten countries at various levels of social modernization show that an average of 26 percent of the economically active population (EAP) in those countries experienced upward mobility in their social status and incomes between 1960 and 1980 (CEPAL, 1989: 31–34). Various measures of poverty showed significant improvement, such as those for extreme poverty.[6]

It is important to emphasize that this period of renewed economic development (regardless of its liberal or illiberal basis) still entailed sharp restrictions on the extent to which elites would allow political liberalization to advance. Much of the period was characterized by the presence of populist or openly authoritarian regimes, many of which gave way to the most repressive authoritarian regimes in Latin America's history. Under populist regimes, political integration was achieved by subordinating popular-sector actors, whereas authoritarian regimes excluded them completely. Moreover, the impressive growth that was achieved did not significantly affect the distribution of wealth, maintaining (or even exacerbating) already high levels of inequality at the same time the living conditions of the popular sectors improved.

It should now be clear that historically the relationship between economic and political liberalism has been quite problematic in Latin America. At best, one could argue that any "predicted" correlation between economic liberalism and political democracy is finally coming true in the 1990s: the region as a whole appears to be firmly committed to new outward-oriented development policies based on market principles at the same time democratic regimes are viewed as the only viable political alternative—although it took well over a hundred years to arrive at this point. It is also important to emphasize that the sudden marriage of neoliberal economic policies and political democracy often came about in the context of an unprecedented economic crisis that belied the most fundamental assumptions relating economic prosperity to democratization. Still, it can be argued that an increasing synchronization of economic and political liberalization processes is occurring. But how long is this likely to last? Is Latin America on a development path that includes both free markets and political democracy? Or will the theoretical conclusions reached in the 1990s prove as ephemeral as those reached in the 1960s, when economic liberalization was linked to authoritarian regimes, or in earlier periods when economic development and social equity appeared to be closely associated with the progressive abandonment of the market?

Why Latin America Has
Not Conformed to Predictions:
The Structural Origins of Social Inequality

To better understand where Latin America might be headed in terms of economic and political liberalization, it is necessary to examine several factors that explain *why* Latin America did not fulfill the expectations in the literature linking economic development more generally with political democracy. Even though that literature was wrong in many senses in its understanding of Latin America, this has more to do with its assumptions regarding causality than with the specific issues of focus. In other words, the distribution of income (i.e., social equity) and class structures are critical to understanding Latin America's development experience, even though actual processes of economic development and modernization did not produce the expected outcomes.

The literature, although often disagreeing on the specifics, has tended to assume that capitalist development would inevitably result in some minimal level of social equity and the appropriate balance of class forces necessary for sustaining political democracy. Whereas multiple paths could achieve this result, all such paths seemed inevitably to lead to the same end point. Some paths were obviously much longer than others and were mired with detours or dead ends, but greater economic development only increased the democratic imperative. The literature failed to take into account the effect the *preexisting* level of social equity and balance of class forces would have on the pattern of development and the future viability of democracy. Moreover, it often sidestepped the question of *agency:* Which social forces would pressure for democratization, and how effective would they be?

Historically, economic development has been associated with declining levels of social inequality in the now developed market economies of Western Europe and North America (Usher, 1981; Portes, 1985; Kuznets, 1955). This link is crucial in explaining the correlation between economic development and democracy. As Przeworski and colleagues (1996: 43) concluded on the basis of World Bank data covering eighty-four countries over time, "People expect democracy to reduce income inequality, and democracies are more likely to survive when they do." In fact, levels of economic inequality may be even more important than levels of economic development in explaining democratic stability. This was the conclusion reached by Muller (1988), who examined the relationship between democratic stability and economic inequality in thirty-three countries during the period 1960–1980. Regardless of the level of development, Muller found that "all democracies with high income inequality . . . were unstable" (p. 63). Significantly, of the nine cases in which democratic regimes were replaced by authoritarian regimes in highly unequal societies during the period, five were in Latin America (Brazil, Chile, Panama, Peru, and Uruguay).[7]

The causal link in this relationship revolves around the distribution of power in a given society. In highly unequal societies, the stakes in politics are potentially high: the preservation of relative privilege for a small minority or greater social justice and equity for the vast majority at that same minority's expense. More concretely, in the case of Latin America, that small minority consisting of the upper and middle classes accounted for less than 10 percent of the economically active population in the 1970s, and in no country did it exceed 15 percent (Portes, 1985). Given democracy's potential for empowering the lower classes, it is difficult to imagine how capitalist economic development can be compatible with democratic institutions without a fundamental trend toward greater socioeconomic equality. Usher (1981), in offering a justification based on democratic theory for the neoliberal economic reforms just beginning to take hold in developed market economies at that time, captured the essence of this dilemma:

> Much depends on whether the trend of capitalism is towards ever greater equality or the reverse. If the trend is towards equality, the incentive to reassign income [from privileged to less privileged classes] would be less than it would otherwise be because part of what might be gained from reassignment can be gained costlessly by waiting. . . . But if, as Marx predicted and his followers have repeated ever since, the distribution of income is becoming steadily worse . . . then it becomes unlikely, almost impossible, for democracy to continue because workers with the political power to displace the capitalist class will eventually be inclined to do so,

and the capitalists or their successors will, at that point, abolish democracy to preserve their privileged position. Democracy would not be viable, in these circumstances, for precisely the reason it was alleged not to be viable in the feudal organization of society in the Middle Ages. (Usher, 1981: 98–99)

From this perspective, a primary source of democratic instability in Latin America becomes obvious. In many respects, Usher's analogy to feudal society is all too appropriate when looking at the region's social structure.

Historically, Latin American societies have been among the most unequal in the world, even compared with countries at similar levels of development (Portes, 1985; Fajnzylber, 1990). This reality reflects the development styles privileged by Latin American elites, which in the ultimate instance have always been socially exclusionary. Import-substituting industrialization, as well as market-oriented policies, have been dependent on a type of social exclusion that "impedes the adequate participation of large segments of the population in modernization processes and in the results of growth" (Altimir, 1990: 12).

The intrinsically unequal nature of Latin American development has been clearest since the early 1950s, when the region as a whole entered a thirty-year period of sustained high growth rates. Looking specifically at the period 1960–1975, the percentage of total income share going to the poorest 60 percent of the population shrank from 18.0 percent to 16.7 percent even as real annual income per household increased from $833 to $1,095. During the same period, the income share of the richest 10 percent of the population increased by almost 1 percent, from 46.6 percent to 47.3 percent. Real annual income per household for that segment of the population rose from $11,142 to $15,829—a real increase per household eighteen times greater than that of 60 percent of the population (Portes, 1985: 22–26).

This trend toward growing income inequality was even more acute in Brazil and Mexico, which experienced the highest and most sustained rates of growth in the region during the period 1960–1975. There, the level of income inequality either remained constant or increased (see Table 1.1). Both countries had the highest rates of inequality in Latin America, with Gini coefficients that ranged from 0.5 to 0.6 (depending on the source), compared with a range of 0.3 to 0.4 for developed market economies.[8]

The historical problem of social inequality has been exacerbated by the tremendous economic dislocations that began with the debt crisis starting in the early 1980s and continued with the various economic policies enacted to restore economic dynamism (Fajnzylber, 1990; Altimir, 1990; Oxhorn, 1998b; CEPAL, 1988). Open unemployment reached double digits in most countries for the first time since unemployment statistics had been

Table 1.1   Income Distribution in Mexico and Brazil, Selected Years, 1960–1975

Income Distribution (percent of total income)	Mexico			Brazil		
	1964	1968	1975	1960	1970	1973
Poorest 20 percent	3.50	3.40	1.90	3.50	3.10	1.80
Poorest 40 percent	10.30	10.50	8.10	11.50	10.00	7.00
Richest 5 percent	28.70	27.90	30.30	27.70	34.90	38.20
Richest 10 percent	41.90	42.10	43.50	39.70	47.80	51.90
Gini coefficient	0.51	0.52	0.56	0.50	0.56	0.61

Source: World Bank, "Balancing Trickle Down and Basic Needs Strategies," World Bank Staff Working Paper No. 335, June 1979, p. 6.

compiled, more than doubling for the region as a whole from an unweighted average of 6 percent of urban EAP in 1974 to 14 percent in 1984. Throughout the decade, industrial wages demonstrated a profound secular decline; by 1991 they were 82.5 percent of what they had been in 1980 (Barrera, 1998). Informal employment increased an average of about 20 percent in Latin America during the decade (Portes, 1989: 24), whereas the income of workers in the informal sector fell 27 percent between 1980 and 1983 alone (CEPAL, 1988: 3).

Even more serious were increases in the levels of poverty and extreme poverty. After declining during the 1970s, the poverty rate again began to climb in the 1980s. Forty-one percent of the population lived below the poverty level in 1980; that figure increased to 43 percent in 1986 and reached 46 percent in 1990 (Altimir, 1993; Torre, 1994). In absolute terms, 71 million more people were living in poverty at the end of the 1980s than had been in 1970, for a total of 183 million people, of whom 88 million lived in extreme poverty—28 million more than in 1970 (CEPAL, 1990).

The predominant policy response to this crisis in the region has not been encouraging from the perspective of the long-term viability of fragile democratic regimes. In practice, short-term considerations have tended to prevail over longer-term considerations of growth with greater social equity, despite a growing recognition that long-term development is dependent on greater investment in human resources (World Bank, 1990; CEPAL, 1988; Fajnzylber, 1990). Public expenditures have generally remained regressive in Latin America (Helwege, 1995; World Bank, 1990: 37). Education, health care, and other programs designed to contribute to human resource development have not been immune from budget cutters' efforts to trim the size of both government budget deficits and the state (Williamson, 1990c; CEPAL, 1988). Instead, policymakers throughout the region have sought to address negative socioeconomic trends by attempting to channel minimal state welfare provisions to those most in need. Although they often contribute to a significant alleviation of the immediate effects of poverty for aid recipients, such policies at best have had only limited impact on changing the underlying structure of poverty. Moreover, they have not reversed the worsening patterns of income distribution inherited from the 1980s.[9]

The privatization of services formerly provided by the state as part of neoliberal economic reform packages has further exacerbated the exclusionary effects of recent economic trends (CEPAL, 1988). In selling off state enterprises that provide the infrastructure for development (energy, transportation, communications, and similar enterprises), the tendency toward excessive concentration of economic resources is reinforced as such services become oriented more toward satisfying the demands of the wealthiest economic actors. Similarly, the privatization of key social services such as social security, health care, and housing favors the middle and upper classes, which have the incomes necessary to pay profitable prices. Perhaps the most dramatic change has come in the area of education. In contrast to its historical role of providing an avenue for social mobility, education has become "a mechanism for the reproduction of social inequality and the introduction of new elitist forms in society" (CEPAL, 1988: 12).

By the early 1990s, Latin America seemed poised to enter a new period of sustained economic growth based on a second wave of economic liberalism. The area was growing again, and a new neoliberal development model seemed in place throughout most of the region. Yet even in the Southern Cone, where historically greater social equity had been achieved, neoliberal economic policies have resulted in a growing income concentration that has exacerbated the negative trends of the 1980s (Altimir, 1993 and 1995; Torre, 1993). Controlling for the different economic phases of each country at particular points in time, Altimir (1993) found that those countries that had recuperated from the crisis of the 1980s and its consequences, completing the process of structural adjustment and implementing important policy reforms, demonstrated a worsening of income inequality compared with earlier periods.

The Chilean experience, which has been much longer and more complete than that of any other country in the region, is important for understanding these longer-term trends.[10] In a six-year period starting in 1987, approximately 1.5 million people escaped poverty as the percentage of those below the poverty line declined from 46.6 percent to just over 30 percent at the end of 1993.[11] Yet, this remarkable improvement was largely the result of job creation. Continual economic growth throughout the period led to a 19 percent increase in employment, bringing unemployment down from 10.8 percent in 1987 to just 5.3 percent in 1992. Given the obviously favorable economic environment during the period and the fact that Chile was quickly approaching full employment, further reductions in poverty will be increasingly difficult to achieve. Despite the dramatic fall in the level of poverty, income distribution did not improve significantly. For example, official statistics showed that the share of national income going to the poorest 20 percent of households remained constant at 4.5 percent from 1987 though 1992 (Ruiz-Tagle, 1993: 643), compared to a 7.6 percent share in 1969 (Barrera, 1998)—a drop of over 40 percent in this segment's share of national income.[12]

Similar conclusions can be drawn from the experience of Argentina. Although Argentina implemented its economic liberalization program much later than Chile, it has had a sufficiently long period of economic growth to see the redistributive consequences of the new economic model.[13] The model has failed to demonstrate its virtues in either promoting development or, even less, generating greater equality. Historically, Argentina has been characterized by more equal income distribution than other countries in Latin America, as well as countries elsewhere in the world at a similar level of development. Beginning in 1975, after economic liberalization had first been attempted by both military and civilian governments, both income inequality and extreme poverty markedly increased. In 1974, the poorest 30 percent of the population received 11.4 percent of the national income; by 1992, that proportion had dropped to 8.9 percent. During the same period, the share of national income of the richest 10 percent of the population increased from 28 percent to 34 percent. According to a World Bank report, the richest 20 percent of the Argentine population received 51.6 percent of the national income in 1993 compared with 46.6 percent in 1980, whereas the income share of the same percentage of the poorest households declined from 5.3 percent in 1980 to 4.6 percent in 1993 (*Pagina 12* [Buenos Aires], September 21, 1994).

The process of impoverishment experienced by Argentine society has no parallel in any other society. Workers as a whole have lost approximately 40 percent of the value of their income since 1980. Between 1980 and 1990, poverty increased by 67 percent in greater Buenos Aires (Minujin and Kessler, 1995). Moreover, the World Bank recently concluded that the distributive impact of state expenditures has exacerbated rather than alleviated social differences. Whereas each person in 1994 in the lowest economic stratum received benefits from public expenditures worth the equivalent of 778 pesos, at the opposite extreme each person in the highest economic stratum received the equivalent of 1,118 pesos. The source of this difference can be found, in order of importance, in expenditures on retirement benefits and social services, university education, housing, culture, and science and technology (*Pagina 12,* September 21, 1994).

In Mexico, the increase in inequality was also dramatic during the same period. Between 1963 and 1977, a slight redistribution of income occurred from the highest income sectors to the middle sectors and between

1977 and 1984 from the highest income sectors to the lowest sectors. Between 1984 and 1989, however, a clear increase in concentration occurred in favor of the most privileged sectors. Statistics show that during that time the richest 10 percent of Mexican households received an additional 5.1 percent of the national income (Lustig, 1992). Lustig also noted that the increase in inequality was even more severe than statistical data can convey because even minimal losses in income can have devastating effects for the poor. Moreover, evidence suggests that the social welfare policies implemented by Mexican president Carlos Salinas in 1989 as part of his National Solidarity Program (Pronasol) have not altered the structure of poverty and inequality (Cornelius, Craig, and Fox, 1994; Graham, 1994; Lustig, 1994; Ward, 1993). According to calculations by Lustig (1992), if the incomes of the poorest 10 percent of households increased at an annual rate of 3 percent (the average growth rate of Mexico's per capita gross domestic product [GDP] during the postwar period), it would take them sixteen years to reach an income level greater than the level of extreme poverty. If their incomes grew at the same rate as per capita GDP during the period 1988–1990 (1 percent per year), it would take forty-seven years to exceed that level.[14]

In sum, Latin America's historically unequal societies have become even more unequal since 1980. Economic growth and new social welfare policies offer the promise of alleviating at least some social consequences through poverty abatement. But the underlying socioeconomic structures generating inequality remain largely unchanged. Ultimately, even poverty reduction remains highly problematic. As the Chilean case amply demonstrates, sustained high growth rates and macroeconomic stability (essentially the situation there since 1984) were sufficient to reduce the poverty level to just under 30 percent—a marked improvement but far short of achievements outside the region and in a context that has been much more propitious for poverty reduction than anywhere else in Latin America.[15] What does this mixed economic record imply for the applicability of any theoretical linkage between economic and political liberalization in the region?

Latin America's Social Pyramid and Weak Civil Society

Latin America's historical (and growing) problems of inequality have undermined any facile relationship between economic liberalization and political democracy through their negative effect on the development of civil society. More specifically, Latin America has been characterized by the emergence of a dominant class and a middle sector concerned more with stability than with growth, and their power has not been effectively counterbalanced by an amalgamation of lower-class groups—Latin America's popular sectors. Instead, the popular sectors remain fragmented and weakly organized. The resultant configuration of social forces and state power has been politically unstable, even though it has produced intermittent but prolonged periods of economic growth and development.

At the upper echelons of the social structure, economic inequality has limited the potential for political democracy in several important ways. First and in many ways foremost, historically, Latin American elites have been concerned more with stability to protect their privileged social position than with promoting, for example, economic growth. This priority dates back to the period of decolonization, when the repressive capacity of the central state was built up to impose the national economic and political integration necessary to take advantage of the economic boom in exports in the second half of the nineteenth century.[16] Ironically (in light of current political and economic trends in the region), the economic opportunities opened by nineteenth-century free trade provided the impetus and resources for the consolidation of strong repressive states firmly under the control of "the class or class alliance that controlled the new circuits of production and circulation of goods under which the export economy was based" (Oszlak, 1981: 28).

As the export trade continued to expand through the second half of the nineteenth century, so, too, did the class structure as new economic opportunities were created in the service sector linked to international trade and the growing state apparatus. In particular, the middle sectors (or middle class) began to emerge as a major social force. The political incorporation of those sectors in the early twentieth century in many Latin American countries mirrored their previous growth in economic power and status and provided the first impetus for democratization in the region (Rueschemeyer, Stephens, and Stephens, 1992; Pinto, 1970).[17] Although conflicts of interest between the dominant class and the middle sectors were not absent (often beginning with the sometimes violent struggle over middle-sector political rights), both groups shared a strong common interest in preserving the status quo from which both benefited, albeit unequally (Portes, 1985). For this reason, middle-sector support was often critical for the success of military coups in many countries during the 1960s and 1970s (O'Donnell, 1973; Garretón, 1989; Valenzuela, 1978).

The relatively high levels of income inequality throughout Latin America gave rise to consumption patterns among the dominant class and the middle sectors that further reinforced structural inequality.[18] "Acute concentration of income" allowed high-income groups to attempt to reproduce "to a caricatural degree a consumption pattern from more advanced societies" (Fajnzylber, 1990: 61). Initially, they could do so because of the lucrative export trade, which could finance high levels of consumption by a small minority. The collapse of the international economy during the late 1920s and the 1930s foreclosed this option, at least temporarily, resulting in the first experiments with ISI throughout the region (Cardoso and Faletto, 1979; Evans, 1979). This policy further reinforced dominant consumption patterns by skewing domestic industrial production toward upper-income groups.

This pattern of consumption contributed to a vicious circle of rent seeking, speculative investments, and declining productivity. Social status and economic power in Latin America became increasingly dependent on access to the economic rents raw material exports provided, either directly through land ownership or indirectly through control of the central state apparatus. Land concentration during the colonial period increased after independence as a result of liberal economic reforms introduced throughout the region to take advantage of the late-nineteenth-century export boom. This concentration drastically curtailed economic opportunities for smallholders—who were unable to adopt more productive agricultural methods—not to mention the growing numbers of landless peasants. The oligarchy's growing economic power was quickly translated into political power as central states were consolidated in most countries in the wake of the same economic boom.

A "pathology of inequity" thus became part of Latin America's historical legacy (Fajnzylber, 1990: 58). Even Argentina and Uruguay—notable exceptions to this pattern because of their relatively uniform levels of agricultural productivity—displayed distribution patterns in 1980 that were comparable to levels reached in industrialized societies in the 1940s. Resources that could have been devoted to productive investment were diverted to consumption and rent-seeking activities (speculative investments, corruption, patronage, and so on). Industrialization under the auspices of a growing state apparatus became a new source of rents—which Fajnzylber (1990: 79) aptly called "rentist industrialization." As renowned Argentine economist Raul Prebisch observed, "The frenetic imitation of the patterns of consumption in the centers [by the upper classes] . . . has acted to inhibit capital formation and, as a consequence, has limited the productive absorption of the workforce" (quoted in CEPAL, 1989: 55).

The ultimate consequences of this pattern of development included the economic exclusion of large segments of society. Although ISI required internal markets, economic dynamism depended on the consumption of no more (and usually substantially less) than 40 percent of the population (Altimir, 1990: 12), which further contributed to a rise in inequality even as Latin America experienced prolonged economic growth and, in a number of countries, rapid industrialization. For example, although per capita income in the region doubled between 1960 and 1980, poverty rates remained intractably high. The relative level of extreme poverty still included 35 percent of the population in 1980 (down from 50 percent in 1960), and the number of people actually living in poverty increased 16 percent during the 1970s alone (CEPAL, 1989: 55).

It is important to emphasize that this period was marked by the dominant class's desire, often with the support of the middle sectors, to severely curtail the possible effects of socioeconomic change and to focus on its own short-term interests. As Fajnzylber explained:

> In the case of [most Latin American countries] where there is a component of rentist leadership, that leadership does not seem to be obsessed with growth nor with the projects of building a future. Its interest lies rather in the maintenance of the status quo, which is particularly favorable to it. (Fajnzylber, 1990: 78)

In particular, there was a lack of concern for the social costs of this pattern of development. There was also little incentive to invest in human capital (education, health care, eradication of extreme poverty, and so on), which explains the regressivity of social expenditures in the region noted previously.

At the same time, relations between various economic interests and the state were not free of tension. Dependent on the state for protection and various forms of rent, business interests were vulnerable to some extent to the specific groups that controlled the state apparatus, including the military (Argentina, Brazil, Chile, and Uruguay, for example) or a single political party (the Institutional Revolutionary Party [Partido Revolucionario Institucional], or PRI, in Mexico). Uncontrolled popular-sector political participation raised the specter of the state adopting policies that would undermine the interests of both the dominant class and the middle sectors. This situation reflected the high stakes of politics in unequal societies and the potential threat that politics itself would become a zero-sum game pitting the haves against the have-nots. Not surprisingly, Latin America's most enduring democratic regimes have resulted from elite "pacts" that limit the threat the popular sectors could potentially pose to elite interests (Karl, 1990). In other countries such as Argentina, Brazil, Chile, and Uruguay, the result has been numerous failed democratic experiments or, as in Mexico, Central America (with the notable exception of Costa Rica), and Paraguay, among many others, little or no experience with political democracy.

Elite fears of democracy, in turn, raise the question of agency: Which groups or social forces will pressure those in control of the state for political liberalization? Although there have been notable exceptions,[19] political liberalization in general has not been entirely an elitist, top-down process. Elites in Latin America (and elsewhere) have been reluctant to expand political rights and have done so only under pressure from various societal forces (Rueschemeyer, Stephens, and Stephens, 1992).

Viewed from this perspective, Latin America's dominant consumption patterns and exclusionary development have affected the popular sectors in two important ways. First and in some ways the more startling, status became so dependent upon consumption levels that even the lower classes aspired to what Fajnzylber (1990: 68–69) described as a "cosmic consumption pattern" and "collective fantasy." More concretely, this hyperconsumerism resulted in "an induced poverty among culturally urbanized popular families that suffered a nutritional deficit by adopting a more elastic demand for foodstuffs than for durable consumer goods" (CEPAL, 1989: 55). A majority of Latin Americans were, in effect, "substituting the demand for 'systematic equity' with the demand for social mobility and the group of expectations that come with it" (Altimir, 1990: 12). Moreover, the cosmic consumption pattern is highly individualistic, exacerbating collective action problems among the popular sectors as each person seeks his or her personal advancement rather than any collective good. Individual frustration, however, can have a cumulative effect as populist leaders appeal to this collective fantasy to further their own interests. The result has been periodic economic instability throughout Latin America caused by irresponsible fiscal policies (Dornbusch and Edwards, 1991). This instability plus the populist mobilization itself have often been critical factors in leading the dominant class (and the middle sectors) to see democratic regimes as an autonomous threat to their interests and thus to support their overthrow (Oxhorn, 1995b; O'Donnell, 1973).

The second effect of this pattern of development that has limited popular-sector agency in pressuring for greater political liberalization has been economic heterogeneity of the popular sectors (Oxhorn, 1998b; Fajnzylber, 1990; Altimir, 1990; Portes, 1985). This heterogeneity reflects historical problems rising from lagging productivity in rural areas and declining standards of living for the peasantry relative to urban dwellers. It also reflects the fact that the economic interests of the peasantry itself are heterogeneous; the group includes small landowners, subsistence farmers, and rural wage laborers who are all part of the popular sectors. Popular-sector heterogeneity is further reinforced by the diversity of Latin America's urban economy, also the product of the exclusionary nature of development. The urban popular sectors include both organized and unorganized workers in the formal economy, the unemployed who are seeking employment, people working in the informal economy, and the *Lumpenproletariat* who are largely outside the formal and informal economies.

Economic heterogeneity creates important obstacles to popular-sector collective action because different segments of those sectors have different, often contradictory, economic interests (Oxhorn, 1998b; Portes, 1985). For example, the urban informal sector is an important source of low-cost consumption items for workers in the formal economy. Improvements in the standard of living for workers in the informal sector could easily translate into lower standards of living for workers in the formal sector through higher prices and loss of desired goods and services. More important, the existence of a large informal sector threatens the job security of workers in the formal sector, particularly those with the fewest skills who are easily replaced by workers willing to receive substantially lower wages, and places downward pressure on wages and other benefits workers might otherwise achieve through collective bargaining. Organization is also a form of power that gives organized labor in the formal sector important advantages over the largely unorganized workers in the informal sector (Oxhorn, 1998b; Portes, 1985). For example, the extension of such benefits as worker's compensation, pensions, health care, and unemployment insurance is closely related to organized groups' ability to pressure the state. The unorganized are generally the last to be included in and are the least adequately covered by such benefits (Mesa-Lago, 1978 and 1989). Such advantages can be seen as coming at the expense of the unorganized, who are deliberately excluded to exacerbate the obstacles to popular-sector collective action.

Induced poverty and popular-sector heterogeneity have helped to dampen societal pressure for sociopolitical change by supporting limited processes of controlled inclusion (Oxhorn, 1995a). At least since the 1930s, elites throughout Latin America have resorted to rigid, hierarchical patterns of popular-sector inclusion that have further divided the popular sectors and ensured some level of political stability by giving relatively advantaged groups at least a limited stake in the status quo. Through state corporatism, populist appeals, and clientelism, political elites have been able to limit popular-sector political participation, subordinating popular-sector collective interests to their own. For example, in different ways and to varying degrees, organized labor became *the* referent for popular-sector inclusion and benefited materially as a result. The specific way in which the working class was incorporated was a crucial turning point in the politics of each country, affecting the subsequent evolution of politics in fundamental and long-lasting ways (Collier and Collier, 1991). When processes of controlled inclusion broke down and were no longer perceived as able to contain rising popular-sector pressures for reform, however, the violent imposition of authoritarian rule resulted, as occurred, for example, in Argentina (1966 and 1976), Brazil (1964), Chile (1973), and Uruguay (1973). Processes of controlled inclusion have maintained relative political stability only in authoritarian Mexico and democratic Colombia and Venezuela, although all three countries have exhibited growing signs of political instability.

The weakness of civil society and its institutions has given the state and political elites in Latin America enormous autonomy that, like a vicious circle, has reinforced civil society's own weakness. Institutional structures and existing power relations reinforce a process of concentration and exclusion. Extremes of income inequality make it virtually impossible to arrive at a necessary societal consensus on the fundamental aspects of the economic system:

> That is, on the property system and on the distribution of income between individuals and social classes. It is this agreement, it is this basic political pact, besides a complex institutional system, that legitimates governments, assures governance and guarantees the effectiveness of economic policies [in developed market economies]. (Bresser Pereira and Nakano, 1994: 12)

In the new democratic context of the 1990s, the dominant classes want popular-sector living standards to rise but only to the extent that the distribution of income is not substantially altered. Economic growth, regulated by the market in place of the state, is perceived as the primary remedy for alleviating inequality.

The economic dislocations racking all of Latin America since the early 1980s have tended to diminish the state's capacity to redress the historical causes of civil society's weakness throughout the region. This problem is reflected in the limited ability of state institutions to guarantee the effective exercise of citizenship, provide moral leadership, and improve income distribution through the allocation of resources and the mobilization of public savings (Przeworski et al., 1995). It is also reflected in the fact that stabilization measures were elaborated and implemented by technocrats without consultation with interest groups or other political institutions that represented different societal interests, particularly those of the popular sectors. The resulting rule by decree, or *decretismo,* is a symptom of the weakness of state institutions in relation to civil society rather than their strength (Przeworski et al., 1995; Haggard and Kaufman, 1995). Unfortunately, *decretismo* has further impeded the reconstruction of the state and the formulation of a democratic growth strategy.

The simultaneous weakening of both civil society and the state in Latin America has affected the interaction of social classes with the state in important ways. At the elite level, states have become increasingly more dependent on business interests (Schneider, 1995). For example, Chile was able to overcome its economic crisis in the early 1980s only by establishing closer links with the business community and modifying its neoliberal economic strategy as a result of new business inputs (Silva, 1992–1993). Similarly, in Mexico the economic crisis and new market-based development policies have led to much closer relations between business interests and the state (Heredia, 1994; Loaeza, 1992; Cook, Middlebrook, and Horcasitas, 1994). Argentina's economic restructuring reflected the emergence of a new ruling coalition dominated by business interests, despite the fact that it was achieved under a Peronist president (Schvarzer, 1998). Even in Brazil, the election of Social Democrat Fernando Henrique Cardoso was made possible by an alliance with conservative business interests, giving him the legislative majority necessary to enact reforms.[20] This suggests that the state, even under a democratic regime, may be less than is commonly thought of a potentially autonomous threat to elite interests. Moreover, economic reforms designed to streamline the state and minimize its capacity to intervene in the economy represent further institutional guarantees for elite interests.[21]

In terms of the popular sectors, many of the old institutions of controlled inclusion are under serious challenge, despite the resurgence of political democracy throughout the region. Latin American citizens are enjoying new and sometimes unprecedented political rights; at the same time, their civil and social rights are being increasingly narrowed (O'Donnell, 1993; Oxhorn, 1998a). Depressed wages, the growth of the informal sector, and changes in existing labor codes have undermined the collective capacity of organized labor (see Chapter 5). The reforms associated with economic liberalism are rolling back many of the rights (and privileges) granted to workers as part of the process of controlled inclusion associated with ISI and state control over markets (Oxhorn, 1998a). The popular sectors' ability to pressure for social and political reform has decreased markedly as a result of the growing fragmentation and atomization of civil society. Historical problems of economic heterogeneity have been compounded by the absence of new collective actors to represent the popular sectors. In a sense, democratization is taking place in the context of social *disintegration* rather than integration, as presupposed by literature linking economic development with democracy.

The broad historical sweep of these arguments should not obscure important differences among country cases. For example, political parties and labor movements, the principal mechanisms for incorporating large segments of the population into the political system, have varied in many aspects that reflect the unique political economies of particular countries. Populist movements, which were responsible for popular-sector incorporation in the majority of Latin American countries, exhibited great mobilizational capacity but little ability to create strong institutions for the political representation of popular-sector interests. But in Argentina, for example, relatively high preexisting levels of social equity and the unique nature of the rich agrarian economy resulted in the emergence of the region's most powerful autonomous labor movement under the banner of Peronist populism. This movement, in turn, contributed to an extreme politicization of the state that undermined both Argentine democracy and further economic development (O'Donnell, 1988; Waisman, 1987). This powerful workers' movement, however, was unable to overcome the crisis of populism by providing a distinct political alternative. The movement confronted the implementation of neoliberal economic policies when it was already experiencing advanced decay of its social and organizational bases tied to the old order. This weakness prevented union leaders from opposing the reforms; instead, they agreed to support the reforms to the extent that their personal interests were taken into account (Palermo, 1995; Murillo, 1997). In practice, this situation privileged clientelism, corruption, and the designation of union leaders to positions of power in carrying out the reforms.

In Chile, by contrast, an economy dominated by mineral exports allowed for the early consolidation of the central state, the most highly developed and extensive party system in Latin America, and increasing levels of political democratization through 1973 that compared favorably with European countries in terms of political stability (Garretón, 1989; Oxhorn, 1995a). Chile avoided the populism and extreme politicization of the state that were ultimately responsible for Argentina's "reversal of development" (Waisman, 1987). Although harsh neoliberal reforms were imposed by a repressive military regime, organized labor survived and has begun to reestablish its organizational bases. Moreover, labor has (with limited but notable success) engaged both the coalition government and business groups in negotiations on issues of central concern to the working class as a whole. In neither case did civil society come to reflect the level of dispersion of power characteristic of civil societies in developed market economies. Even Chile's apparently consolidated democracy ultimately succumbed to the harsh limits of controlled inclusion.

At another extreme, Mexico and Brazil represent cases in which the weight of the state combined with extreme social inequality quashed most autonomous organizations among the popular sectors until relatively recently. Institutions of state corporatism dampened, with very different degrees of success, the societal pressures that emerged in the wake of rapid but highly unequal industrialization in the postwar period. Both countries experienced strong populist movements (Cardenas in Mexico during the 1930s; Vargas in Brazil intermittently during the 1930s, 1940s, and early 1950s) that laid the foundations for their strong central states. But only Cardenas was able to consolidate the hegemony of a single political party, the PRI. Although it has been under increasing strain, this hegemony has survived for over half a century and still commands the allegiance of the bulk of Mexico's labor movement. As in Argentina, Mexican labor leaders loyal to the PRI have tended to support neoliberal reforms in exchange for protection of their personal prerogatives (Zapata, 1998).

Brazil represents the only case in Latin America where civil society has actually become stronger in recent years. This situation has been reflected in the political party system with the emergence of the Partido de los Trabalhadores (PT). The strengthening is also reflected in the growing power of the labor movement, which has become more independent of state corporatist institutions, gained more members, and strengthened its organizational structure in both the private and pubic sectors.[22] Still, the party system is characterized by extreme fragmentation. Moreover, the sheer magnitude of the social inequalities endemic in Brazilian society raises the real danger that democracy will exclude half of the population, that Brazilian society will, in effect, be sharply divided in two—one half very "civil" and the other increasingly less so.

In sum, even if no agreement exists on which social classes (if any) are necessary for the emergence of political democracy, it is clear from almost any perspective that Latin America's class structure has not been conducive to stable democratic regimes. Historically, structural inequality has created an assemblage of class interests and incentives that makes the kind of class compromise associated with democracy in developed market economies fragile at best and impossible in the worst case (see, for example, Przeworski, 1985). Whereas social mobility and the power of numbers have been able to compensate for disparities in wealth and social status in developed market economies, making political resources noncumulative (Dahl, 1961), initial disparities in wealth and status present since the colonial period have tended to grow rather than diminish in Latin America. When the numerical advantage of the popular sectors has threatened to transform itself into real power, the reaction of the more privileged groups has been increasingly violent; thus, political power has tended to be cumulative throughout the region. In Latin America at least, liberalism has thus tended to be far more exclusionary than inclusionary.

Economic Liberalism, Political Democracy, and the Civil Society Nexus

Earlier literature was clearly wrong in suggesting that economic liberalization requires authoritarian governments. But does this mean successful economic liberalization requires political democracy? The short answer is no. As China since the late 1970s, South Korea and Taiwan during most of the postwar period, and Latin America during the late nineteenth century all attest, markets (and capitalism more generally) can prosper, if not thrive, without competitive and participative political systems. Economic freedom and political freedom are not synonymous. Regardless of any long-term association between economic development and democracy, there seems little reason to assume that such a relationship will hold for any particular country at any particular point in time or at any specific level of development.

Democracy, however, should be the goal of development (Bresser

Pereira, Maravall, and Przeworski, 1993). Even if (to say the least) an uneasy relationship exists between economic liberalization and political democracy in Latin America, this situation has little to do with markets per se; rather, it is the result of the *kinds* of markets (and capitalism) that have emerged in Latin America. To take political democracy for granted or to assume that it is inevitable once appropriate market-based reforms are in place assumes this interrelationship does not exist. This is exactly what much of the recent literature on economic restructuring has done: it has ignored the ways in which Latin America's "new" markets and development model may perpetuate and even exacerbate the structural causes of the historically problematic relationship between economic liberalization and democracy in the region.

The discussion here has emphasized the ways in which capitalist development has generated a highly unequal distribution of power within Latin American societies during periods of both economic liberalization and high levels of state regulation of the economy. The economic and political power of relatively small minorities in each country has been cumulative, reinforcing and reproducing over time a stratified social structure that, at best, has provided for only limited integration of select segments of the popular sectors. This situation is the exact opposite of the pluralist ideal in which the power of numbers can counteract the advantages of wealth and status through liberal democratic politics. It is also very different from the experience in the industrialized countries, where capitalist development has supported a genuinely inclusionary form of liberalism. Instead, throughout Latin America the stakes in any political game involving the popular sectors are raised dramatically in a struggle over the preservation of privilege versus greater social equity.

As a basis for attempting to (re)construct a critical theory of Latin American political economy, this focus on unequal power structures and social classes underscores the historical weakness of civil society in Latin America. As defined earlier, civil society is the social fabric formed by self-constituted groups representing distinct societal interests and identities. It is characterized by a dual dynamic in which those groups simultaneously resist subordination to the state and demand inclusion in national political structures.

It is important to emphasize that this dual dynamic of resistance and inclusion demonstrates why political democracy is often the result rather than the cause of a civil society. Historically, civil society emerged in Western Europe, for example, through a process of struggle among self-constituted units competing for jurisdiction and pursuing collective interests. Its emergence there reflected a relatively more equal preexisting distribution of power dating back to struggles over the establishment of the first medieval craft guilds and towns (Hall, 1995; Oxhorn, 1995a). This case illustrates how the strength of civil society reflects the dispersion of political power throughout polities, which ultimately contributes to the advent of stable democratic regimes supported by already strong, vibrant civil societies whose component elements struggled for democracy in the first place.

To the extent that capitalist development contributes to the emergence of strong civil societies, it also contributes to the correlation between development and political democracy, at least in developed countries. At the beginning of the industrialization process, general levels of social equity were significantly higher than has been the historical norm in Latin America. Similarly, industrialization created relatively larger working classes that could organize collectively into self-constituted units that altered the relative distribution of power within society to their benefit (Rueschemeyer, Stephens, and Stephens, 1992; Przeworski, 1985; CEPAL, 1989). Workers (and other collective actors) demanded inclusion in state policymaking processes and successfully resisted being subordinated to an all-powerful state. Numbers became a source of power, although not necessarily (and not exclusively) according to the pluralist ideal of one person, one vote but rather through workers' ability to constitute themselves into collective actors capable of defining and defending their collective interests. Civil society thus expanded and became stronger.

In Latin America, in many ways economic development has had the opposite effect: rather than contributing to the growing strength of civil society, it has reproduced preexisting levels of social inequality. Power has not been effectively dispersed throughout Latin American societies; instead, it has been concentrated at the level of the state and among members of the dominant class and, somewhat later and to a lesser degree, the middle sectors. For much of the twentieth century, the dual dynamic of resistance and inclusion that defines civil society has (often forcibly) been displaced by processes of controlled inclusion. Populism, corporatism, and clientelism have effectively limited the ability of different groups and social classes to constitute themselves into collective actors capable of defining and defending their collective interests in relations with other actors. Important exceptions, such as Chile, Uruguay, and Argentina, have allowed different societal groups to express themselves collectively, but the real redistribution of power central to the concept of civil society has proved an impossible goal over the longer term.

The argument that emerges from even this very schematic comparison of developed market economies and Latin America is that the strength of civil society mediates the relationship between economic and political liberalization. Where civil society is strong, economic liberalism is likely to be inclusionary and to lay the foundations for viable democratic regimes. At the extreme, one might even argue that economic liberalism then will ultimately *require* political democracy for continued economic dynamism, as seems to be the case in countries with the most highly developed market economies. Where civil society is weak, however, economic liberalism is likely to be exclusionary. The same factors that inhibit the growth of civil society are likely to reproduce themselves in highly segmented social structures that reflect varying extremes in the concentration of wealth and power. Democracy at best will remain fragile and will be limited to certain political rights (particularly the right to vote) at the expense of important civic and social rights of citizenship.[23]

Beyond comparing Latin America's experience with that of developed market economies, the concept of civil society is also useful for understanding important differences among countries within the region. By arguing that historically civil society in Latin America has been weak, we do not mean to imply that civil societies in specific countries are either equally weak or weak in the same ways.[24] As explained earlier, important differences exist in the structure and organization of civil society within the region that reflect each country's unique political economy. This proposed focus on civil society is valuable because it helps to highlight important differences and their consequences and allows for causal inferences that go beyond the simple correlations between economic liberalization and/or development and political democracy, however robust such correlations may be statistically.

As we stated at the outset, the current effort is only preliminary. The relationships and concepts developed here require more research and elaboration. In particular, future research needs to be directed toward three areas.

First, country-specific differences must be explored. Although a general Latin American "pattern" clearly exists, there are many important exceptions, and the history of each country is necessarily unique. More specifically, work needs to be done on the relationship between development policies or models and class structures in the particular context of each national economy. Similarly, the nature of collective actors and their relationships with each other and with the state must be explored in greater detail. In particular, the evolution and composition of the dominant classes in different Latin American countries and their changing relationship with the state merit more investigation.

Second, alternative ways of organizing civil society to overcome the collective action problems caused by the heterogeneity (and poverty) of the popular sectors need to be explored (Oxhorn, 1998b). Although we have emphasized the historical nature of both inequality and the weakness of civil society in Latin America, we do not wish to appear overly deterministic. Our emphasis on the need to study specific cases reflects our belief that alternatives do exist; one just needs to be creative in looking for them.

Similarly, the fact that almost every country in the region has a democratically elected government and at least some of the political and civic rights associated with democratic regimes suggests that new forms of collective action among the popular sectors might possibly emerge. The extreme nature of the economic dislocations since the early 1980s also appears to have generated new forms of popular-sector collective action in attempts to cope (Oxhorn, 1995a and 1995b).

Finally, the changing world economy and the demands of international economic competitiveness in the 1990s may offer new possibilities for converging interests among Latin America's social classes. Research should be directed at discovering (or creating) a societal consensus based on common interests in promoting more equitable development. Only then can a positive relationship between economic liberalization and democracy be taken for granted.

Notes

1. The correlation between economic development and democracy was first demonstrated by Lipset (1959). That conclusion has been the subject of countless subsequent studies. For recent reviews of that work, see Rueschemeyer, Stephens, and Stephens, 1992; and Lipset, 1994.

2. We are indebted to Pamela Starr for the neomodernization label.

3. We are borrowing this concept from Marshall (1950).

4. Argentina, Brazil, Chile, and Mexico experienced a period of political instability between 1889 and 1893 as positivist authoritarianism was openly challenged by liberals. In Chile, a civil war broke out in 1891 and ended with a liberal victory (Dabéne, 1994).

5. Uruguay, which temporarily adopted a variant of the new authoritarian-progressive credo beginning in 1880, was unique in incorporating subaltern classes at the beginning of the twentieth century. This incorporation took place, however, under a regime (*batllismo*) in which economic liberalism was replaced by a strong interventionist state.

6. For example, the incidence of extreme poverty in Mexico fell from 69.5 percent in 1963 to 57.7 percent in 1977 and 29.9 percent in 1984. See Lustig, 1992.

7. Argentina, which experienced two military coups during the period, was not included because of a lack of data on income inequality. The other four examples were Lebanon, Malaysia, the Philippines, and Turkey. It is also worth noting that historically Chile and Uruguay, as well as Argentina, have been among the most equal of all Latin American societies.

8. Gini coefficients vary between 0—perfect equality—and 1. High levels of income inequality exist not only between classes but also between regions in both countries. The disparity in wealth between the richest and poorest states in Brazil was eight to one; even among the relatively richer states, the disparity was three to one. In Mexico, this regional disparity was six to one. In contrast, the disparity in wealth between rich and poor regions in countries such as the United States and even India is no more than two to one (World Bank, 1992).

9. A large body of literature now exists that examines the basic elements of this approach throughout the region. See Oxhorn and Ducatenzeiler, 1994; Graham, 1994; and Ward, 1993.

10. The following discussion is based on Ruiz-Tagle (1993). See also Muñoz and Celedón, 1993; Vergara, 1994; and Garretón, 1994b.

11. This figure compares to a rate of 36 percent in 1979 and was significantly higher than the 28.5 percent rate reached in 1969. See Barrera, 1998.

12. Some slight discrepancies are found in the statistics reported by Barrera (1998) and Ruiz-Tagle (1993) that reflect different data sources. Those discrepancies, however, do not alter the conclusion that the income shares going to the poorest 20 percent of Chilean households dropped by about 40 percent between 1969 and 1992. The income share of the bottom 60 percent of households declined by over 25 percent during the period, whereas that for the upper 20 percent grew by approximately 25 percent, reaching 55.1 percent of total income in 1992.

13. The following section is based primarily on Beccaria (1993).

14. It is worth noting that Lustig arrived at these conclusions in 1992 before the current crisis exploded in December 1994.

15. Chile's recent experience also contradicts the basic economic logic behind the trickle-down theories of growth undergirding the neoliberal approach to development. Sustained economic growth should have led to a redistribution of income as the economy approached full employment because market pressures would have led to a rise in real wages. In Chile, unemployment levels and inflation (which can erode real wages) reached historic lows, and real wages even increased (see Chapter 5). Yet, these developments did not produce the expected income redistribution. Ironically, the reason for this failure has much to do with the severity of the preceding economic crisis: the income share of the poor and near poor was so low that even dramatic changes in the circumstances of individual families did not alter the overall distribution of income (conversation with Alvaro Díaz, May 1995).

16. The arguments in this paragraph are drawn largely from Oszlak (1981). Also see O'Donnell (1988) for the case of Argentina. In Chile, a strong centralized state was established much earlier than was the case in most of the region and with considerably less development of the state's repressive apparatus, which Oszlak attributes to the higher level of elite homogeneity in Chile than in other countries. In any event, the economic expansion made possible by growing export opportunities had the same effects as in other countries in terms of the state's expansion and penetration of national territory, as well as of the configuration of class forces. Militarization also played an important role, especially during the War of the Pacific (1879–1883) in which Chile's national territory expanded by more than one-third to include the mineral-rich Atacama Desert. See Oxhorn, 1995a.

17. To some extent, the incorporation of the middle sectors corresponded to Latin America's first wave of democracy. But middle-sector incorporation did not necessarily entail political democracy, even if it did increase political participation. For example, Mexico's revolutionary process can be seen as essentially middle class in terms of which social groups benefited most. See Hamilton, 1982; and Eckstein, 1988. Similarly, middle-sector incorporation in Brazil is more closely associated with the authoritarian *Estado Novo* in the late 1930s and early 1940s than with Brazil's subsequent experiment with liberal democracy from 1945 until the 1964 military coup.

18. The following discussion is drawn from CEPAL, 1989; Fajnzylber, 1990; Altimir, 1990; and Pinto, 1970.

19. These include cases of "preemptive" political liberalization, such as Brazil

in the early 1970s (Skidmore, 1989). They would also include (even rarer) instances in which the dominant class experiences expanded suffrage in its interests as its different factions compete peacefully for political power (Valenzuela, 1985). In these instances, however, elites attempted to impose strict limits on political liberalization that were later undermined through social mobilization.

20. Brazil is unique because the current government must confront powerful interest groups that developed during the latter years of the dictatorship and preceding democratic governments. Both business groups and the labor movement have become more active and more autonomous of the government. Labor in particular has increased its strength significantly by organizing public-sector workers since the adoption of the 1988 constitution. This increase in the power of interest groups contrasts with the weakening of executive decisionmaking capacity as the executive must continually negotiate with political parties (there are currently nineteen in the parliament) and interest groups. See Chapters 4 and 6 in this volume.

21. State reforms have also hurt large segments of the middle sectors who have lost their jobs and opportunities for social mobility.

22. Unions were given the right to organize in the public sector by the 1988 constitution.

23. Marshall (1950) distinguishes among civil, political, and social rights of citizenship. It is worth noting that Marshall's discussion of the evolution of citizenship rights illustrates the increasingly inclusionary nature of liberalism in Great Britain. The exclusionary aspects of liberalism in Latin America today are analyzed in O'Donnell (1993); Oxhorn (1998a and 1998b); and Acuña and Smith (1994).

24. This is also true regarding the general decline in state institutional capacity in recent years.

2

Civil Society, State Capacity, and the Conflicting Logics of Economic and Political Change

Carlos H. Waisman

In this chapter I focus on the crucial role played by civil society and state capacity in the determination of the outcomes of the economic and political transformations under way in most of Latin America. I make two claims. The first is that a clash between the conflicting logics of economic and political liberalization has been prevented so far by inhibiting factors, some of which are likely to lose their effectiveness in the long run. When that happens, the outcomes of the resulting transformation will depend largely on the strength of civil society and the capacity of the state. The second claim is that economic liberalization and the consolidation of democracy are affecting civil society and state capacity in complex ways. Even if these two factors can sustain a continuation of the double transformation, the outcome is likely to be a dualization of society and polity. My discussion will be theoretical, but the empirical reference will be the most heavily industrialized countries of South America—those of the Southern Cone.[1]

Too often, civil society is left undefined in the transitions literature. Frequently, it is vaguely understood as the realm of social life outside the state or sometimes, more specifically, as the network of social movements in a society or as a property of social intercourse. I think civil society is best conceptualized as a slice of society, the other slices being the economy, the state, and the family and community structure (neighborhoods and other nonassociational groups, informal networks). Its core is the web of voluntary associations of all kinds, which stands between the economy and the family-community structure on the one hand and the state on the other. The relationship between civil society and the state is best understood on the basis of two dimensions: autonomy and capacity for self-regulation. Both are relative: even in the most democratic societies, the autonomy of private associations is limited by institutions—the state in particular—and the self-regulation of conflict among representative associations is constrained by the legal, administrative, and political frameworks within which they operate.

Civil society is strong when the web of voluntary associations is large, the associations in question are highly autonomous from the state, and the web has a high capacity for self-regulation through bargaining among its units. A strong civil society requires not only de Tocqueville's "art of association" but the institutionalization of that art as well. This situation differs from three others in which civil society is not present or is very weak: the case in which autonomous groups do not exist (either because the society is atomized or because of repression), the instance in which they exist but are controlled by the state (the state corporatist pattern), and the condition in which powerful autonomous associations exist but conflict among them is intense and occurs outside institutional channels (the praetorian case).

State capacity refers basically to the effectiveness with which policies are made and implemented. State capacity is independent of political regime: both democratic and authoritarian regimes vary in terms of the effectiveness of their states. Low effectiveness may result from factors such as the sheer incompetence of the staff in the state apparatus, lack of adequate material resources, the inadequacy of the laws or rules within which the state works, corruption, or insufficient autonomy vis-à-vis elites and other strategic groups in the society.

The political consequences of a weak state capacity vary according to the extent of state control of the society and the strength of civil society. Obviously, the larger the scope of the state, the more devastating the consequences of its ineffectiveness: an incapable state may bring havoc to a Manchesterian capitalist society but would be lethal to a state socialist one. If we restrict the discussion to the liberal democratic model in a contemporary capitalist society in which the state has limited functions, the consequences of weak state capacity would depend on the strength of civil society. When civil society is strong, nothing will save defense, security, and justice from state incompetence, but society may still manage large areas of education, health, and social security with a minimum of effectiveness. When civil society is weak, an incompetent state contributes to the erosion of the social order, a process whose consequences might be fatal in the extreme case not only for democracy but also for the nation-state itself.

The range of possible outcomes in such a situation would vary according to the type of weak civil society that exists. When society is atomized or fused with the state through corporatist mechanisms, possible outcomes would range from a vicious type of privatization of state functions (which should be distinguished from the virtuous type discussed earlier in the case of a strong civil society)—carried out on the basis of mechanisms that could include clientelism, corruption, and even organized crime—to outright despotism. In the praetorian instance of a weak civil society, a state with limited capabilities would facilitate a dynamic leading to mass praetorianism and eventually to an intense level of polarization that might trigger demobilizing forms of authoritarianism, as occurred in the Southern Cone in the 1970s. In extreme situations, the confluence of either of these varieties of a weak civil society with a low-capacity state might even trigger scenarios in which the very unity of the nation-state is called into question.

The strength of civil society and the capacity of the state are central factors in all of the sociopolitical processes that make up the economic and political transformations I discuss. These transformations include the decay of the economic and political institutions that made up the "old regimes" (autarkic capitalism in the economy and, recently, authoritarian regimes in the polity), the modalities of the transitions away from those regimes, and the characteristics of the economic and political transformations under way.

In what follows, I briefly discuss the contradictory social logics that guide the economic and political transformations in question and present hypotheses to explain why these logics have not yet clashed. I then examine the current state of and prospects for civil society and state capacity in the region.

The Conflicting Logics
and Inhibiting Factors of Change

Industrialized countries in South America have been undergoing large-scale economic liberalization in the context of recently established democracies. Economic and political liberalizations are governed by opposing social logics, a fact that might hinder one or both processes.

This potential for a clash between the contradictory logics depends greatly on the sequence in which economic and political liberalizations have taken place, but it exists in all cases. There are three possible sequences for economic and political liberalization. The first corresponds to the case in which privatization, deregulation, and the opening up of the economy precede democratization; Chile is an example. A second pattern is one in which the sequence is reversed, as, for instance, in Venezuela. The most frequent situation is one in which economic liberalization and the consolidation of democracy take place more or less at the same time; Argentina and Brazil are cases in point. This last sequence is the least favorable because the potential for conflict between the logics that govern the two processes is the highest. Let us examine the logics in question.

Privatization, deregulation, and the opening up of the economy are instances of the logic of differentiation. These processes increase the differentiation within a society in both the vertical and horizontal senses: polarization between the affluent and the deprived widens, as does the gulf between winners and losers within each social class and that between sectors of the economy and regions of the country. Both upward and downward mobility intensify. The Marxist image of affluence and misery growing at the same time in different poles of society is eminently applicable to this situation. Competitive sectors, or those shielded from foreign competition (for example, producers and providers of nontradable goods, such as many services), expand, whereas the least competitive branches of the economy, or those most dependent on strata negatively affected by economic liberalization, contract. Regions that house the expanding sectors are likely to thrive, whereas those that have specialized in activities that now appear nonviable will turn into rust belts or their agrarian equivalents.

The consolidation of democracy is governed by the logic of mobilization. In a recently established democracy, the activation and organization of groups hurt by the liberalization of the economy are facilitated by two factors. First, democracy allows for and induces mass political participation; moreover, in the new conditions the potential costs of mass political action are usually much lower than was the case under the preexisting repressive regime. Second, a young democracy induces political entrepreneurship: access to the political elite is now open to those who represent social and political constituencies. Activists and militants rush to service already mobilized groups and try to form and mobilize potential power bases. Economic liberalization is an ideal environment for group formation, for it gives competing political entrepreneurs inventories of grievances that easily translate into political agendas. Thus, from both below and above, institutional factors are conducive to articulation by movements of resistance to economic liberalization.

These two logics have the potential for inhibiting each other and, consequently, for blocking or derailing economic liberalization, the consolidation of democracy, or both—which is why the simultaneous pattern is less favorable than either of the other two. In the Chilean sequence, the political effects of the social dislocation produced by economic liberalization were contained by an authoritarian regime; in the Venezuelan pattern, the social order undergoing disarticulation could draw, at least for some time, from the capital of legitimacy accumulated by democratic institutions over several decades. In any case, the potential for collision between the logics remains in all three sequences.

And yet, the great transformation in economic and political institutions is occurring. Substantial conflicts have been attributable in part to these logics (outside the Southern Cone, examples include the Chiapas uprising and the turmoil in Venezuela, both of which had other important institutional causes as well), but thus far no blockage or breakdown has occurred as a consequence of the interaction between them. I argue that the clash between the opposing logics has been avoided thus far because of the operation of three "cushions," or moderating factors, that have inhibited political mobilization. These factors can be called the structural, the institutional, and the cognitive-ideological.

The structural cushion consists simply of the fact that economic liberalization weakens and destroys the power bases of the coalitions supporting the "old regime" (entrepreneurs, unions, and in some cases public-sector managers and workers) and, in general, those of all the groups hurt by trade liberalization, privatization, and deregulation. The processes of economic transformation generate insecurity and economic deprivation and thus discontent. Impoverishment and marginalization, however, also reduce the groups' capacity for organization and mobilization in defense of their interests.

The relationship between impoverishment or growing insecurity and capacity for mobilization varies according to the intensity of the threat. Three levels can be distinguished in this connection. The first corresponds to the case in which substantial danger is perceived. Workers, businesspeople, and middle-class groups facing threats to their standard of living or economic security will usually be able to deploy the power resources under their control (numbers, organization, wealth) whenever the threat is intense but its materialization is not perceived as inevitable. The second level involves the situation in which the threat is extremely intense, and its materialization appears not only inevitable but also imminent. In such a case, mobilization capacity may be inhibited by two factors. First, people start focusing their energy and attention on survival and on the search for individual exit options. Second, specifically for the working class, is the deterrent effect of the formation of a large labor reserve army that usually emerges in such a situation.

The third level is that in which individuals have already been expelled from their regular positions in the working or middle classes. In this case, their capacity for collective action is very limited, again for two reasons— one psychological and the other structural. The first reason is the sheer demoralization that usually follows downward mobility. The second has to do with the fact that except in company towns and similar settings, people in this situation are likely to weaken or cut ties both among themselves and with their class of origin. Lower classes in this condition are characterized by political apathy punctuated by infrequent, highly inorganic (although not usually spontaneous), and very short-lived outbursts of activity that is sometimes violent.

The second cushion is the institutional. New institutions inhibit mobilization—either indirectly, by legitimating economic liberalization, or directly, by blocking the activation of some of the groups hurt by privatization, deregulation, or the opening up of the economy.

New or recently reformulated institutional mechanisms are a central aspect of economic and political liberalization, and some have a legitimating potential. In the economic sphere, this is obviously the case with the privatization of pensions, for instance, or the establishment of a safety net for the poorest strata. Advocates of economic liberalization could claim that the new pension policy, in addition to strengthening capital markets, converts citizens into stakeholders and that the new safety net alleviates some of the strongest negative consequences of the collapse of the "old regime" (and perhaps of the instauration of the new one). These mechanisms might give the entire transformation process (which is widely perceived as an indivisible package) legitimacy. But changes in economic institutions may also block collective action. The flexibilization of labor markets is the most conspicuous case: it reduces trade union strength, as well as workers' job security.

In the political sphere, the reestablishment of competitive politics (even where democracy is limited, inefficient, and riddled with corruption) has had a legitimating effect not only on political institutions but on economic policies and institutions as well. Constitutional and legal reforms, which have been extensive in many societies undergoing transitions, have also contributed to the legitimation of the new political regime and, indirectly, of its economic policies.

The final cushion is the cognitive-ideological one, whose sources are both external and internal. The exogenous sources are international demonstration effects: economic nationalists and leftists have been affected by the collapse of communism and the apparent success of the Thatcher-Reagan economic policies in the 1970s and 1980s. The endogenous factor is the process of political learning experienced by state, political, economic, and cultural elites, which was triggered by the economic and political consequences of the "old regime."

In Argentina, Chile, and Uruguay, the institutions of autarkic capitalism, which appeared so promising when they were implemented during the Depression and World War II, led to modern societies and stagnant economies in the 1960s and 1970s. In the 1970s this explosive mixture triggered revolutionary situations, with highly repressive military regimes as their aftermath. Those experiences led strategic elites to conclude that autarkic capitalism was simply not viable. The case of Brazil is interesting, for because of the sheer size of its internal market and the state's greater capacity to steer the economy, the long-term economic consequences of autarkic capitalism were not yet evident when it embarked on large-scale economic liberalization. In this instance, political learning and international demonstration effects fused, for elites interpreted the evolution of Argentina and Chile as the writing on the wall: if the long-term effects of autarkic capitalism in those countries had been stagnation and illegitimacy, the same would surely be the case in Brazil.

Everywhere in the world, the cumulative effect of these cognitive processes has been both the abandonment of autarkic capitalism and acceptance of the liberal model. In some cases, this acceptance took the form of active support (sometimes as a result of surprising conversions, as was also the case in Central and Eastern Europe), whereas in others it was the product of the ideological paralysis caused by the exhaustion of alternatives. Essentially at the same time, state socialism and autarkic capitalism—two forms of neomercantilism[2]—failed, and open market capitalism, apparently triumphant, was the only option left. One can speculate that the conversion to this radical alternative in both South America and Eastern Europe was caused by the simultaneity of the demise of autarkic capitalism and state socialism. If one of these regimes had appeared viable when the other was collapsing, one can hypothesize that substantial segments of the strategic elites in the other regime would have oriented themselves toward the kindred neomercantilist alternative.

The Weakening of Inhibiting Factors

I believe the efficacy of two of the inhibiting factors, the institutional and the cognitive-ideological, is likely to decrease over time. The structural cushion will continue to dualize society and block the mobilization of those hurt by economic liberalization, but the effectiveness of the other two factors will become contingent on the perception by different social groups that the reforms under way are in their interest. That perception depends, in the last instance, on economic performance: if the open economy does well, social expenditure could expand, and the institutions of the mature welfare state could be established, thus strengthening the existing consensus. On the other hand, if economic performance is unsatisfactory, social inequality would increase, the welfare state would remain rudimentary, and consensus on the continuation of economic reform would eventually erode.

Social behavior, however, is a reaction not to the facts themselves but to the interpretation of those facts. For this reason, the future of the double transformation will be a function not only of economic performance but also of the strength of civil society and the capacity of the state. This is the case for two reasons. First, the successful institutionalization of an open market capitalist economy and a stable and effective liberal democracy requires both a strong civil society and a satisfactory level of state capacity. Second, during the transformation process these factors could compensate for the negative consequences of the possible erosion of the institutional and ideological cushions. Only a strong civil society would be able to prevent either mass apathy or mass praetorianism, institutionalize consociational patterns of bargaining, and develop a long-term horizon for satisfying interests within which consensus on the continuation of economic reform and the distribution of its costs could be processed. The performance of basic state functions, including those connected with social policy, in a way the most important social forces would consider acceptable presupposes a state with a reasonable level of competence.

None of the relatively industrialized Latin American countries looks like an East Asian "tiger," even though Chile approaches that model in several respects. The countries in the region also vary in terms of the size of their competitive or easily convertible sectors, their location in relation to export markets, their endowment of natural resources that have favorable market prospects, and their stock of human capital. For these reasons, the outlook for economic growth is variable.

In the rest of the chapter I will focus on the other two determinants: the strength of civil society and the capacity of the state. The vigor of these factors is generally more limited than that of countries in Western Europe, the best performers in Central Europe, and the newly industrialized countries of East Asia, but differences are found among the countries under consideration.

In focusing on the need for these two factors, I am not making a functionalist argument in the sense that they would be "prerequisites" for (and their absence an "obstacle" to) the institutionalization of capitalist democracy. I see the strength of civil society and the capacity of the state not as attributes but as ordinal variables. A functioning liberal democracy does not require high levels of either, but it would not operate very effectively or legitimately without adequate levels. For example, it is difficult to conceive of a strong liberal democracy in which most of the population is apathetic and marginal to politics, is involved in associations controlled by the state, or participates in organizations that engage in the acute social conflict Samuel Huntington has called "mass praetorianism" (Huntington, 1968). That is also true for a state that is incapable of extracting from society substantial revenue through taxation or of imparting justice and managing public health, education, and social security with minimum effectiveness.

Current Civil Society and State Capacity

In South America today, significant differences exist between countries: civil society seems to be stronger in Argentina than in Peru, and state capacity is higher in Chile than in Argentina. Some commonalities can be discerned, however, especially in the Southern Cone.

Typically, the state is contracting at the same time it is shedding, where they exist, the corporatist mechanisms through which it has controlled labor and other segments of society. Government effectiveness, however, remains questionable in most policy areas.

Understanding changes in civil society is more complicated,[3] for that society is stronger in some senses and weaker in others than was true in the autarkic capitalist period. On the one hand, civil society has less capacity than was the case in previous democratic or semidemocratic stages to resist attacks by the state (as is seen in labor's inability to confront neoliberal economic policies), but on the other hand, some sectors are more autonomous vis-à-vis the state and show a greater ability for self-regulation. Two indicators of this phenomenon are the consensus among substantial segments of the elites (economic, political, and, in some cases, trade unions) about the desirability of a shift to open market capitalism and the fact that since the reestablishment of democracy, most forms of social conflict have been managed within institutional channels.

The weakness of civil society in relation to previous democratic or semidemocratic periods can be understood through two factors. The first involves the changes in the social structure produced by the crisis of autarkic capitalism and the beginnings of economic liberalization in many countries under authoritarian rule. The second factor entails, for labor and the Left, the effects of repression suffered under the military regimes.

For the bourgeoisie in almost all countries, the slowdown and stagnation under autarkic capitalism led to a crisis in the sectors most dependent on mass consumption. Further, economic liberalization weakened the sectors most threatened by foreign competition while strengthening the most competitive ones. Labor was weakened directly by the deindustrialization that followed the crisis of autarkic capitalism and the beginnings of economic liberalization and by repression, but the most important factor has been the change in the social environment within which unions operate: as poverty, job insecurity, and unemployment grew among the labor force that had stable jobs, labor's mobilizational potential plummeted.

On the other hand, the new maturity of civil society, again in relation to previous democratic periods, has been the result of the cognitive processes discussed earlier—the political learning from the economic and political crises in which autarkic capitalism floundered and the international demonstration effects. The collapse of communism and the statist and nationalist ideologies that also circulated in the region (from doctrinaire corporatism and right-wing nationalism to the CEPAL [Comisión Económica para América Latina y el Caribe] Doctrine and dependency theory) have contributed to this maturity but not because the presence of those ideologies would inherently lead to intense confrontation among social forces. Consider, for example, the strength of civil society in Italy and France, which had large and disciplined Communist parties and labor movements controlled by those parties during the Cold War.

Mass praetorianism in the 1960s and 1970s was less the result of radical ideologies as such than of the long-term structural consequences of autarkic capitalism mentioned earlier: stagnation in the economy and modernization in society—that is, the processes of industrialization, urbanization, and growth of education that generated large working and middle classes, the intelligentsia included. Rather than direct causes of the intense social and political conflicts of the period, those ideologies were intervening factors. They provided the prism through which middle and working classes interpreted the self-limited nature of autarkic capitalist development.

The collapse of those ideologies left ideologically oriented actors disarmed and without frameworks for understanding the new state of affairs. Many reoriented themselves toward formulations that were social democratic or even liberal (in the Latin American and continental sense of the term), which contributed to the disappearance of the fear of revolution that in the past had been a dominant factor in the political action of elites.

The consequences of economic transformation on civil society are complex. On the one hand, such transformation produces the social dislocation discussed previously; on the other, it solidifies autonomous associations in some areas of social life (both vertically and horizontally, among the class segments and regions that are the "winners" in the process of economic differentiation) and decreases state penetration of society. These processes may help to generate a system of bargaining and peaceful conflict resolution among interest groups—that is, help to enhance societal self-regulation. This, as we have seen, is what the nebulous formula "a strong civil society" so popular among students of transitions actually means: the existence of strong networks of autonomous associations that represent interests as well as values and that limit the power of the state because of their ability to manage social processes through interaction within institutional channels.

Regarding the strengthening of state capacity, it should be clear that an open market economy and an efficient democracy presuppose a state not only smaller but also stronger than the one that existed under autarkic capitalism. The state would be smaller not only because it would encompass a more limited proportion of the labor force and produce a more modest share of the gross domestic product (GDP) but also because its ability to regulate society and control its organizations would be drastically reduced. But it would be stronger vis-à-vis society, for it would have enhanced capabilities—again, compared with the autarkic capitalist state—to extract resources through taxation, administer justice, and manage defense, health, education, and social security in a more effective manner.

The current period represents an inflection point in the relationship between state and society. The danger is that the social dislocation produced by economic liberalization could either increase the atomization of society and lead to mass anomie or facilitate praetorian mobilization. The first outcome would entail a deterioration of the already modest quality of the new democracies, whereas the second would lead to disturbances ("social explosions," such as those that occurred in Argentina and Venezuela in the early 1990s) that might trigger the autonomization of the armed forces and, in extreme situations, set in motion a process that could culminate in authoritarian regimes, with or without a constitutional facade. Neither extreme scenario appears (so far) to be on the horizon for the Southern Cone societies.

Prospects for Civil Society and State Capacity

The strength of civil society and state capacity differ in terms of their amenability to agency, particularly to government intervention. Whereas political or governmental action might lead to improved state capacity, the strength of civil society is primarily a function of the broader social institutions and the culture of the society. This differential susceptibility to agency results in part from the fact that improved state capacity and the strengthening of civil society imply contrary changes in the relationship of power between the state and society. Increased state capacity often entails a higher concentration of some kinds of state power, which is a condition for greater autonomy and managerial effectiveness. On the other hand, the strengthening of civil society involves not only a relatively low level of centralization of social power but also an enhanced self-regulatory capacity of these autonomous social actors and thus a reduced jurisdiction of the state.

This argument does not imply that civil society is impervious to institutional design. The difference is one of degree, not of kind. Institutional design may enhance state capacity (for example, by professionalizing the higher civil service, streamlining procedures, reducing state functions to the basic ones, generating incentives for compliance with the law, and so forth), but it may also contribute to strengthening autonomous associations and increasing their capacity for self-regulation. This is what happens, for instance, when state and religion are effectively separated or when corporatist mechanisms for regulating labor relations are replaced with collective bargaining procedures that minimize government involvement.

Economic Liberalization,
Democratic Consolidation, and Civil Society

I will now look in more detail at the effects of economic liberalization on civil society in the institutional context of a recently established democracy. As I argued earlier, some aspects of this complex transformation strengthen civil society, whereas others weaken it.

The positive effects include, on the one hand, the removal of constraints on the operation of interest groups and, on the other, the generation of incentives for strengthening civil society. The removal of constraints includes, first, the reduction or disappearance of obstacles to group organization by dismantling the repressive apparatus of the authoritarian state and, second, the relaxation or elimination of "positive" corporatist controls (co-optation mechanisms) over interest groups and other voluntary organizations.

In the area of incentives, the economic and political transformation contributes to strengthening civil society, also in two ways. First, democratic institutions nurture the associations and movements that make up civil society, for, as we have seen, they promote group formation and impel political and interest groups to develop and represent specific constituencies. Second, the functioning of an open market economy requires periodic bargaining over wages, conditions of employment, and prices in response to changing market conditions. Thus, it is conducive to the emergence and consolidation of a bargaining culture among interest groups and to the gradual institutionalization of non-zero-sum conflicts among them, which facilitates the spread of mechanisms for the management of social conflict that do not involve the state as a decisionmaker (a situation that is compatible with a governmental role as a regulator or last-instance adjudicator). This is the institutional environment in which societal self-regulation is likely to grow.

We also know, however, that economic liberalization and democratization weaken civil society in two ways. First, economic liberalization produces economic and social fragmentation, as pointed out earlier. What I called the logic of differentiation continues to operate; its cumulative effect is likely to be the dualization of society into a "civic" pole, characterized by strong associations and capacity for self-regulation, and a "disorganized" or marginalized one, with a low level of autonomous group organization and a low capacity for sustained mobilization—a description that fits one of the weak civil society cases discussed previously. The ensuing forms of political action would be citizenship in the first case and either apathy, perhaps punctuated by short-lived mobilization, or subordinate participation in the second case.

Second, democracy facilitates the development of protest groups and movements, but its main effect in this regard is likely to be the reinforcement of dualization. Marginalized strata and regions have lower rates of political participation and fewer resources that could be converted into political influence. Political parties and government agencies will be more likely to interact with and engage the civic segment; therefore, democracy will become a game whose strongest and most permanent players will be the organizations and groups within that pole. Parties and governments may build constituencies within marginalized groups and regions, and those constituencies may jump to the center of the political stage in some situations (especially when they display noninstitutionalized forms of behavior). The relationships between them and the government and parties, however, are likely to be clientelistic or state-corporatist and thus not conducive to the strengthening of civil society.

The overall effect of simultaneous economic liberalization and consolidation of democracy is, therefore, the segmentation of society into an organized and autonomous sector that looks very much like a strong civil society and a disorganized or dependent sector susceptible to political marginality or subordination to the state. Such a partition has always existed in the Southern Cone (much less so in Uruguay and Argentina than in Chile and especially Brazil), but it is intensifying and will further intensify as economic liberalization advances. Such a gulf is found in all democracies, and Ralf Dahrendorf (1988) has argued that the cleavage between the "organized" and "disorganized" sectors is becoming the central one in advanced capitalist countries. In those richer and more internationally competitive societies, however, the civic segment is much larger than that in the poorer, emerging countries that are in the midst of transformation.

In some countries, the spatial organization of the economy into cores and peripheries will likely lead to a situation in which the civic and disorganized fragments are territorially based, essentially like the Italy described by Robert D. Putnam (1993). In other cases, "strong" and "weak" kinds of civil society and "northern" and "southern" types of social structure would be adjacent to each other and would interpenetrate, basically like the pattern that exists in many large metropolitan areas in the United States. The proportions would be reversed in those societies, however; civic spots would exist in a background of marginality and state corporatism.

In the first of these cases, the cumulation of territorial cleavages and social fracture could lead to a deepening of dualism and in some instances to intense regional polarization. This situation might produce either the emergence of centrifugal political movements in the "rich" regions, as in Italy, or the breakdown of public order in the "poor" ones, as in Mexico. Such polarization will be more likely when the economic and social segmentation is also correlated with cultural or ethnic differences (whether real or imagined) or with distinct historical trajectories. Several South American countries, including Argentina and Brazil, have substantial potential for developing inducements to political entrepreneurship along these lines.

In the second case, that of interpenetration, the prospect would be the decay of democracy and its transformation into a mere facade. The exclusionary and clientelistic pattern of the relationship between state and society characteristic of the weak civil society would submerge the autonomous and pluralistic participatory model prevailing in those segments with a strong associational life.

Economic Liberalization, Democratic Consolidation, and State Capacity

As was the case with civil society, state capacity is also enhanced in some respects and weakened in others by economic liberalization and the consolidation of democracy. Two of the positive consequences stem from economic liberalization and a third from democratization. In the first economic liberalization case, privatization, deregulation, and the opening up of the economy reduce the functions of the state, which may allow the state to concentrate its organizational and human resources on the functions that remain—security and defense, the administration of justice, public health, education, and social security. Second, economic liberalization weakens or eliminates rentistic segments of the capitalist class and their labor counterparts, which ends the colonization of the state by distributional coalitions.

Democracy promotes state capacity by canalizing demands toward the basic functions of government. Therefore, the fulfillment of those core functions becomes critical; it becomes something that might contribute to improving government effectiveness. Nothing concentrates politicians' minds more than the threat of nonreelection because of poor performance, and in open market capitalist societies the standard for evaluation of politicians by the electorate is performance in these areas. Management of the economy in particular remains paramount, and the state is likely to focus its resources in that area to maintain "business confidence" and therefore enhance the likelihood of politicians' reelection.[4]

Economic liberalization and democratization may also have consequences that hamper the growth of state capacity. Economic liberalization by itself does not reduce state capacity as such, but its social effects discussed earlier increase the need for effective government action in some areas (social policy in particular), which is likely to increase the gap between actual and expected outcomes of state action. The consequence would be a reduction of perceived state effectiveness and thus of the legitimacy of the state, especially among people in the marginal or disorganized sector, even if their demand-making capacity is limited. This situation would increase their apathy and alienation.

Regarding the effect of the new democratic institutions on state capacity, the selective institutionalization of incentives for improved effectiveness, discussed earlier, has its downside. Such institutionalization might also mean that the functions most critical for reducing social segmentation will not be considered central by state managers. The stewardship of the economy (especially the levels of inflation and unemployment) and the maintenance of law and order (the physical security of citizens in particular) are likely to be more central criteria for the electorate's evaluation of politicians than performance in areas such as health and education. For that reason, state failure in fulfilling these other functions is less likely to produce intense, generalized social demands and therefore to create a sense of urgency among politicians and government officials.

The operation of two mechanisms explains this situation. The first is the contradiction between individual and collective interests, which applies mainly to taxation. Most taxpayers perceive more effective taxation to be against their interests; this is especially true for groups with greater capacity for organization and mobilization. Therefore, they are unlikely to demand greater efficiency in this area. People who pay little or no tax, however, would benefit objectively from more effective tax collection, and improved government efficiency in this area would cost them little individually. They are also the people, however, who have less ability to mobilize and organize. In fact, even taxpayers for whom efficient taxation would entail a major cost will likely profit from the expected benefits in areas such as public health and education. But costs for those taxpayers would be definite and immediate, whereas gains would be uncertain and mediate; thus, they are likely to focus mainly on costs.

The second mechanism is a typical collective action problem that applies to health, education, and social security. Most citizens are aware of serious deficiencies in state management of those areas, and improved state performance would obviously be in their interest, but such issues are seen as more distant and less urgent than those that deal with economic and physical security. Therefore, they are less likely to trigger intense, generalized mobilization.

Thus, the overall effect of economic liberalization and democracy on state capacity is also complex: the great transformation may increase the autonomy of the state, but it may also focus the state's energies on macroeconomic policy and the maintenance of law and order to the detriment of education, health, and social policy. These effects are likely to interact with those I pointed out earlier in connection with civil society: not only are social demands unlikely to induce this partially effective state to carry out policies aimed at diminishing the segmentation of society, but the balance of societal demands might lead to policies whose unintended consequence is the widening of the gap between the civic and disorganized segments of society. Again, such processes are also at work in advanced capitalist countries, but the effects are less intense in those societies because their internal differentiation is weaker, their civil societies are stronger, and their states are more effective than is the case in the new South American democracies.

The New Political Cycle in the Southern Cone

Even if the workings of civil society and the effectiveness of the state can prevent a clash between the logic of differentiation and the logic of mobilization, the outlook in the sociopolitical sphere is for the persistence of the dual or combined pattern of development most Latin American societies have experienced in the socioeconomic sphere throughout most of their history. But this outcome is contingent rather than the ineluctable consequence of structural determination. There is no reason to think social and political segmentation is necessary or that it will be permanent. Assuming civil society and state capacity are strong enough for the double transformation to continue until the economy has found its new place in the international division of labor, the interplay of these two factors and economic performance will eventually determine the extent to which civil society and autonomous democratic participation broaden and thicken.

In any case, this will be a long process. A new political cycle is starting in the Southern Cone, the third since the Depression and World War II. The first was that of statist democracy, whose institutional forms were populist-corporatist in Argentina and Brazil and pluralist in Chile and Uruguay. The relationship between state and society in that period was dominated by the dynamics of incorporation and praetorianism. In all countries in the area, the second cycle was the authoritarian one, whose political dynamics were those of demobilization and exclusion. The cycle opening now is that of mass liberal democracy, and its politics will be governed by the dynamics of association and autonomy. Unlike the previous cycles, this one is not grounded in inherently self-limiting institutions (economic in the first case and political in the second) but allows for the institutionalization of very different kinds of polities.

Notes

1. In the early 1990s, the industrial share of GDP was 31 percent in Argentina, 38 percent in Brazil, 36 percent in Chile (1985), and 32 percent in Uruguay.

Industry comprised 28 percent of the labor force in Argentina, 28 percent in Brazil, 29 percent in Chile, and 29 percent in Uruguay (1980–1985). See World Bank, 1995a and 1995b.

2. Autarkic capitalism and state socialism can be called neomercantilist because they shared two central characteristics pointed out by Jacob Viner in his classic treatment of the subject: high levels of statization and regulation of the domestic economy, and relative isolation vis-à-vis the world capitalist economy. Both values were higher under state socialism. See Viner, 1958.

3. For a discussion of the background and current state of civil society in Latin America, see Oxhorn (1995a).

4. On "business confidence" and politicians' strategies, see Block (1987). On politicians' self-interest in the great transformation in Latin America and Eastern Europe, see Geddes (1996).

3

Social and Economic Transformations in Latin America: The Emergence of a New Political Matrix?

Manuel Antonio Garretón

I argue in this chapter that current transformations in Latin America cannot be characterized as a transition to a market economy.[1] In doing so, I place the discussion of structural adjustment policies and their effects in a broader analytical framework that emphasizes the ways the structural, political, and cultural transformations of the last few decades have affected the patterns of collective action. This process has created new challenges for social and political actors trying to ensure stable conditions for governability and development. Drawing on earlier work, I conceptualize this process as a change in the sociopolitical matrix that defines relations among the state, the system of representation, and social actors. This process accounts for a transition that is much broader than the passage from one kind of political regime to another or from one economic model to another. The transition configures a new set of relations in the political, economic, cultural, and social spheres.

Structural Adjustment: Its Progress and Limits

Latin America has not, as neoliberals would like us to believe, been experiencing a transition to a market economy in recent years. Instead, the region has been undergoing a complex change in the mode of development as a result of the process of globalization, the crisis of the previous development model, and the need to reinsert national economies into the worldwide economic system. We are not witnessing the emergence of what has been called a "market society" (which does not exist anywhere) or even a coherent new mode of development but rather a situation of rupture and tentative reorientation.

This rupture has been marked in part by structural adjustment policies tested in various Latin American countries since the mid-1980s (Chile, Mexico, Colombia, Argentina, Bolivia, and Peru, among others). These policies were oriented mainly toward controlling inflation, reducing public expenditures, eliminating tariffs, and privatizing public enterprises and services. But in reality they were accompanied by a long-term vision that has had important effects on redefining the role of the state, disarticulating the ways in which social demands are processed, and changing the way social actors attempt to influence their living conditions. In this sense, three dimensions of structural adjustment should not be confused. First are the technical measures necessary to overcome a short-term economic crisis, which has also been reflected in the general loss of dynamism in the economy. Second, for the medium term, the need exists to lay the foundation for a new development model that could replace the state-led model of import-substituting industrialization that prevailed for more than four decades. Finally, there is the ideological vision that transforms instrumental and short-term measures into the utopia of a new development model in which the new and good society would have the market as its only paradigm; this was the role of neoliberalism.

These distinctions make it possible to differentiate between what can be considered the "objective necessity" of adjustments and the long-term socioeconomic proposals that have tended to become dominant. These proposals turned a transitory policy into an ideological and political model, generically called neoliberalism.

The objective necessity consisted of adjusting public expenditures to the capacity of the national economy, as well as to the new productive and economic contexts created by both technological change and the globalization or transnationalization of the market. The so-called neoliberal structural adjustment, in turn, consisted of (1) the transfer of economic initiative to the private sector, which would increase private-sector autonomy and control over the direction of growth; (2) a change in the state's protectionist policies toward entrepreneurial sectors and wage earners, leaving an important portion of the latter vulnerable concerning the satisfaction of their basic needs and creating a massification of those sectors excluded from the market; (3) the expansion of market mechanisms (considered the only legitimate ones) into a great variety of areas of social life; and (4) a weakening of the state's integrative, distributive, and regulative functions, as well as a reduction of its size—despite the initial strengthening of the state that is necessary for redefining macroeconomic policies and equilibriums, understood principally as providing a favorable context for development of the private sector.

The adjustment carried out with a neoliberal orientation has uncovered two dimensions of its contradictory effects. On the one hand is the efficacy of measures for confronting the crisis and, in some cases, achieving stability and growth. On the other hand, there is a lack of equally efficacious solutions for alleviating the social effects of reforms and ensuring the productive, social, environmental, and political sustainability of development.

An accumulated experience allows us to observe critically the voids and disarticulations structural adjustment has left behind in the social and political spheres. In every case where structural adjustment policies have been implemented, the role of social actors, both classic and new, has been severely limited. It is sufficient to note the weakening of labor unions and the virtual disappearance of the so-called new social movements that were so visible in recent decades and that were supposedly the carriers of emergent general demands relating to human rights, the environment, generational categories, women and gender relations, ethnic diversity and rights, regionalization, and so on (Garretón, 1996; Escobar and Alvarez, 1992).

Latin American and international debates have been dominated by the perception of the inevitability of the adjustment that has taken place and its success with respect to stabilization and growth. This apparent success has hidden the negative effects adjustment has had on the population. The current challenge is to implement a "social adjustment" to the economic adjustment that has been completed, thereby reestablishing the macrosocial and environmental balance. More fundamentally, this will require rethinking the relationships among democracy, integration, and social equity and development, which until now have been marked by simplistic views and mechanistic determinism.

There is an increasing consensus within the Latin American political class, as well as among the technical cadres and, no less, the business sectors, about the necessity of having carried through the structural adjustment (or about doing so if it has not yet been done), given the new conditions in which the world economy is developing, with open and competitive markets. This is the point of departure from which the countries of the region can confront the pending tasks of development. It can be said, too, that consensus exists regarding the negative evaluation of the social dimension (equity, equality, social costs, national integration), the political dimension (loss of state capacity, the disarticulation of already precarious systems of representation), and the cultural dimension (the disarticulation of identities, ways of life, and social relations). In other words, if the separation of the economy and politics was a necessary step, the appropriate regulation of the economy by politics and the rearticulation between the two have not yet been accomplished. No consensus equivalent to the former exists on how to alleviate the social costs of adjustment or on how to do so to keep social concerns from being divorced from the requirements of economic reform.

Strategies for combating poverty or, more generally, strategies for conducting development with equity that correct the perverse effects of exclusion and the deterioration of the living conditions of broad segments of the population face key unresolved dilemmas concerning the future of Latin American societies.

The first attempt at structural adjustment took place in Chile under the Augusto Pinochet dictatorship in 1975 and failed completely in 1981–1982. A similar attempt also failed under the Argentinean dictatorship. Now, more than a decade after the new structural adjustment in Chile (which was also carried out under the military regime) and several years after other countries began the process (Bolivia, Mexico, and Colombia, among others), a diagnosis of the social situation demonstrates the incapacity of the neoliberal formula to confront poverty and, in general, to address the needs of large segments of the population that are the most dependent on market mechanisms to satisfy their basic needs. The ideologues who created the formula argued that economic growth would automatically generate the resources necessary to raise the standard of living of the population. The idea of the subsidiary state that prevailed during the first phase of adjustment had as its corollary the paternalistic policies that during the most acute moments of the adjustment process served as mechanisms for social control over the most marginalized sectors. Minimum employment programs intended to alleviate high unemployment rates are an example. This explains why, in cases like Chile, authoritarian regimes introduced substantial changes in state institutions to carry out social policies. This authoritarian and technocratic paternalism also generated a cultural change regarding the way the state and society view the poor. The poor are transformed from the "subjects" of social policies (with mechanisms for processing their demands and, in some cases, for their participation) into the "beneficiaries" of targeted policies.

Analyses comparing social policies in various Latin American countries show that public social spending in the region dropped radically during the adjustment period. This was particularly true in health care and education, which dropped from 14.90 percent of public expenditure to 13.69 percent between 1980 and 1987. The decline was even greater in countries such as Mexico, which experienced a reduction from 16.42 percent in 1980 to 9.79 percent in 1987 (CEPAL, 1994). In the early 1990s, however, several countries (Argentina, Bolivia, Chile, Mexico, Uruguay, and Venezuela) reversed the tendency of the 1980s and reduced poverty levels. This reversal was largely the result of growth, decreased inflation, and rapid increases in employment and wages (in some cases in minimum wages). But this improvement is only one step in recuperating losses from past decades. Rates of inequality (except in Uruguay) and the percentage of households classified as poor are higher now than they were at the end of the 1970s.[2]

For the region as a whole, compensatory policies have become governments' dominant policy option, preventing the integrated restructuring of social policy. Criticism of the inefficiency of the welfare state under the misleading principle of subsidiarity has given way to targeting social policies toward so-called vulnerable groups, as demonstrated, for example, by the proliferation of emergency funds stimulated by international cooperation. The current tendency in the countries of the region is to give targeted policies a permanency that gradually replaces traditional state social institutions. This policy hides the need for integral reform of the state to better combine policies that can address emergent necessities (pockets of poverty and vulnerable groups more generally) with a long-term view in which the so-called hard goals of social policies are guaranteed (for example, better income distribution, health care, education, social security, and housing). Such goals are rarely the main objective of emergency funds.

In this way, an important challenge in the current period—what some authors call "post-neoliberalism"—is to recuperate the efficacy and legitimacy of state redistributive policies that are structural in nature. This would mean assigning social expenditures to traditional institutions (for example, Ministries of Education, Health, Labor, and Housing). Those institutions should be modernized through the application of greater technical criteria, decentralization, and more flexibility. At the same time, this modernization should be coordinated with the new institutions (emergency funds, for example) that enjoy certain advantages vis-à-vis traditional structures. The new targeted entities have greater visibility for the target groups; they have more flexibility in their procedures and provide a stronger link to intermediate and nongovernmental organizations. They can also generate new mechanisms for participation among the so-called beneficiaries. At the same time, the policy of emergency funds risks creating a new form of clientelism and permanent dependency of the beneficiaries, as well as duplicating state efforts or, given the lesser controls they are subject to, promoting open or disguised cases of corruption (dos Santos, 1994).

The coordination of structural policies with targeted ones is still far from effectively crystallized because of resistance from business sectors and the political Right to open the theme of state reform, their fears of the danger of increasing public spending, and their unwillingness to accept higher taxes. This situation creates a paradox in which there are demands for increasing the social responsibilities of the state but no adequate means for financing them, which redounds in a criticism of the state's weight and inefficiency.[3]

Thus, the central problem today is not the necessity of adjustment, the need to separate economics from politics, or the creation of freer or more autonomous markets; all of these things have been done or will be done in the near future. The real question is how to avoid or correct the negative effects these changes have had on the population. Above all, it is about how to establish a new relationship among the economy, the state, and society that can provide social and political control of the economy without affecting its dynamism and relative autonomy. In other words, it is about how to reconstruct the sociopolitical system in terms that go beyond the exclusive issue of democratic transition and consolidation. In some ways, the situation can be compared to the challenge Latin American countries faced after the 1929–1931 world economic crisis. This means the problems derived from past or future adjustments, along with the general issue of a transition to a new model of economic development, cannot be addressed without rethinking them in terms of the new Latin American context, or problematic, at the end of the twentieth century.

The New Latin American Problematic

In Latin America the idea of development has always been associated with the idea of social and national integration. The state represented unity and therefore played a central role both in assigning resources through redistributive social policies and in articulating social demands. This situation had two consequences. On the one hand, social concerns (including economics) were subordinated to politics, as was expressed through a strengthening of the mobilizational dimension of political actors at the expense of their representative dimension. On the other hand, collective action was important for processing social demands as long as it had an organizational basis and was politically oriented. For example, recall the policy of promoting social organizations in Chile and Peru during the 1960s or the strong position labor movements enjoyed in Argentina, Brazil, Mexico, and populist states more generally in negotiating mechanisms for integration.

Today, the landscape is very different. The Latin American versions of welfare states (certainly incomplete and inefficacious) have not been replaced by modern state forms that can provide solutions to the challenges of deepening political democracy and increasing social and economic integration, much less to problems of poverty and exclusion, which have increased, first, because of the crisis and then as a result of adjustment.[4]

The governments or, in more general terms, the democracies of the region must confront two themes that have been insufficiently debated. As a result, consensus around them is weak, if not nonexistent. The first involves the role of the state in its relationship with society and how to deal with state reform or modernization when concerns over its size have dominated questions of function (Garretón, 1995b). Second, what kind of modernization is associated with what I call the emergent matrix, a debate in which a pragmatic and restricted idea of "growth" has dominated a vision of a coherent development model and alternative paradigms of modernity? This requires a reformulation of the Latin American problematic at the end of the twentieth century in terms of four processes that are interrelated but relatively autonomous of one another: the construction of political democracy, social integration or social democratization, the redefinition of the pattern of development and international insertion, and the redefinition of the model of modernity.[5]

The first process is the *construction of political democracy.* Transitions from military dictatorships or authoritarian regimes to democratic regimes were the fundamental political processes of the 1980s. They dealt with establishing a basic nucleus of democratic institutions to solve the problems faced by all political regimes: by whom and how a society is governed, relations between people and the state, and the channeling of conflicts and social demands. All of this was done in the process of replacing explicitly dictatorial mechanisms and institutions. In general, the central aspects of these processes have been completed in the sense that they have formally ended authoritarian or military regimes. Although a new wave of authoritarian regimes or military dictatorships seems unlikely, however, all of the transitions led to the creation of incomplete democracies with important authoritarian enclaves among their institutions and actors, as well as unresolved ethical problems (for example, the violation of human rights under the dictatorship). In some cases they also led to partial regressions. In other cases, the result has been unstable formulas in which a democratic regime does not consolidate itself or brings on successive political crises.

But however important the remaining problems of transition and consolidation are, the main challenges to democracy in the region today can be better defined in terms of the *deepening, relevance,* and *quality* of democratic regimes. In many cases, these problems are superimposed upon the still pending problems of democratic transition and consolidation. Democratic deepening refers to the extension of certain mechanisms and, above all, of the ethical principles of the democratic regime to other dimensions of social life. Relevance refers to those problems a democratic regime, by definition, must resolve (problems of government, citizenship, and the institutionalization of conflicts and demands). These problems must be resolved through, not outside of, the regime. We speak of the "irrelevance" of democracy when it exists formally as a regime, but the real or de facto powers within or outside of the national society predominate in the resolution of regime problems. The quality of democracy is related to the phenomenon of expanding citizenship, which I refer to later. It deals with problems of participation, representation, and citizen satisfaction with decisionmaking processes at the local, regional, and national levels. In resolving problems of the democratic regime's deepening, relevance, and quality, the democratic fate of Latin American societies is at stake. In the end, these phenomena will determine regime stability and the possibilities for new waves of authoritarianism.

The second process is *social democratization,* which should not be confused with political democracy. In Latin America, social democratization was the ethical principle on which political democracy was based. Three different issues are at stake. First, there is the problem of exclusion and social cohesion; second is the phenomenon of expanding citizenship; finally, there is the theme of participation.

Problems of exclusion and cohesion or social integration must be redefined in terms of the new characteristics of exclusion. The problematic of exclusion versus integration, or fragmentation versus cohesion, has not only been important but has served as a foundational element of nationalities, identities, and the principle of stateness in Latin American societies. Whether it is part of the body of ideas associated with the original colonization or of the twentieth century's modernization and development processes, the ethos of integration has always been contradicted by the practice of exclusion. What appears new today is that this exclusion or fragmentation of society is no longer expressed in terms of class or of a specific social category that generates actors struggling for integration, as was characteristic of industrialization or modernization and agrarian reform. The line of exclusion penetrates all social categories and sectors that have produced identities and collective action (rural, urban, business sectors, workers, women, ethnic groups) and divides them all into "insiders" and "outsiders." Thus, the excluded—which in some cases includes more than half of the population—emerge as an internally fragmented mass without ideological referents or organizational resources to allow them to become actors engaged in conflict with other actors. They simply appear superfluous. The central problem is whether the current development models can allow for the integration of those sectors or whether they are condemned to be permanently elitist, with subordinate incorporation of small groups in each social category. And all of this is taking place in a period when past revolutionary pressures that to a certain extent had forced more inclusive patterns of development have disappeared.

Today, social democratization has a different character from the one Karl Mannheim called "fundamental democratization" and Gino Germani described in terms of certain countries' passage from restricted democracy to extended or mass democracy. Social democratization now deals with the normative expansion of citizenship through the transformation of the concept of polis. If we understand citizenship as the recognition of rights vis-à-vis a power, that power no longer refers exclusively to a territorial polis or a single dimension of polis. Globalization, mass communication, gender relationships, the accumulation of knowledge, environmental protection,

citizen (especially urban) security, the transparency of politics to deal with
corruption, generational conflict, social identities, and self-determination—
to list only some of the dimensions of what have been called "emergent
issues" (CEPAL, 1994)—all redefine what can be considered part of the
quality of life. Above all, these dimensions define new forms of power and,
as a result, new fields of citizenship that are no longer reducible to T. H.
Marshall's trilogy (1950). People want to be citizens not only by having
civil, socioeconomic, or political rights.

Social democratization is also associated with the theme of participation. In part, this theme goes back to the problem of local democracy and
the reformulation of the role of politics. But I want to underline here that
participation was classically defined in Latin American societies as incorporation, integration, and inclusion; in other words, participation was con-
ceived socially as "access to" and politically as mass mobilization. Today,
in social terms the egalitarian or integrative ethos cannot be identified with
access because it deals with a demand that defines equality of opportunity
in terms of the quality of different goods and services with different contents. This is especially evident in education. In turn, equity defined in
terms of equal quality but with a content that varies according to the specific demand challenges policies based on the market or on self-regulation in
diverse spheres of society and complicates the tasks of state and public
policies. Politically, participation has been redefined in terms of representation, thus questioning traditional forms of social organization and politics
based on mobilization.

In relation to the third process, *economic development and international insertion,* we face an overwhelming myth: Latin American societies, and
certain countries in particular, have resolved the age-old problem of the
economic model by implanting an open market economy, replacing the statist and closed economy that supposedly prevailed during most of the twentieth century. Adjustment processes have played a significant role in the
euphoria associated with the change of models in the direction of the market, competitiveness, and an open economy. Independent of the political
conditions under which those adjustments took place, I have suggested that
they only partially resolved a short-term economic problem and that they
also contributed to the resolution of a longer-term problem relating to the
necessity for greater separation of the economy from politics. But in general, there has been a tendency to confuse adjustment with a broader model of
development—one, with practically no exceptions, that has resulted in an
increase in poverty and, above all, in social inequalities. The error is in
believing that a development model can be reduced to a model of accumulation and that the international insertion of a country can be reduced to a
question of markets or economic exchange. In this sense, the Comisión

Económica para América Latina y el Caribe (CEPAL) has aptly posed the depth of the problem by referring to issues of productive transformation, equity, sustainability, and cultural identity (CEPAL, 1992).

The fourth process is what can be called the dispute over the appropriate *model of modernity*. Modernity is understood here as the way in which a society constitutes its subjects. Modernity is the affirmation of subjects, individual or collective, who construct their history. The Latin American type of modernity, revolving around the national-popular matrix, is in crisis. In the face of this crisis, a simple copy of the model of modernity identified with the specific modernization processes of developed countries, particularly emphasizing the North American model, emerges as an alternative. Neoliberalism and the so-called new authoritarianisms (which were basically military) identified their historical project with "modernity." The democratic transitions of recent years rectified only in part the political dimension of modernity. At a time when the model of modernity associated only with its rationalist-instrumental dimension is in crisis all over the world, it seems that model is just being discovered in Latin America, like children with new toys. The problem is that only a few children have access to those toys.

Opposing this model of modernity, also in a primitive and one-sided fashion, is the vision of a Latin American modernity identified with a social base or root in racial mixture (*mestizaje*) and a particular subject, which is the Catholic Church. The constitutive moment of this identity and subject would have been the initial evangelization of the continent, with its current equivalent in the pontificate of John Paul II. The church's positive face showed when it placed "the preferential option for the poor" and, in some countries, the issue of human rights against dictatorships in the center of sociopolitical and economic concerns. Its more critical face seems to show in the cultural field, where its opposition to a model of modernity it considers materialistic has led the church to oppose necessary processes of secularization, moving closer to old integralist conceptions and new fundamentalisms.

Both extremes claim to define modernity and its alternative once and for all, either independent of any subject or based on a transcendent essentialism. Both visions are ahistorical and therefore cannot account for the syncretism, hybridization, or ruptures in Latin American forms of everyday interaction that combine—sometimes confusedly, sometimes creatively—rational-scientific and expressive-communicative dimensions with collective historical memory (Canclini, 1989; Garretón, 1994a).

As I have pointed out in other publications, globalization today means we are moving from a basically geopolitical world to a basically geoeconomic and, above all, geocultural one (see, for example, Garretón, 1996). Today, space and power are defined less in terms of territory or military might; the market has been unable to fully replace them, and possession of the means of production does not exclusively determine power. All of these elements matter and are important to the same degree as the diversification of social dimensions we are witnessing. But in this diversification space is increasingly defined by communication. Models for the appropriation of communication space are models of creativity, innovation, and knowledge. To the extent that this is true, geocultural space in the twenty-first century will be dominated by whoever proposes a model of creativity or modernity that simultaneously combines scientific-technological rationality, expressive-communicative rationality, and historical memory. Those who cannot combine these three elements will lose.

New Relations Between State and Society

If we want to identify a concept that can account for these four processes from a more general perspective, we could say we are in a situation of the disarticulation and recomposition of the Latin American sociopolitical matrix. I have argued that this situation is the relationship among the state, the system of representation, and the socioeconomic basis of social actors, institutionally mediated by the political regime. The fundamental idea is that we are passing from a classical, political, or state-centered national-popular (and so on) matrix characterized by the fusion of its components to a different pattern for constituting society and its subjects and actors. I believe both the positive signs of economic growth and political maturity in some places and the spectacular nature of the negative aspects of the continent's current situation (profound social decomposition, social explosions, and political violence or depoliticization, according to the case) are basically related to this disarticulation and change in sociopolitical matrices.

This transformation can develop in diverse alternative directions, such as permanent decomposition, an attempt (although rather unviable) to reconstitute the classical matrix, the juxtaposition of the diverse dimensions of society from the classical and emergent forms, and the emergence of a matrix characterized by the simultaneous strengthening, autonomy, and complementarity of its components mediated by a democratic political regime. It is not clear which alternative will prevail, and the current landscape is contradictory in this regard. In turn, the rearticulation of the sociopolitical matrix in terms of the hypothesis of the autonomy, strengthening, and complementarity of its components implies four dimensions not reducible to one another (Garretón, 1994a).

The first dimension is *reform of the state*. The reaffirmation and strengthening of the "stateness" principle imply the reform of the state, not only its modernization, reduction, or increased functions. The state has diverse functions to which diverse principles of transformation correspond. The reform or transformation of the state must also be placed in the perspective alluded to earlier of building a sociopolitical matrix characterized by the strengthening, autonomy, and complementarity of its components.

State reform cannot be restricted to the dogmatic issue of its size and reach; the principles and functions that make the size of the state a relative variable must be considered. It is necessary to abandon the tradition of trying to solve problems by adding new departments and agencies to the state without altering existing ones. It is also necessary to move away from the neoliberal argument that the magic solution to all problems lies in reducing the state's apparatus. This could mean that in certain areas, such as justice and redistribution, an increase in human, institutional, administrative, and bureaucratic resources beyond the necessary reforms of existing structures should be considered. In other words, the size of the state apparatus may need to be increased. Conversely, it is necessary to think about reductions in the state apparatus dealing with certain economic functions and, above all, reductions in some military functions. More generally, when referring to state size, those functions relating to the redistribution of wealth and integration should follow a pattern that is the inverse of the one corresponding to the state's coercive functions.

To reinforce the principle of a state or stateness, we must make a clear distinction between what constitutes state policy and what constitutes government policy. The first is based mainly on consensus, whereas the second follows the majority principle. New problems—such as those related to human rights, the environment, and, in particular, the exclusion produced by poverty—should be included as part of national state policy.

Reform of the state does not mean a uniform transformation of all areas of state action. In some areas, such as justice, a profound reform that affects norms and personnel is needed. In others, reform should be directed mainly toward modernization, a smaller bureaucracy, decentralization, and the retraining of state employees. Finally, the state will have to deal with some new matters, sometimes by playing an active, direct role and sometimes through its capacity to regulate the activities of other actors. This will require new structures (for example, for dealing with problems of the environment and innovation), new regulations (for example, in the areas of communication and information technology), or the restructuring of existing agencies by giving them new responsibilities (for example, in the areas of culture and education), which will perhaps be related more to regulation, orientation, and evaluation than to administration.

I have pointed out that the terms under which the access of individuals, as well as of society more generally, to the state is understood to have changed. Regarding state services, the issue (even for the most marginal sectors) is not only one of coverage or access to services; today, the issue is the quality of the service or good. This means quality has become a condition of equity and that we can no longer separate these two dimensions. This observation concerns not only housing and health care but also, in particular, education and the judiciary.

Regarding decisions made by the state, the principles of state autonomy and stateness should not be forgotten. But the institutionalization participation by individuals and society at the central and decentralized levels of the state makes it necessary to introduce principles of direct democracy in some areas and, in other cases, to reform the state's structure to allow for the presence of noncorporate representation on commissions and national councils in various fields of state action.

The second dimension is *representativity.* There are at least two aspects to strengthening the system of representation. One has to do with decentralization and the strengthening of local and regional democratic spaces and collective authorities. The other aspect, which I want to discuss in some detail, relates to political parties and the political class.

In the old sociopolitical matrix, the triple function of a party system—representation, the formulation of societal projects, and recruitment of leadership groups—was fused in "catch-all" or "vanguard" parties. Political parties oscillated between excessive reliance on ideology and their lack of identity, between irrelevance and excessive interference in society, between absorption or destruction of one another and compromise without a project. But beyond the crisis of old party forms, the very idea of the political party is in crisis everywhere as the concept of representation, as we shall see, is being redefined. It is in this adverse context that strong party systems must be built.

A strong party system is the necessary counterpart to a strong state. This implies inclusiveness along the political spectrum, internal democracy, negotiation and concerted action, and the capacity to form large coalitions and establish connections with society to ensure that new themes, conflicts, and social cleavages can be expressed. All of this is what constitutes the representativity of the party system. In turn, the possibility of forming majority government coalitions in multiparty systems implies institutional changes in the system of government, which suggests the need to introduce certain elements of parliamentary systems. This is true not only from the point of view of responsibility, as has been widely argued, but also from the perspective of constructing majorities and strengthening political parties (Haggard and Kaufman, 1994; Linz and Valenzuela, 1994).

The third dimension refers to the *autonomy and reinforcement of civil society and social actors,* which has two subdimensions. First, this implies the separation of the economy and politics. In this regard, the risk is no

longer the politicization of earlier periods but economicism and the myth of
self-regulation that reproduce the power relations of the market.

Second, there is the question of strengthening social actors. The reinforcement of the principles of stateness and representativity implies a transformation in politics. At the same time, it requires that civil society—the
social actors that are autonomous from the state and the party system—
must grow in strength and density. The growth, diversification, and
strengthening of social actors allow for an increase in participation levels,
which should not be limited to a symbolic dimension but should also be
directed to the effective solution of problems. Again, this poses the question of the decentralization of state power and the advancement of local
democracy.

Today, we seem to be witnessing a general weakening of collective
action and social movements. The classical sociopolitical matrix was characterized by a type of collective action centered on political objectives and
thus on the state, as well as by a type of social movement founded on principles of development, modernization, nationalism, populism, and social
integration. The paradigmatic expression of such action was the workers'
movement, to which other movements were allied, at least in ideological
terms. Military regimes and various other authoritarian regimes, as well as
the economic crisis of recent decades, finally ended this form of action.

Now that the classical matrix has been disarticulated and the transitions that unified social movements in the democratic struggle have
reached their zenith, the unifying principle of social action has disappeared.
The principles and orientations of action (freedoms, equalities, identities,
national independence, self-realization or expansion of subjectivity, social
belonging, and interactions) and actors, if they exist, have diversified and
are often contradictory. In effect, all principles seem to have diversified,
sometimes in contradictory ways, and are now expressed through totally
distinct actors. At the same time, social mobilization and organization seem
to have been replaced by public opinion measured in polls closely tied to
the media, sporadic group explosions, and individual demands. All of this
is combined with the remains of the old matrix, giving social action a very
ambivalent meaning. This ambiguity can be seen in the Chiapas movement
in Mexico since 1994.

Yet, the constitution of social actors faces a problem even more serious
than the diversification of principles of action and struggle and the lack of
unifying principles or themes—social exclusion. I have suggested that all
social categories are currently experiencing the division between insiders
and the excluded, as well as conflicts among the included regarding models
of modernity. The first does not define a conflict but a type of exclusion.
The second defines a conflict in which the subordinate actors are very weak
and face a high risk of exclusion at any time. In these situations, no actors

are organized on a regular basis; instead, we find sporadic mobilizations and fragmented, defensive action.

The problem now is to rethink the configuration of actors. No social or political actor is capable of constituting a general field of action or articulating the various principles of action that emerge in the process of modernization and social democratization. The paradox of state action stems from this inability. One cannot expect the state to be a unifying agent in the life of a society and the diversity of its actors, but state intervention is indispensable for the generation of spaces and institutions in which actors can act autonomously. If the state and, in some cases, political parties do not assume that role, the absence or weakening of actors and the crisis of representation can last indefinitely.

The fourth dimension in the recomposition of the sociopolitical matrix refers to the *strengthening of the democratic regime and politics.* I argued earlier that the democratic issue no longer seems to be part of the authoritarianism-democracy cycle that characterized most of the twentieth century in Latin America but that it is part of a change in epochs. At the same time, democracy is no longer called upon to achieve what it cannot accomplish as a regime, which corresponds to other spheres of society. In other words, democracy is accepted for what it is—a particular dimension of society and not a totalizing or global form for the organization of society. But it is in terms of a regime that more is demanded from it. Today, demands are focused on the representative dimension of democracy, but the very idea of representation is being questioned by deep transformations in the nature of what should be represented in the political sphere.

All of this indicates that the installation and reproduction of traditional institutions are not enough, however indispensable they may be. This problem calls attention to the enormous difficulty of inventing institutions, in particular of imagining and creating new institutions to confront the two great problems that will threaten democracies in the future: the irrelevance of institutions in relation to the de facto or real national and transnational powers and the incapacity to take into account the social demands created by the exclusion of vast sectors of society. In other words, institutional creativity must be applied to solve the problems of who governs society and how it will be governed and, above all, to confront the most deficient aspect of democratic traditions, especially in Latin American countries: the content of "good government," which implies but goes beyond the concept of accountability.

I have insisted on a concept of democracy that is restricted to a political regime—that is, to the institutional mediation between the state and society for solving only the problems of government, citizenship, and the channeling of conflicts and social demands. This limitation makes it possible to clearly define the democratic problem and avoid demanding from a political regime something no regime can provide. But it is necessary to remember that a regime is more than a set of institutional mechanisms (although it cannot exist without them): it is founded on profound social agreements concerning specific ethical principles. It has been said that in many Western democracies this agreement was made around the principle of liberty and that in Latin America the ethos of democracy was more egalitarian than libertarian. The historical institutional, representational, and liberal deficits of diverse Latin American regimes in the face of the strength of populisms and extrainstitutional mobilizations stem from this egalitarianism. Authoritarian experiences have strengthened the libertarian ethos, and the structural transformations associated with a specific vision or model of modernity have eroded the egalitarian, solidary, or integrative ethos of Latin American democracies. But there will be no viable democracies if they do not combine those two ethical principles and if those principles are not embodied in representative and efficacious institutions.

The central element that fused the components of the classical matrix was politics. But politics had a mobilizing character with weak institutional and representational systems. In the current situation of decomposition and recomposition, politics apparently loses its centrality to social life as reinforced by the fact that globalization from "above" and the reassertion of particularisms and identities from "below" seem to generate uncontrollable forces that dominate the scene and demolish the concept of national community as the privileged locus for collective action and politics. The totalizing, ideological, statist, confrontational, and mobilizing character seems to be giving way to the opposite characteristics, which makes it impossible to express the true social conflicts in official politics. The distance between politics and society will grow, leaving the former locked in an elitist game with a high proclivity toward corruption and the latter at the mercy of either the natural forces of the market or the symbolic forces of particularistic interests.

The redimensioning of politics, however, does not mean the loss of its importance but rather the restoration of its basic role in the articulation of diverse processes if the idea of a national society or community is to be preserved. This would be its natural space. It is no longer possible to think in terms of political projects that are contained in only one of the four processes discussed earlier; every political project must include each of these processes. This does not mean their contents are fixed, since they tend to be autonomous from politics and are determined in part in civil society. Rather, it is to ensure that actors and subjects have a role in each process and to permit articulation among them. This situation contrasts with what politics was in past decades. The creation of institutions, the notion of representation, and the construction of alliances and coalitions take on crucial importance in Latin American politics.

Conclusion

Three main conclusions can be derived from what I have discussed here. First, the classic model of development in Latin America during the twentieth century, based on the intervention of the state, was very successful in economic development and social integration for long periods. The model was ambiguous concerning political democracy and was unsustainable in the new globalizing epoch. Yet, no simplistic or easy relationship exists between the introduction of market mechanisms that try to end the economy's past subordination to the state and the deepening of political democracy. In the case considered the most successful, Chile, structural adjustment and the emergence of a new model took place under a harsh dictatorship, producing a high level of disarticulation of the society and increasing inequality and poverty. Contrary to the widespread ideology, economic liberalism, democracy, and development have not followed a cumulative and linear relationship but have been very contradictory in Latin America.

Second, what is changing is not only the nature of modern society but also the predominant mode of modernization and development based on the role of the state and the mobilization of social actors. It seems the dominant factors will be the globalization process and international market forces that lead to a separation of the economy and politics. Structural adjustment has contributed in part to this rupture, but if that adjustment is not accompanied by a reinforcement of the links among the state, social actors, and the economy, countries will experience not only economic stagnation in the long run but an increasing disintegration of society.

Third, the emerging development model, in which international market forces play a central role, has destroyed the material, political, and organizational bases for social actors and will tend to permanently weaken them. The crucial issue today is the reconstruction of a political system that allows for the simultaneous strengthening of the state and the autonomous capacity of collective actors to define the type of modernity they want. Such a system requires the construction of a new sociopolitical matrix. The issue is therefore not one of the transition to a market economy but rather a reconstruction of society and politics that in each case will allow the nation-state system to survive.

Notes

1. This chapter draws on the report "From the Adjustment Policies to the New Relations Between the State and Society," written by the author with Malva Espinosa for the Independent Population and Quality of Life Commission, Paris, 1994.

2. During the period 1990–1993, Chile, Uruguay, Argentina, Costa Rica, and Brazil had higher social expenditures, which reached more than 10 percent of GDP. But increasing per capita social expenditures did not mean such expenditures were progressive. Social security, which accounted for much of the growth of public expenditure, was regressive. With some exceptions, only public health and basic education were effectively targeted toward the poorest sectors. See CEPAL, 1994.

3. The Chilean case during the period of democratic government (1990–1994) illustrates positions that at least reveal a preoccupation with the long term. To reverse the paternalistic wave that prevailed under the authoritarian regime, actions have been taken that claim to create more equitable conditions and that necessarily include a combination of structural policies and policies targeted to emergent groups. Thus, social policy has been oriented to achieve an important increase in public expenditures and, at the same time, to create specific state agencies such as the Solidarity and Social Investment Fund, the National Women's Secretariat, the National Youth Institute, and other local and communal development entities, in addition to the Ministry of Planning and Cooperation, dedicated mainly to poverty.

4. Analyses of the effects of adjustment in the majority of countries in which it has been carried out show that it generated an increase in social inequalities linked to a drop in average and minimum wages, which translated into an increase in poverty, reverting the tendency of the first three postwar decades. Today, the urban poor are more numerous than the rural poor, and the decline in living conditions in cities is greater than that in the countryside. See Díaz, 1994a.

5. The description of these four processes draws on Garretón (1995a).

Part 2

Market Constraints to the Consolidation of Democracy

4

Political Participation and Social Exclusion of the Popular Sectors in Chile

Manuel Barrera

In this chapter I attempt to link the phenomenon of social exclusion with the political life of the popular sectors and the vicissitudes of "popular" civil society in Chile. Although it is impossible to do so without continually referring to the country's experience during the military regime, the central focus of these reflections is the political period called the "transition to democracy." Chile lived through two decades of great social conflict between 1970 and 1989, which not only caused a traumatic historical transformation but also created strong pressure on Chile's viability as a national society. The transition government, which assumed power on March 11, 1990, represented the institutional translation of social processes that can be traced back to earlier struggles in search of a legitimate resolution for the tensions and social rifts created by a dramatic historical period.

As is natural, the Chilean transition was characterized by economic and political processes that originated during the period of military government and continue to this day, coexisting with new economic orientations and political realities. This combination of processes that endure and emerging processes forced the first transition government to manage the political situation with skill and ingenuity. The "democracy by agreements" (*la democracia de los acuerdos*), the politics of consensus, and political and social concertation are all distinct expressions of a fundamental phenomenon: Chile is trying to progress toward a democratic order identified by general agreements that could be superimposed on potential social conflicts generated by persistent authoritarian elements in the democratic order and the high levels of social inequality that are part of the new economy.

As is well known, during the military regime Chile experienced a powerful restructuring of its economy driven by neoliberal policies. The structural adjustment began in 1975. Two phases can be identified in its development: a transitional, or initial, phase that lasted from 1975 to 1985 and one of consolidation from 1986 on. Chile endured the longest initial phase of any country that implemented adjustment policies in Latin America. The prolonged duration of the transitional phase of adjustment can be explained by the 1982–1983 recessionary crisis, which unraveled earlier processes of economic change. The popular sectors—workers in the formal and informal sectors and the unemployed and their families—paid a high price in terms of unemployment, a fall in real wages, and political and social exclusion during the first fourteen years of economic reform implemented by the military government (Barrera, 1994).

The economic change that resulted from this strategy was so great that it could be characterized as foundational in relation not only to economic restructuring but also to the creation of a new social order. A modernizing bourgeoisie class was created that has played a leading role in the economic growth and modernization that have resulted from the imposition of a program of radical changes—including a reorientation of the economy's productive structure, a decreased role of the state in the economy, an opening to the international economy, and deregulation of markets, including the labor market.

In this social order, the popular sectors have a new status and social position. The changes are profound and reflect, among other things, the insertion of popular organizations into society and the relationship of those organizations with the state and political parties.

In effect, neoliberal economic reform has been taking place in Chile for more than twenty years. From 1974 until 1989, it took place under the military government of General Augusto Pinochet. Since 1990, it has taken place under a regime of a transition to democracy. Obviously, this distinction is important for an analysis of political and social phenomena.

Another significant distinction during this period of economic change can be made between a first stage, which lasted from 1974 until the 1982–1983 crisis, and a second stage from 1984 on. Díaz (1994b) describes these phases as the "social deconstruction of the seventies" and the "social reconstruction of the eighties," a distinction that has strong sociological implications. The data Díaz provides to support this distinction make it possible to capture, in a synthetic way, the initial phenomena of growing unemployment, the unraveling of wage guarantees, the growth of the informal sector in urban areas, the spurious tercerization of the economy, the growth of poverty, and, later, the process of recuperation (until 1988) that was eventually transformed into a process of economic expansion (Table 4.1).

The social deconstruction, subsequent recuperation, and initial economic expansion took place during the military regime. But that does not mean other important areas of social and political life have been completely

**Table 4.1   Social Deconstruction and Reconstruction in Chile, Selected
Years, 1972–1992 (percentage)**

	Social Deconstruction		Social Reconstruction
Changes in the Occupational Structure (percent of EAP)	1972	1982	1992
Unemployment	4.3	19.6	4.4
Regular wage earners	60.2	39.2	60.4
Tercerization of the conomy	50.9	61.8	51.5
Informalization	22.9	32.7	22.1
Emergency employment programs	0.0	11.0	0.0
Public-sector employment	12.0	8.0	6.0

Source: INE, Mideplan, Ministerio de Hacienda, calculated by Díaz (1994).

restructured, even today. On the contrary, at the level of both civil society and the political system, equilibriums have not been reestablished that would allow for popular participation through organizations and movements; further, the values, mechanisms, and practices that would allow for popular-sector representation in the political system have not been recreated. Although these economic and political phenomena affect social organizations and movements as a whole and the political system in general, in this chapter I refer only to the popular segment of civil society and its links with political institutions. I emphasize the actual social and political situations of the popular sectors in the context of consolidated economic reforms and successful macroeconomic performance at the same time the democratic regime is moving toward consolidation, despite its various restrictions.

Limits of the Democratic Transition

The experience of five years of democratic transition demonstrated that democratization in Chile has important limitations that are the result of the constitutional norms established in negotiations between the military government and the political opposition at the time, the Concertation of Parties for Democracy (Concertación de Partidos por la Democracia), or Concertation. Obviously, the Concertation did not voluntarily subscribe to those limitations; they were the result of negotiations with the dictatorship that made it possible to reach a larger political agreement that included holding free elections.

Limitations to the democratization process have also emerged from the political party system and parties' activities. A principal limitation has been the separation of political parties from civil society, as manifested in Chileans' lack of interest in politics and their tendency to negatively evaluate political parties, the Parliament, and politicians in general. The distance between the citizenry and political parties and citizens' lack of interest in public affairs have led to a crisis of representation. Citizens have been left in the role of electors, and political rights have been reduced to the vote. Today, it is difficult to say with any certainty who represents whom. The activities of political parties exhibit an excessive concentration of party governance and decisionmaking in a leadership elite that reproduces itself.

Other limits to the democratization process are derived from the neoliberal model for managing the economy. Although the unemployment rate has decreased in recent years to 5 to 7 percent and the so-called informal urban sector has been reduced to approximately 22 percent of the economically active population (EAP), a segment of the population remains excluded. Whereas employment is important for determining the dimensions of inclusion versus exclusion, so is the level of income. In that sense, the Chilean economy tends toward a growing concentration of wealth among a minority. The 1994 CASEN survey of total income distribution found that the three poorest deciles (30 percent of households) received less income in 1994 than in 1992; they received 8.4 percent of the country's total income in 1994 compared with 9.0 percent in 1992. This greater relative impoverishment[1] of the poorest 30 percent of households compared with all other households indicates the existence of structural factors that have consolidated the situation of inequality (MIDEPLAN, 1995). This concentration of wealth—of which the distribution of income is only one indicator—contributed to the existence of a large number of poor people: 28.5 percent of the population in 1994, or a total of 3,916,475 people (MIDEPLAN, 1995).

This situation is made more difficult by the fact that the state is small, economistic values impregnate the culture of society, and no political utopias exist with any social force for dramatically overcoming marginality and exclusion. No revolutionary utopia—and its concrete manifestations in parties, movements, militants, and revolutionary actions—has political, social, or cultural significance.

This limitation to the democratization process is obviously not totally the result of the neoliberal economic model. Poverty has always existed in Chile, income has always been concentrated, and exclusion has always been present. These phenomena, however, are occurring simultaneously with sustained economic growth, and revolutionary messages—the "utopias" that foresaw and promised an abrupt change toward equality and full participation—have disappeared from the political system. The state has distanced itself from social actors. The parties that allegedly have popular social referents in their programs propose a decrease in poverty now and its eventual elimination through social policies such as education and health care, which will show success very slowly. More specific social policies involve targeted action, which largely prioritizes individual rather than structural strategies for overcoming economic and social subjugation.

The institutional and economic limitations to the democratization process mean the transition to democracy has not yet allowed for a level of inclusion and citizen participation similar to that reached in 1973. If, as some argue, the transition has ended,[2] that means the level of democratization achieved—that which we now have—is normal and relatively stable for a certain period. It implies no expectation exists of more democratization as a result of the dynamic intrinsic to transition. One could thus conclude that Chile has a political regime of limited, restricted democracy.

State, Political Parties, and the Popular Sectors

Neoliberal reform has drastically changed the relationship between the state and the popular sectors that existed under the import-substituting industrialization development model. The expression "compromise state" reflected a particular equilibrium among social classes under an economic model in which the state played the central role in the economy and was committed to incorporation of the popular sectors into the economy and the political regime. The compromise state has ceased to have force under the model of a free market, economic opening, and limited democracy. On the contrary, the market has assumed the principal role in the economy, and the state plays a subsidiary one. The popular sectors have lost their main source of "protection" and are left exposed to the vicissitudes of a market governed by objective laws with respect to this ample social segment.

To the extent that there is a consolidation of the free market and economic opening, there will also be an objective distancing between the state and the popular sectors. State employment opportunities, subsidies, and protective legislation will become increasingly scarce, as will all types of material gains emanating from political clientelism. In the past, important groups of workers, *pobladores* (shantytown dwellers), and political activists from the lower and middle classes had been constituted as clients of political parties or the government and sometimes of parliamentary representatives who helped to obtain favors for their electorate through legislation and assistance with the state bureaucracy. Today, the loss of the state's influence in the economic sphere places powerful limits on possibilities for engaging in legislative or bureaucratic clientelism. Clientelistic practices interfere with the free functioning of the market, and private economic actors do not offer clientelistic favors to groups that are socially weak. Workers (especially those who are organized), *pobladores* (especially those organized in territorial associations), middle-class white-collar workers (especially those employed by the state), and some groups of agricultural workers (such as the beneficiaries of agrarian reform) had constituted clienteles—sometimes powerful ones—of the government and the political parties and, on occasion, constituted personal clienteles of individual political leaders.

Clientelism greatly influenced the pattern of relations between the popular sectors and the state and between voters and politicians. For many social leaders (of labor, *poblador,* and professional and student organizations, among others), this mode of relations enabled them to obtain resources for both their groups and themselves in exchange for their political loyalty, reflected principally (although not exclusively) in the vote.

For large groups—some identifiable in terms of employment and geography (such as the mining enclaves), others in terms of their position in the state apparatus (such as those employed in the central administration of the state) or their professions (such as teachers and doctors), and others as a result of their strategic position in the economy (copper miners, port and railroad workers)—clientelism took the form of an alliance between the group and a specific political party that was in power or that exercised strong influence in Parliament. In this manner, for example, the coal miners of Lota and Coronel established a solid and prolonged alliance with the Communist Party. Copper miners did the same with the Communist Party, the Socialist Party, and later the Christian Democratic Party. Railroad workers established a similar relationship with the socialists, whereas employees in the central administration of the state, teachers, and doctors were allied first with the Radical Party and then with the Christian Democrats. *Pobladores* on the periphery of Santiago established an alliance with the Christian Democratic Party in the 1960s and later with the revolutionary Left.

Each party protected particular segments of the popular sectors through favorable legislation, administrative prebends, and solidarity during times of crisis—whether economic, natural, work related, or political. The parties also used the strength of their political influence to support their petitions and hopes.

This pattern of relations between social sectors and politicians left many in the popular sectors untouched by its benefits. In particular, those sectors that lacked organization because they had no clear social, employment, or political identity were excluded because it was impossible to negotiate their electoral support. Socially amorphous groups, such as small peasant landowners, self-employed workers, housewives, and domestic servants, did not enter into such political relationships. Those citizens who for diverse reasons could (or would) establish personalistic relations with their "patron" only on an individual basis were also excluded from such clientelism; this group included tenant farmers, domestic servants, and the various providers of services for private homes such as gardeners, seamstresses, and those who took in laundry, among others. This individualized particularism remained outside any political relationship, although in many respects it substituted for one.

This clientelism was based fundamentally on the opportunities provided by the state to offer favors to client-citizens who were part of a social aggregate. Given its powerful role in an economy in which it was the owner of large enterprises, its role in providing social security, and its quasi monopoly over health care and education, not to mention that it employed large numbers of people, the state was in a material position to be the object of demands and a subject in the provision of prebends.

This model accommodated the middle- and lower-class political parties that began to strenuously challenge the political, social, and economic power of the oligarchy beginning in 1920. The state became organized and evolved from then on to assume, beginning in 1940, the promotion of industrialization and its corresponding infrastructure. The government soon controlled the economy, which served as the basis for the mass incorporation of people into political life that came with universal suffrage, into cultural life with the widening of school coverage, and into urban life with the heavy migration from rural areas. In any case, this inclusion was always partial: the country continued to perceive of itself as a dual society.

The Radical, Socialist, and Communist parties, along with the Christian Democrats beginning in the 1960s, utilized clientelistic relations with an intensity and an amplitude that were in tune with the economic and political changes. In this manner, the political elite used the resources at its disposal to obtain popular support, sacrificing the autonomy of collective actors and subordinating them to its interests.

Clientelism has lost its force with the type of state that emerged from the authoritarian period, as well as with neoliberalism. Political parties were incorporated into state institutions with the election of the president and the Parliament beginning in 1989, when the period of transition to democracy formally began. During that period, clientelism disappeared. Further, there has been no opportunity for the populism that existed in Chile (although it was weak compared with that of Argentina and Brazil) under the governments of General Carlos Ibàñez (1952–1958), Eduardo Frei Montalva (1964–1970), and Salvador Allende (1970–1973). Populism and clientelism were two modalities through which the popular sectors established relationships with the state and political parties in a democracy. Both sides received immediate benefits. For the popular sectors, those benefits included practices that facilitated their economic incorporation and political participation. The leaders of social movements and popular organizations easily obtained personal benefits in relation to their status and life chances.

In Chile and in Latin America more generally, populism ignored the structural causes of the popular sector's problems and, as a result, reinforced the subordination of that group by offering it apparent and ephemeral solutions. Even worse, this situation inhibited any possibility of popular-sector autonomy. Therefore, the group could not constitute itself into a political subject.

Did populism by the state and political parties, as well as clientelism, only represent a type of relationship between those groups and the popular sectors, or were they mechanisms that allowed the formation and ensured the survival of social movements and organizations? In Chile's recent history, both popular and middle-class social movements have been notoriously weak, not only in the period prior to 1973 but also in relation to the military government. That weakness is seen in the disappearance of some of those movements from the social scene, including the shantytown, student, and peasant movements. The so-called new social movements—such as the feminist movement, for example—that were allegedly emerging in the 1980s disappeared in the 1990s. Many of their leaders became members of Parliament or civil servants in the state apparatus, breaking their ties with the emerging social movements, which then disappeared.

With respect to organized labor, rather than a movement there is a union organization that specializes in making demands and negotiating issues relating to the economic interests of its members. This type of organization defends its members' economic interests almost exclusively, as if they were those of the country as a whole. It is characteristic of middle-class professional organizations, such as those made up of teachers and doctors.

Organized labor as a whole now focuses on pressing demands based on workers' alleged rights. But a distinction must be drawn between those workers' organizations that do so in a confrontational manner and those that seek to do so through negotiation and compromise. The former are found among professionals and employees of the state and public enterprises; the latter are found in the private sector and are on the way to becoming a trade union movement based on negotiation and collective bargaining.

If it is generally true that (as I believe) a Latin American sociopolitical model exists whose central characteristic is the interdependence between social mobilization and political intervention, as sustained by Touraine (1987), that is not the case in Chile today. The confrontational labor organizations found within the state and its economic enterprises are what remain of state corporatism in relation to popular sectors, which contradicts the actual socioeconomic tendencies in Chile. The most important corporate entity in the country is the military, which has become largely autonomous from the rest of the state.

The social situation in Chile during the period of transition to democracy has been characterized by the absence of social movements and, as a result, the lack of social mobilization. The existence of trade unions based on demands related to their economic interests and committed to negotiation rather than confrontation in the private sector of the economy—the sector that leads economic growth—has led to the atomization and fragmentation of the social organization of workers.[3]

In sum, populism (which was never as important in Chile as in other countries on the continent) has exhausted itself, as has the clientelism that had been very important to Chilean democracy for the economic and political incorporation of the popular sectors. Only partial manifestations of state corporatism—which was part of the political life of Latin America during the period of inward-looking growth—remain. The transition to democracy led to a political regime of limited democracy, as the compromise state ceased to exist. To this scenario must be added what I said earlier about social movements and organizations, as well as about the concentration of wealth and the economic exclusion of many popular-sector families. The compromise state was replaced by a neutral state. Populism was replaced by political objectives and rationales, and clientelism with targeted social expenditures. Passivity took the place of social mobilization, and participation in the market replaced political participation. The labor movement was divided into trade unions concerned with collective bargaining and public employee unions. The political representation of the popular sectors—like all political representation—is ambiguous. No one knows who represents whom.

What kind of democracy can develop under these conditions? O'Donnell (1992) provides a good answer: delegative democracy. The person who wins a presidential election wins the authority to govern the country as he or she feels is appropriate. The president is the incarnation of the nation, the arbitrator of the national interest, which he or she defines. And in Chile this occurs within the limits of a restricted democracy. Is such a limited, delegative democracy the inevitable result of Chile's authoritarian experience and its transition from an economy centered on the state and the nation to an economy centered on the market and the external world?

The Question of Representation

Perhaps the political situation in Chile can best be understood in terms of the concept of a limited democracy—that is, democracy with heavy authoritarian connotations—in which social mobilization and participation are surpassed by the distance and apathy of the citizens. In this type of democracy, fundamental political institutions function within certain conservative limits. The principal act of citizenship is voting. Between elections, the electorate forms the audience for a performance on which it will give its opinion by voting. This public audience expects political actors to play their roles in a rational manner so the economic system and political regime will function with efficiency and without sudden changes. It informs itself regularly through the written press and television; it rarely emits opinions, although to send signals to the authorities it will respond to public opinion polls that protect its anonymity. Only some public roles are important to this public. Increasingly, the roles of parliamentarian, state minister, and party activist are losing status. The president, high court judges, the highest officer of each branch of the armed forces, the leader of each of the four or five principal political parties, and the highest dignitaries of the Catholic Church are the positions this citizenry considers important. In that sense, O'Donnell's concept of delegative democracy is applicable.

This political regime of restricted and delegative democracy—without populism and clientelism, in which corporatism takes refuge in the last redoubts the compromise state can provide—is functional for the affirmation of a national capitalism that is powerfully expansive and that grows through a new mode of accumulation whose most characteristic feature is the exclusion of sectors that cannot integrate. Thus, the surplus that would have gone to the reproduction of those sectors under other circumstances is freed for accumulation. What happens to the political representation and social participation of those popular sectors in this kind of democracy? The state is clearly separated from social actors and, therefore, from the movements and organizations of the popular sectors. The political forces that have parliamentary representation—four parties of the Concertation and three opposition parties—do not define their political platforms with reference to social classes. As a result, the parties of the Left and center are not considered representatives of the popular sectors, the working class, or the middle class; the fundamental reference for their actions is the preservation of democracy and economic growth. They want modernization to be accompanied by social integration; neither social mobilization nor widespread deliberative and activist political participation interests them. The revolutionary path was replaced by a reformist one. Appeals to the people, the workers, and the masses were replaced with attention to a public that at an appropriate moment will assume its citizenship (albeit incompletely) to cast its vote.

Who, therefore, represents the popular sectors? The state and political parties do to the extent that they represent the common good of society. If what is appropriate for the country—especially in terms of the preservation of democracy and economic growth—coincides with the interests of the popular sectors, then the politics of the common good favors those interests up to the limit of that coincidence.

The politics of the common good is incompatible with clientelism. The scrutiny of citizens' political activities, the reduction of the state's role in dispensing employment and running public enterprises, and the consciousness of the economic need for public saving and, in general, for budget equilibrium and sobriety in fiscal expenditures make clientelism nonviable.

Given that populism and clientelism have disappeared from the political scene and that corporatism has been minimized, a phenomenon that has always been present can now be seen clearly. That phenomenon is a certain type of patrimonialism—the form of domination characteristic of the oligarchy—that certain, albeit few, political leaders can exercise. Generally, those leaders are the heads of factions or the principal leaders of each government party. Using a Weberian definition, patrimonialism is not based on the obligation to serve an impersonal and objective "end" in obedience to abstract norms; on the contrary, it is submission in virture of a strictly personal devotion. The personal authority of a *dominus* within a domestic community is charactistic of partrimonialism. Only he or she decides who gets what. The relationship between the *dominus* and those he or she protects is based on the loyalty of the latter and the protection provided by the former (Weber, 1944).

Although this type of relationship is common in any system of domination, the fact that the main leader of a faction or the leader of a party (if there is one) has a high probability of assuming whatever government position is available to the party regardless of the leader's personal interest (and that the leader could surround himself or herself in this position with a small personal following that is not necessarily partisan or part of the bureaucracy) makes this relationship similar to patrimonialism. The head of a faction is the "lord" par excellence; he or she does not serve the electorate. The exercise of the lord's influence in the state apparatus to obtain prebends for followers is limited to a small circle of close family members (children, brothers, in-laws) and a few other followers. The entire group of supporters is very small and is not necessarily formed by party activists, given that the lord exercises influence according to what is personally convenient without taking either the electorate or the party into account. This is the model of an essentially patrimonial relationship.

Patrimonialism has a much broader significance than that discussed here in local systems of power where power tends to be privatized. Only with great difficulty can this kind of practice—which extends to parties of both the center and the Left in Chile today—favor the popular sectors as was the case with populism and clientelism. Party representation of the popular sectors has yet to be created. If it actually comes about, such representation will develop out of the formation of autonomous social classes that will unfold with the consolidation of an expanded, independent capitalist economy. The subaltern classes (people in the informal sector, peasants, wage earners with precarious job security) have not clearly constituted themselves as autonomous social classes, both because the capitalist economy is not yet an independent and expanded national system and because of the political regime of limited democracy.

The lack of structurally constituted subaltern classes also implies the absence of a "class for itself"—that is, of autonomous organizations and social and political projects. This structural and ideological ambiguity in a historical period when workers', or popular, political parties have modified their conceptions of the economy and society, changing their political practices with no specific social referents, has resulted in the ambiguous representation of the popular sectors.

The Response of Popular Civil Society

During the period of inward-oriented development and the compromise state with its populism and clientelism, a politics of controlled inclusion prevailed. In effect, with the authoritarianism of the 1970s and 1980s, a pattern emerged that has been called "coerced marginalization" (Oxhorn, 1995b). Paradoxically, during this period the popular segment of civil society expanded into areas from which it had been absent, and it did so with higher levels of autonomy.[4]

This paradox has not disappeared, although it has diminished to the extent that political and social elites control democratic institutions in a manner increasingly distant from the common people. The potential for the popular associational tendencies that flourished during the authoritarian regime to continue to develop will depend largely on the role political parties play in the relationship between the state and civil society.

Popular civil society is understood as the rich social fabric formed by a multiplicity of units constituted on territorial and functional bases. It constitutes what one historian has called *bajo pueblo* (underclass; see Salazar, 1990). The strength of this society resides in the peaceful coexistence of those units and in their capacity to resist subordination to the state and simultaneously demand inclusion in national political structures (Oxhorn, 1995b). This dual dynamic of resistance and inclusion characterized popular civil society during the authoritarian period. Resistance was highly successful, and the coercive exclusion was offset by demands for inclusion in the most general aspects of political life, although not in the areas closest to the popular sectors.

The capacity generated by popular civil society was so important in Chile that its mobilization opened political space. The popular organizations were not animated by the search for a representative democracy, however; instead, they were searching for a direct democracy that sought to create a popular subject outside of the institutional system, which implied that they avoided institutionalized relations of power. Valenzuela (1993) used the concept of *populism* (in the Russian sense of the term) to characterize this cultural and social alternative. Although popular civil society demanded the end of authoritarianism and the democratization of society at the national level, at the level of grassroots organizations—which constituted popular civil society—actual practice valued a certain culture of the excluded: horizontal relations of power, an economy of solidarity, and self-education. This practice corresponded to concepts such as liberation theology, popular education, and the popular economy developed by intellectuals from different spheres in a vigorous process of "going to the people" who were free of all leadership "from above."

This culture of exclusion differed from the culture of poverty to the extent that the latter included disintegration, conformism, hopelessness, and apathy. During the authoritarian period, popular civil society lived a daily alternative experience and represented an associational pattern parallel to that of the national society.

This popular associational pattern should not be confused with that of either new or traditional social movements. The pattern involves a large number of communitarian organizations that run a wide gamut and are not unified; they are generally territorial and functional organizations with a local reach. They have certain advantages over classical social movements, such as labor movements, that allow them to function in conditions of extreme exclusion because they lack the political visibility that converts classical movements into easy targets for repression. Their sheer number is appreciable. Whereas official statistics sometimes overestimate the number of members who actually participate in the organizations, Tables 4.2 and 4.3 provide a good approximation.

The deliberate atomization of civil society, the destruction of networks of political representation, and the emphasis on centralized, technocratic political decisionmaking during the period of authoritarian rule favored the existence of organizations based on tightly circumscribed territorial domains. In this territorial sphere, popular organizations endeavored to offer collective solutions for alleviating social problems that were alternatives to those controlled by the authoritarian state—solutions for problems such as hunger, unemployment, and housing that, therefore, conflicted with the individualistic logic of the neoliberal model. They also contradicted the heterodox logic of controlled inclusion associated with the compromise state, given the autonomy of popular action.

The weakness of this type of organization, however, lies in its organic precariousness. Thousands of popular economic organizations are

Table 4.2   Communitarian Organizations, 1990 and 1991

	Number of Organizations		Number of Members	
Type of Organization	1990	1991	1990	1991
Territorial organizations				
Neighborhood councils	6,582	7,477	1,024,462	1,400,277
Mothers' centers	4,582	5,068	87,224	125,911
Community gardens	100	285	19,241	19,241
Total territorial organizations	11,264	12,830	1,130,927	1,545,429
Functional organizations				
Parents' centers	317	1,859	14,656	290,583
Cultural centers	144	434	5,151	27,835
Youth centers	49	321	987	18,263
Sports clubs	6,318	8,561	298,120	623,894
Other	2,667	3,387	130,656	220,314
Total functional organizations	9,495	14,562	449,570	1,180,889
Total communitarian organizations	20,759	27,392	1,580,497	2,726,318

Source: Statistics cited in SECC, 1996, *Zona Pública,* no. 11.

Table 4.3   Communitarian Organizations, 1996 (July)

Communitarian Organizations	Number of Organizations	With Information[a]	Number of Members	Average Membership[b]
Territorial organizations				
Neighborhood councils	10,849	4,611	693,406	150
Mothers' centers	2,306	849	23,777	28
Communal gardens	23	11	415	38
Homeowners' associations	39	20	813	41
Neighborhood council coordinating bodies	190	70	34,921	499
Mothers' centers coordinating bodies	7	1	32	32
Subtotal, territorial organizations	13,414	5,562	753,364	135
Functional organizations				
Sports clubs	5,472	2,600	168,440	65
Parents' centers	255	67	12,159	181
Cultural centers	455	213	8,357	39
Youth centers	344	142	11,383	80
Youth cultural centers	37	6	273	46
Sports clubs coordinating bodies	48	10	3,850	385
Subtotal, functional organizations	6,611	3,038	204,462	67
Total communitarian organizations	20,025	8,600	957,826	111

Sources: Departamento de Información, División de Organizaciones Sociales (DOS), Ministerio Secretaría General de Gobierno. Statistics cited in Secretaría de Comunicación y Cultura del Ministerio (SECC), 1996, "Juntas de Vecinos: Claves de la Participación," *Zona Pública,* no. 11 (Santiago: Secretaría de Comunicación y Cultura, Ministerio, Secretaría General de Gobierno).

Notes: a. Number of organizations for which information concerning their membership is available.

b. For those organizations for which information concerning their membership is available.

subsistence entities that do not go beyond the nuclei of a few extended families. Despite this, productive workshops, microenterprises, soup kitchens, and consumer cooperatives have functioned successfully for prolonged periods within their tight limitations.

The sustainability and vitality of many popular organizations have depended on external agents, such as nongovernmental organizations (NGOs), that receive financial resources directly from foreign agencies. The educational and organizational activities of middle-class professionals during the many years of military government were also decisive. The NGOs see themselves as strengthening the popular segment of civil society. Despite financial difficulties, the number of NGOs has increased in recent years. With the governments in transition, they have won not only security—because of the lack of repression—but also respectability. Currently, some NGOs fill an indispensable role in linking the state's social programs to the popular sectors. Although that role entails a cost for those state programs (even though they have a high level of social consciousness, Chilean NGOs tied to the popular world do not work for free), without their existence it would be difficult for those programs to fulfill an indispensable precondition for their success: to reach the poor. Although the observation by Figueiredo and Rogers (1994) that NGOs are led "by the nonpoor for the poor" and that this reality will diminish their viability in the long term is correct, in Chile the majority of NGOs have assumed a role of accompanying rather than representing the poor.

Few of these institutions, however, are located in places where the poor live. For the state, it is impossible to directly reach the nuclei of poverty without intermediation or if the poor are not organized. It is unclear whether the appearance in Latin America and Chile of a multiplicity of small organizations democratically structured with participatory practices can lead to a type of popular organization that will be effective in establishing a functional relationship with the state. Some writers have expressed an optimism that could appear ingenuous concerning the emergence of a democratic civil society directly connected to such popular organizations because those organizations facilitate direct participation by their members in the decisions that affect their lives (Oxhorn, 1995a). The organizations' organic precariousness does not appear to warrant such open optimism, although the issue is still being debated.

The popular organizations that have been studied most are the economic organizations oriented toward what Razeto (1993) has called the "popular economy of solidarity and work," which constitutes a genuine survival strategy. This economy extends from workers in the informal sector, street vendors, and people connected to popular markets to small enterprises run by their own workers, including a variety of family, individual, and collective microenterprises. The organizations entail production, distribution, and consumption carried out with an abundant labor force and financial, material, and technological resources of diverse origins and quality. They have had the support, first, of NGOs and, later, of state social programs. This popular economy of solidarity and work emerged under the military regime and continues under the transition regime in an urban informal sector (which has grown throughout Latin America but not in Chile), where it accounts for approximately 22 percent of the urban labor force.

This economy has become a genuine informal network for social protection. The permanency of this type of economy has much potential, given that the economic opening and the free market have generated a process of rationalization and modernization of economic production in only one part of the economy. This situation creates opportunities for popular civil society to develop with a logic that is contrary to the economism of neoliberalism. If that happens, communitarian activities that affect the popular sectors, such as soup kitchens (group preparation of food), family gardens, home-building co-ops, and consumer co-ops (which in Chile have the suggestive name of "buying together," or *comprando juntos*), might be able to consolidate. According to some authors (for example, Razeto, 1993), this may be the way to advance toward a popular-sector sociopolitical project supported by the democratization process. But this concept may only be an exaggerated perception of the political potential of grassroots organizations. Table 4.4 shows the variety of these organizations in Chile and their persistence over time.

This survey of popular economic organizations has been carried out systematically for a number of years (Programa de Economía del Trabajo [PET], various years). Although their number is fairly substantial, they are far from constituting a massive response to the situation of exclusion and poverty. Obviously, popular organizations oriented toward education, neighborhood organization, sports, and recreational activities must be added. These popular organizations as a whole could be the basis for the creation of a *poblador* movement. As is known, however, discontinuity of collective action by the poor has been a historical constant. The current absence of a social movement of *pobladores* is a result of the imposition of a market economy at the same time the state's integrative role ended. For poor families, this has meant the assumption of survival strategies as an unavoidable requirement (Espinoza, 1993).

At the same time, research on the relationship between the *poblador* movement and the labor movement highlights the way the societal character of the latter—that is, organization and mobilization based on interests tied to rational motives—is distinct from the "communitarian" character of the former (a feeling of belonging to a whole that reacts to economic and political exclusion), which makes articulation between the two difficult. This difference has impeded not only the emergence over time of common

Table 4.4   Popular Economic Organizations, Selected Years, 1982–1991

Organization	1982	1983	1984	1985	1986	1989	1991
Solidarity employment workshops	151	198	215	338	411	691	494
Consumer cooperatives	57	87	115	214	223	122	101
Community gardens	—	—	—	27	67	152	12
Popular cafeterias[a]	121	99	93	30	20	16	9
Soup kitchens[a]	34	42	41	232	201	279	189
Housing cooperatives	27	28	18	17	22	63	14
Home-building cooperatives	5	28	51	8	32	51	20
Committees of people seeking housing	—	—	—	52	104	2	86
Debtors' committees	12	18	—	4	115	1	—
Health care groups	22	22	72	114	137	105	70
Committees of unemployed	21	35	33	—	25	—	—
Trade unions for workers in the informal sector	8	12	21	—	22	27	11
Coordinating bodies for popular economic organizations	7	10	13	30	30	102	73
Other	29	24	33	30	—	70	238

Source: Programa de Economía del Trabajo (PET).
Notes: Commercial microenterprises are not included.
a. Popular cafeterias normally distribute food with minimal community participation. Soup kitchens generally emphasize members' participation in buying, preparing, and distributing food.

spaces for struggle but also the construction of the "national and popular" political project longed for by the Left (Baño, 1985).

These organizations represent the response of the popular sectors to the extreme social exclusion they experienced during the military regime, which persists, albeit with less intensity, during the transition. The regime of limited democracy in Chile has not incorporated into its political institutions the capacity to politically represent the popular sectors because of the convergence of two opposing views. The political Left wants to represent the interests of the entire society, above all those of respect for human rights and the strengthening of democracy. Popular organizations prefer actions that are more autonomous and social than political, those through which civil society can be reinforced. Both positions favor democracy in that they tend to separate the state from civil society, thus avoiding making the state the exclusive depository for all societal interests. This philosophy overlaps with neoliberalism's demand for a reduced state. Democracy must always be social. Touraine (1995) noted that it is the separation of civil society and the state that allows for the creation of a political society. One necessary condition for the existence of democracy, therefore, is the recognition of civil society's autonomy.

After eight years of democratic government, the *poblador* movement has not been reconstituted, but popular organizations have not disappeared. Neighborhood councils (*juntas de vecinos*) were legally recognized by the military government under the same concept of freedom of association that was applied to trade unions both outside and inside business firms. This policy stimulated their dispersion because any group of neighbors that wanted to form a neighborhood council could do so. In addition to promoting parallel neighborhood governing bodies, the policy also resulted in the emergence of small entitities with little representational capacity. Moreover, the golden rule of authoritarianism was applied to them: leaders could be designated by local authorities who, in turn, were designated by the central government. This control was maintained until the end of the military government. Only in December 1989 was a new law dictated that allowed the leaders of these organizations to be elected by their members.

Given their legal recognition (which other organizations did not have) and their objectives, during the transition neighborhood councils could have been transformed into a pole of attraction for all communitarian organizations—economic, cultural, youth, sport, and health—but that did not happen. Why did the neighborhood councils and other communitarian organizations not disappear; why, on the contrary, have some even grown? This has occurred because despite their organic weakness, these organizations constitute the only possibility for popular families to confront, through solidarity, problems of subsistence, housing, and their relationship with society. At the same time, they are the only means by which local governments and decentralized state programs have an organized counterpart in the community. The organizations allow antipoverty programs to be carried out with some contact with community groups. In effect, educational and training programs for young people and female heads of households, antidrug programs, employment promotion programs, and other programs financed by the central government and carried out by NGOs and private institutions in connection with municipal governments mobilize the diverse groups in the community to carry out the programs.

This relationship linking local governments and the central government's targeted programs with popular communitarian organizations has developed over the years of democratic government. It has been strengthened to the extent that local governments—in which previously the dictatorship had intervened heavily—have been democratized. The relationship presumes that a change of attitude has occurred among local officials, a large percentage of whom are those who were in office during the authoritarian regime. But it also assumes a change of attitude among *pobladores,* which varies from distancing and rejection to participation.

Government promotion of neighborhood participation is manifested not only in the democratization of legal structures that had strong authoritarian elements through new legislation adopted in 1996 but also through the investment and social programs of different ministries. As Ricardo Brodsky, director of the government's Division of Social Organizations, noted:

> If one analyzes housing, street pavement, health and education programs, or the National Plan for Overcoming Poverty, you will find many forms of citizen participation. Programs of Health Care with the People, Committees for Hospital Development, participatory street paving, collective applications for housing subsidies, anti-drug programs or programs for the aged with a strong participative component are indicators that favoring the participation of communities in key decisions is part of the political matrix of this government. (SECC, 1996: 19)

Popular organizations' linkages with government programs and local governments stimulates their evolution toward a higher level of formalization within the framework of democratization in Chile. For that reason, organizations that have survived since the authoritarian period and become involved in these programs are organically stronger, a prerequisite if they are to be effective participants in antipoverty activities. As a result, the persistence over time of targeted and decentralized social policies will tend to make popular organizations more stable.

Economic organizations will probably tend to incorporate themselves more solidly into the local market, based on the benefits derived from the government programs in which they participate. To the extent that popular economic organizations strengthen their organizational structure and successfully incorporate themselves into local markets, they will increase productivity and generate higher incomes, which is how they will demonstrate their viability and eventually achieve autonomous development. Such development will probably be a condition for their continued survival, given that targeted antipoverty programs will slowly diminish in line with their own success. In parallel, popular participation in the local institutions of a democratic state will increase in tune with the consolidation of the democratic regime. Elections of neighborhood councils, city councils, and mayors and the activities of local governments elected by the population favor increased participation by popular organizations in the local community. This is the process that is now unfolding.

Conclusion

The context for this discussion of political representation of the popular sectors has been the process of creating an expanded and independent capitalist system in Chile. In effect, since 1986 the economy has developed at a rapid and sustained rate.[5] The development strategy privileges private enterprise at the expense of the state and cooperative mechanisms. The nature of this strategy, on the one hand, and the characteristics of the political regime—which combines democratic and authoritarian elements in its institutions—on the other have meant the popular sectors have not regained the status they had achieved in society prior to the military regime (before September 1973). One of the most salient characteristics of the democratic period following military rule has been the gradual decrease in the mobilizational capacity of social movements and the disappearance of most of those movements from the social and political landscape. At present, only part of the labor movement has any mobilizational capacity.

This situation implies that the popular sectors, especially the poor, do not channel their political potential through social movements. Given that they also do not do so through political parties, communitarian popular organizations appear to be important because of their potential to be transformed into mechanisms for the representation and participation of the popular sectors. If this is true, one question is particularly important: What are the possible ways in which these organizations can develop?

In concluding this analysis of the political situation of the popular sectors, I offer my hypothetical vision of the possible evolution of the phenomena discussed. Communitarian popular organizations will begin to form part of the local, decentralized political system that has been emerging through the activities of municipal governments elected by popular vote. That system is decentralized because it has no organic or functional ties to the larger political system as a whole, since neither the state nor political parties have adequate mechanisms for exercising political influence in hundreds of communities and thousands of small entities with very specific goals.

To the extent that government and private economic programs reach the popular sectors, popular economic organizations will gradually be incorporated into the market economy according to their capacity. This has already begun to happen with microenterprises that link themselves with the commercial banks managing their credit programs. At the same time, those organizations will distance themselves from the solidarity economy. The organizations will probably participate in local markets with some ties to the national market, although their sphere of activity will be principally local. This incorporation into a local market will allow successful organizations not only to survive as organizations but also to strengthen themselves organically; thus, they will achieve stability.

In the same manner, noneconomic popular organizations will tend to be consolidated as a result of their contacts with municipal governments and the central government's programs targeted at the poor. The extension of democratic practices throughout society will stimulate this process.

If all of this happens, Chilean society will be on the path toward a dualism that is less severe than has been the case until now. It will be a more restrained dualism. This dualism would represent a more advanced stage in the process of national integration, one in which social exclusion would not have the same characteristics it has had since 1973. It would pave the way for an initial process of autonomous inclusion, one not controlled by the state or political parties.

This moderate and nonexclusionary dualism would be both economic and political. On the one hand, the capitalist economy would operate in the national market with strong linkages to the international economy. On the other would be a precapitalist (in the process of development) economy that would operate in multiple, relatively autonomous local markets that would include popular economic organizations. Organizations that failed to incorporate would disappear. Those that became linked to one of the markets would be integrated into a capitalist logic and be cut off from a logic of solidarity and communitarianism.

In the political system, a dualization can also be foreseen that differs from authoritarian exclusion. Two relatively autonomous spaces would exist. One would be a national space corresponding to representative democracy that would continue to increase its liberal democratic qualities. This space would be formed by fundamental political institutions, including political parties. The other space would be a local one of participative democracy; it would revolve around local life rather than national politics. Political parties and the political elite would be found in the national space, which would be responsible (along with the state as a whole and business interests) for maintaining sustained economic growth and an emphasis on social policies and democratization.

The sphere of action for popular organizations would be the municipality and the local neighborhood—that is, the more immediate community. That community, however, will be strengthened by national capitalist development and state social policies. The organizations that survive will be more efficient in achieving their goals. They will be less numerous but better organized. One should not expect them to be concerned with national politics.

The two poles of these dualisms, economic and political, may move closer with the success of antipoverty efforts. If over the next ten years sustained economic growth occurs averaging 5 percent or more a year—as is probable according to the data currently available—and the current effectiveness of social policies continues (a 1 percent decrease in the poverty rate for every 2.7 percent increase in GDP), the poverty rate will reach single digits. Social integration would then be viable, and social inequalities could be reversed. Economic and political dualisms would gradually disappear. Chile would have an independent and expanded national capitalist economy. Its democracy would be representative, and the participative practices of popular organizations would have an impact only at the local level. The distance that would exist between politics and the average citizen would be the cost that would have to be paid for the disappearance of populism and clientelism from the political system. If all of this comes to pass, the popular organizations that helped the popular identity to survive during long years of dictatorship and during the democratic period will have facilitated popular-sector integration into a national society that is more complete in terms of its capitalist development but less participative in terms of its democratic practice.

Notes

1. Absolute for the poorest 10 percent.
2. In a speech in 1992, President Patricio Aylwin concluded that the process had ended during his presidential term.
3. According to statistics from the Ministry of Labor, in 1994 there were 12,109 legally autonomous unions in Chile, with 661,966 members. Their average size was 54.6 members.
4. On this theme and the corresponding discussion, see Oxhorn (1995b).
5. The average increase in GDP has been over 6 percent a year since 1986.

5

Restoring Governance:
Has Brazil Got It Right (at Last)?

Philippe Faucher

> If Latin Americans are not prepared for what is coming, they will see
> transformed into junk yards not only many of their machines and indus-
> tries but also many of their cities, entire regions, and quite possibly even
> whole countries.
> —Francisco C. Weffort, "America Astray"

This pessimistic statement by Francisco C. Weffort dates back to 1991,
when Brazil and a number of Latin American countries were in the midst of
their worst economic crisis since World War II. The disillusionment concerning Brazil, however, had more profound roots. For the period 1985–
1990, Brazil was governed by José Sarney, the first civilian president after
twenty-one years of authoritarian rule. Despite hopes for change, politics
remained a nefarious game played by second-rate politicians (the same personalities tolerated by the military), debt service reached unbearable levels,
and the government—easy prey to populist temptations—suspended its
obligations to the international financial community. As the public deficit
exploded and international credit disappeared, inflation accelerated, and the
economy seemed on the verge of collapse. Nevertheless, corruption was
rampant; the government continued to openly buy support from constituents.

In this context, serious doubts were voiced about the viability of
Brazil's democracy. Would economic chaos produce such instability that it
might undermine the political transition? Could the society hope for anything better than a hybrid system of "delegative democracy" (O'Donnell,
1994)?[1] As the 1990 presidential elections approached, many saw the
Workers' Party (Partido dos Trabalhadores, or PT) and its leader, Luís
Inácio "Lula" da Silva, as the only chance for change. Others feared the

polarization of an organized socialist workers' party, notoriously infiltrated by radical left-wing factions, could provoke in such a highly unegalitarian society. Fear prevailed, and Fernando Collor de Mello was elected president by a close margin. Although he was an outsider and something of a dissident from the traditional right wing, Collor was nevertheless very much a member of the oligarchy. After only eighteen months in power, the newly elected president was paralyzed by his own incompetence. A special commission of the Congress found him and his close political associates responsible for numerous counts of corruption. On the eve of being voted out of office by the Senate, Collor resigned, to the nation's relief.

The transitional government of President Itamar Franco (1992–1994) proved more productive than expected. The economic stabilization program introduced by his finance minister, Fernando Henrique Cardoso, demonstrated resilience. Inflation was sharply reduced and consumer confidence restored.[2] Riding the popularity wave produced by his *coup-de-maître,* Cardoso was elected president in 1994 by a clear majority in the first round of voting. During its first two years in office (1995–1996), the Cardoso government preserved economic stability despite making only limited progress in controlling the budget deficit, and Congress approved several important amendments to the constitution—a task that had appeared insurmountable under the previous administration.

In this chapter I argue that until 1994, for both fundamental and systemic reasons, Brazil was perilously close to witnessing the collapse of its institutions. The success of the stabilization program initiated in 1994 and the country's apparent economic turnaround since Cardoso's election, however, have forced an alteration in the preferences of major economic agents and a partial realignment of the governing coalition. These changes have permitted the introduction of a number of reforms and the emergence of a political agenda that together have begun to address directly the sources of ungovernability in Brazil, although this challenge remains far from fully resolved.

What are the reasons for this impressive, although still fragile, success? It is not enough to say that the right person applied the correct policies at the right time in a social and political environment that was ready to accept them as a consequence of previous failures. Certainly, much of the credit should be given to the individuals involved. The institutional trauma caused by the corruption charges that led to the 1992 impeachment of President Collor (Montclair, 1994) also increased the audience for those advocating reform. But we must look beyond the anecdotal and circumstantial forces in the Brazilian case to better understand the factors that have contributed to the restoration of governance.[3]

Governance refers not only to government operations but more widely to the relations among state, market, and society. In this respect, governance can be measured by the ability of the state to maintain order in the face of normal disruptions and by the capacity to adapt in response to changes in its environment. Concern about governance is not directly related to a regime's relative strength or to the reliability of its institutions. As defined here, governance measures the capacity of the state to implement policy, to act within a set of predictable rules, and to maintain order.

For almost ten years, beginning in the mid-1980s, Brazil's civilian governments had been plagued by a declining capacity to implement policy because of three related factors: the fragmentation of the political elite, which led to weak and fragile governing coalitions; a decline in both the resource base of public administration and its capacity to deliver services; and a generalized weakening of public authority as a result of blatant corruption and the illegitimate use of violence. The most tangible manifestation of this ungovernability was the government's inability to deal with economic instability, which was augmented by a strong minority coalition of interests whose members were either protected from the costs of inflation through indexation or were able to profit from monetary instability. Ungovernability was thus magnified by repeated failures to stabilize the economy. Government ineffectiveness on this critical issue deepened the economic crisis, creating a vicious cycle that increased ungovernability.

The institutional crisis in 1992 produced by the disclosure of a massive corruption scheme under the Collor government and the impeachment procedures that followed, combined with the acceleration of inflation, which prevented all but a few Brazilians from insulating themselves from the negative consequences of economic instability, created an atmosphere conducive to the introduction and successful implementation in 1994 of a new stabilization plan, the Real Plan. The success of that program allowed President Cardoso to build a political coalition whose strength was enhanced by his solid electoral victory. These forces produced a high degree of legitimacy for the Cardoso government, which enabled it to rally state governors and build a majority in both houses of the Congress. Restored economic stability and high government legitimacy established a window of opportunity for the newly elected government to push for an agenda that would address the structural sources of ungovernability in Brazil. The Cardoso administration now faces the challenge of consolidating economic stability while carrying out the reform of the state and the restoration of public authority needed to further augment governability in a democratic environment.

In this chapter I first consider the factors responsible for the repeated failure of Brazilian authorities to implement a successful economic stabilization program during the first decade of civilian rule. At the market level, this failure reflected a lack of support for stabilization throughout Brazilian society. A minority of Brazilians, who were either protected from inflation or who benefited from it, formed a small but powerful coalition opposed to stabilization and its recessionary consequences. The majority, meanwhile, was too concerned about having to pay the high costs of yet another failed stabilization program (rising unemployment without price stability) to support a new plan. At the political level, failure resulted from a weakly institutionalized party system and the absence of an aggregative agenda, which exacerbated the fragmentation of interest representation in Congress and thereby limited the government's ability to build stable majority coalitions. The persistent fiscal hemorrhage thus could not be brought under control through legislative action, leaving authorities no alternative than to impose unpopular cuts by executive decree. Such abuses of executive power, however, were easy prey for the opposition and its allies in the bureaucracy and enabled them to force reconsideration of the cuts. The joint impact of the fiscal crisis and pressures for market liberalization pushed political leaders to engage in a mostly negative agenda designed to shrink the size of the state and, ultimately, its capacity to implement policy. The outcome was Brazil's version of a "disintegrated state" apparatus (Nelson, 1994a: 20). Finally, the shift from clientelism to corruption, arising from the blurred boundaries between the public and the private spheres (Martins, 1993), combined with systemic human rights violations and the impunity of those who perpetrated those crimes to further undermine the authority of public institutions and, thus, their ability to implement policy.

In the second section I argue that the unexpected success of the Real Plan was the result of the emergence of hyperinflation, the exposure of President Collor's corruption schemes, and the manner in which the Real Plan was implemented. Hyperinflation eroded the effectiveness of indexation and thereby augmented the economic risks of market instability for a large segment of the Brazilian populace, which undermined the membership and, thus, the strength of the coalition of actors who had no interest in stabilization and rallied those who feared the economic costs of another failed attempt. Following the congressional and judicial investigations of President Collor's corruption schemes, it became clear to the general population that those involved in overpricing practices, unwarrantable price increases, and speculation were the ones who profited most from economic chaos. Public disclosure of the large profits realized by banks, financial institutions, and firms at a high cost to society undermined Collor's policy influence. Finally, the Real Plan was designed and implemented in a gradual and negotiated manner that helped to minimize the costs of stabilization for the majority of fixed-income earners.

I then show that because economic stability translated into an unprecedented level of political support for President Cardoso and his allies, the victorious electoral coalition was transformed, through well-established practices of "political engineering," into a broad, although fragile, majority in the legislative assemblies. The Cardoso government attempted to exploit this legislative majority to initiate reform of the Brazilian state and to reestablish public authority—to rebuild governability in Brazil. After eighteen months in office, as the administration struggled to contain the fiscal deficit while avoiding a recession, the population became increasingly dissatisfied with the government's performance. Municipal elections in the austral spring of 1996 created an opportunity for allied parties, hoping to capitalize on the growing impatience for change, to renegotiate the terms of their cooperation with the government. By this time, however, the direction of change had been clearly set by Cardoso's administration. The "reform of the state" initiative and the concrete actions taken to restore the authority of the judicial system acknowledge the fact that markets, social distribution, and citizenship depend largely on a state that has the authority and the resources to deliver services efficiently. I believe these orientations are the most significant and enduring initiatives of the current administration, as they are likely to enhance democratic consolidation in Brazil.

The Enduring Failure to Stabilize

The evaluation of an economic stabilization program should be conceptualized in terms of an economy's ability to exhibit growth under democratic conditions (Bresser Pereira, Maravall, and Przeworski, 1993). Brazil struggled with high inflation and low growth for most of the 1980s and early 1990s; thus, compared with other countries of the region, its attempts at stabilization can be considered a case of marked failure. Enduring high levels of inflation are expressions of an acute distributional war between social groups that occur when powerful economic interests are in a position to profit from market disruptions either in countries with weak states, where democratic institutions have been disrupted, or in authoritarian regimes. This characterization certainly applies to the Brazilian situation during the civilian transition from military rule. The repeated failure to implement stabilization programs illustrates the government's loss of capacity to steer the economy, decide on an economic policy, and oversee that policy's effective implementation.

For many years, economists debated the policies required to stabilize an economy plagued by hyperinflation. The debate subsided as inflation was tamed, leaving behind a deceiving incantation dubbed the "Washington consensus," a magical formula by which future generations might avoid renewed economic instability (Williamson, 1990c). Policy success, however, relied on more than a sterile set of policy prescriptions and also rested on the considerable creativity of successive economic teams facing extremely demanding situations that stretched markets well beyond their predicted limits. The need to construct a coherent set of policies that enjoyed the support of a sufficient fraction of economic agents and thereby could be implemented effectively ensured that the experts' conception of what ought to be done was ultimately of limited use. The solution did not lie in technocratic control by the experts but instead in matching policies with an extremely complex set of assumptions about the behavior of economic agents and the expectations of the market. Economists' initial explanation for the failure of stabilization efforts was to blame the "economic populism" of politicians (Bresser Pereira, 1991). Although superficially accurate, this explanation leaves unexplored the reasons economic populism was so common in Latin America and, for the purpose of my argument, in Brazil.

Although history provides occasional evidence to the contrary (such as the Vargas regime of the period 1930–1945), where democratic institutions are weak and income distribution is highly concentrated, governments will tend to lack the political capacity to implement policies that negatively affect dominant economic interests. In Brazil, a coalition of politically influential economic actors had no interest in stabilization, whereas those who would have gained from price stability had limited political influence until the 1992 political crisis. The lack of support for stabilization from the political and economic elites, the faltering legitimacy of the government, and the government's incapacity to rally the population behind its objectives ensured that the political problem posed by stabilization was intractable.

Weakening of the State

Stabilization not only requires a well-designed program, political courage, and government determination; it also needs the support of civil society and of a country's political and economic elites. Facing fragmented political representation and lacking a clear, stable, and coherent majority in Congress until 1994, the Brazilian executive was not in a position to obtain the clear vote of support necessary to impose the transitional costs of stabilization on a skeptical population. The transition from authoritarian rule took more than ten years to complete. In 1985, the civilian alternative to the military regime was made up of a loose coalition of moderate reformers, liberal democrats, and a large number of last-minute opportunists—many of whom had been associated with the authoritarian regime for years. Faced with the responsibilities of power, the coalition rapidly exploded into opposing factions, enjoying, in the name of democracy, their right to dissent.

Ten political parties were represented in the Congress that wrote the new constitution in 1988. The internal heterogeneity of each party, the absence (with few exceptions) of programmatic or ideological identification among party members, and the difficulties of enforcing party discipline made any coherent and stable majority difficult to establish.[4] Approval of any legislation required that ad hoc coalitions be formed to produce an instant majority. These majorities were based on personal tradeoffs among members of Congress and extended beyond party affiliations and across ideological lines (Martins, 1993: 22). During the Collor administration, the formation of legislative coalitions was even more difficult because of the presence of twenty parties in Congress, none of which held more than 20 percent of the seats. Without a defined and stable majority, the government frequently faced nearly paralyzing opposition within the legislative assemblies.

The lack of legislative support for stabilization measures was compounded by a disorganized state apparatus increasingly incapable of providing even the most basic services (such as sanitation and education) to the population. By eroding state capacity to borrow funds when needed, the fiscal crisis deprived the state of the resources either to fund development policies or to introduce reforms aimed at producing significant structural change in the productive system. Much as Brazilian society for too many years had ignored its fiscal crisis, it also refused to question the developmentalist state's structure and plethora of public enterprises. Lacking the resources and, in all but a few isolated sectors, the competence required to carry out its expansive portfolio of tasks, the bureaucracy lost its capacity to implement government policies. Furthermore, widespread corruption, institutionalized violence, and an underfunded and ineffective judicial system combined to increase the cynicism of the population and to undermine confidence in public institutions to the point of destroying public authority and plunging society into an atomic state. In the next three sections I look at the forces that have crippled the Brazilian government's capacity to implement policy—fragile and fluctuating political coalitions, the erosion of the state, and corruption and institutionalized violence—and that together have undermined the legitimacy of the political class and public institutions within the Brazilian population.

Fragile Coalitions and Pervading Clientelism

In the transition to an effective democratic regime, consolidation comes through practicing the formal rules of political democracy and through the resulting progressive penetration of democratic practices into other spheres of society. In Brazil, however, that process of consolidation was restricted. The transition from military rule extended for more than ten years,[5] throughout which civilian governments relied on cabinet-level politicians with ministerial experience obtained under military rule. This situation gave the political elite both the time and the access needed to influence the transition process and thereby preserve its power. The consequent permanency of the political elite helps to explain the persistence of old political practices in democratic Brazil.

Elite continuity means the traditional clientelistic networks either survived or recomposed themselves (Hagopian, 1992). The perpetuation of the patrimonial style of politics, as illustrated by O'Donnell (1992), has produced a paradoxical blend of government omnipotence and impotence. Both military and civilian governments have resorted to "government by decree" (permitted in cases of emergency by the 1988 constitution), which involves "handing down decisions which are not subjected to the institutional and legal procedures of a constitutional system" and is an expression of omnipotence (O'Donnell, 1992: 39). Indeed, most Brazilian stabilization plans, as well as broader economic reforms (such as privatizations), have been imposed in such a technocratic fashion.[6] The repeated failures of those measures, however, caused in many cases by resistance from within the bureaucracy, also point to the impotence of this style of governance.

Another characteristic of Brazilian politics that both underscores the weakness of democracy and helps to explain the political instability that impairs governance there is the "fluidity" of the partisan structure. Three characteristics of that structure portray its fluidity. First, parties appear and disappear to suit the electoral ambitions of prominent members of the political oligarchy. Labels are constantly changed for no other purpose than to create a convenient instrument to channel support from a given clientele to a specific candidate in a particular election. Second, the change of allegiance from one party to another is not only common but is guided by the opportunistic motives of political actors. Although party leaders have the capacity to enforce discipline within their clientele through control of the distribution of resources, members of Congress encourage competing parties to bid against each other for their support and regularly change allegiances to benefit from the best offer.[7] No ideological barriers limit passage from one political formation to another, and ideological consistency is not a required or a valued political asset.[8] Third, because the game is about controlling more resources as part of either the opposition or the government, it has not been uncommon for parties to "transform" themselves from part of the opposition into members of the governing coalition (Hagopian, 1992: 282; O'Donnell, 1993: 1360). In fact, some parties have succeeded in getting members appointed to cabinet positions while they are formally part of the opposition. Such political practices both create and heighten institutional instability and, as such, tend to reproduce themselves through time.

Political coalitions are fragile and can change shape very rapidly. The challenge for the executive has been to negotiate simultaneously with parties, special interest groups, and state governors to create and maintain the necessary space to carry out its political agenda. In this setting, votes in Congress are exchanged for favors such as government contracts and the nomination of political allies to government posts. The consequent political and institutional instability has forced the executive to adopt a very short-term policy perspective. Negotiations produce ad hoc coalitions that eventually lead to the formation of a congressional majority for a specific piece of legislation but with no guarantee that this coalition will be maintained to pass another piece of legislation. The vote on a particular date is not indicative of the support the government will enjoy the next day. The legislative agenda is thus limited to projects that fall within the lines of least resistance. More controversial proposals—namely, most decisions dealing with economic stabilization—could not generally muster a legislative majority and thus have to be issued by decree.

If tensions between the executive and Congress increased, the chance of having legislation approved would diminish significantly. The policy consequence of this situation was made evident during the Collor administration. As an outsider to the political elite, Collor, who was elected by a broad coalition of more than 35 million votes, did not enjoy the support of any large national party. He created his own political formation, the National Renovation Party (PRN), but was unable to translate his electoral coalition into a governing majority. Of the twenty parties represented in Congress in 1990, the PRN held no more than 10 percent of the seats. Only by forming broad, unstable, and costly coalitions was the government able to have parts of its legislative program adopted.

As President Collor's popularity faded in the wake of mounting rumors of corruption, dissent raged among the parties that had initially supported his administration's legislative program. In March 1992, Collor asked every member of his cabinet to resign in an attempt to rebuild an effective governing coalition. Even after reshuffling his entire cabinet to accommodate as many political parties as possible and using the full weight of the government's budgetary prerogatives, Collor was unable to rally a majority in each house. The Collor administration thus felt compelled to force through a number of policy changes by decree, which further infuriated the opposition majority in the Congress. Constitutional amendments needed to enact essential reforms but that required the support of 60 percent of the Congress were irremediably out of reach. As the cost of maintaining a majority coalition became unbearable, Collor's fragile base of congressional support collapsed in a spectacular way: the Congress voted to impeach the president. Collor's vice president, Itamar Franco, assumed the presidency in the wake of the impeachment vote, but the political elite—considering him an interim president—was hesitant to make a commitment to his administration. By maintaining its distance, the elite gave the new president no choice but to govern through provisional measures issued by decree.

Erosion of the State

The erosion of the state can be traced back only in part to the fiscal crisis; it is more fundamentally a crisis of the state apparatus. Without adequate resources, the Brazilian state was unable to manage its own administration or implement its policies. Even the means designed to enforce respect for laws and regulations became dysfunctional. That is, the administration had lost not only the means but also the authority to act. Widespread patrimonialism and clientelism also led to a peculiar form of privatization of the state. Most of the nation's collective resources were appropriated by particularistic interests in the form of rent. Social struggles occurred more to defend the privileges of specific groups—such as workers, bureaucrats, or professors—than to ensure a more equitable distribution of resources.

As pointed out by Tavares de Almeida (1995), the fiscal crisis further enhanced those features of the structure and procedures of the federal administration that accounted for its internal fragmentation and institutional fragility. Under military rule, the executive branch adopted a pattern of financial centralization combined with structural and decisional decentralization. Government agencies, public enterprises, and foundations thereby acquired considerable autonomy from the central government, which further fragmented decisionmaking. But they also acquired low levels of institutionalization, discretionary methods, and high personnel turnover, which made the federal bureaucracy both flexible and weak.

The bureaucracy also suffered severe blows to its human and financial resources. The most damaging of these was the radical and indiscriminate dismissal of thousands of public servants by the Collor administration. Drastic cuts to the administration were made on the basis of the political strength and support of powerful policy communities. Agencies responsible for economic regulation were abolished—such as the National Superintendency for Supplies (SUNAB) and the Inter-Ministerial Price Council (CIP), which were responsible for monitoring prices—and public investment in health, housing, and education was choked, yet subsidies for industry were maintained. Clientelistic pressures took advantage of those cuts and victimized the remaining agencies. Under the control of particularistic interests, the institutional autonomy of the sectoral bureaucracies was dramatically reduced. Both demoralized by the disorganization of the administration and concerned about the probable loss of their generous retirement privileges, many senior bureaucrats retired. As a result, within months the administration lost much of its expertise. The operational capacity of the Brazilian state thus collapsed because of a loss of resources (both human and financial) and increasing penetration by clientelistic interests, which blurred the distance between private and public space and opened the way for corruption.

The erosion of the state reduced its capacity to implement policy. The state no longer had the proper instruments or adequate operational conditions to fulfill its assigned tasks. These limitations caused the deterioration of the state's capacity to collect taxes, provide services, and enforce regulations. Consequently, major policy shifts, such as trade liberalization and privatization, were rendered largely insignificant by a weak and divided bureaucracy lacking both the political leadership and the institutional capacity needed to carry out reforms.

Weak Institutions Allow for Impunity and Anomie

Beyond the fragility of ruling coalitions and the erosion of state capacity, the government's ability to implement policy was further undermined by a loss of legitimacy born of corruption and human rights violations. Corruption is hardly new in Brazil, and it is widely accepted by the private sector as part of the price of doing business. Rumors of corruption concerning President Sarney, his political associates, and members of his family were constant throughout his term in office. With the Collor administration, however, the scale of the network and the amounts of money involved reached unprecedented levels.[9] Further, the new, inexperienced government made the mistake of displacing the bureaucrats who had controlled policy networks in previous administrations and instead channeled the government's wealth to its friends (Montclair, 1994). Those who were displaced were among the first to denounce abuses by the new administration, as evidenced by the corruption scheme involving directors of Braspetro, the trading subsidiary of the national petroleum company, Petrobrás.

One defense of these wrongdoings further illuminates the source of the problem. P. C. Farias, who managed the Collor corruption network, argued that he was handling the affairs of the presidency and the party in the same manner as his predecessors had. He argued that because the campaign financing law did not enable parties to raise the resources required to finance increasingly expensive campaigns (legislation forbade contributions from juridical persons [Martins, 1993: 42]), all candidates were forced to commit abuses. In other words, when laws are badly designed they are unenforceable, which inevitably leads to abuses. As it becomes clear that those abuses will go unpunished, abusers grow bolder. As the state's inability to make the law stand becomes visible, standards of public morality become confused, and the collectivity drifts into anomie.[10]

Corruption during the Collor administration took its toll on government legitimacy. In March 1990, at the beginning of Collor's term of office, polls revealed that 71 percent of the population supported Collor and his cabinet. Despite the recession caused by a disastrous stabilization plan, the president continued to enjoy a high approval rating (about 60 percent) for a number of months (Weyland, 1996: 196). In the ensuing year and a half, however, a succession of scandals involving various ministers and some of Collor's close associates sapped the administration's popularity and legitimacy.

To corruption and tax evasion one should add the multiple forms of violence and exploitation endured by the victims of abuse by official security forces and private militias. When the state has no recognized authority or is incapable of exerting its authority, as occurred in Brazil, collective space becomes a "brown area" (O'Donnell, 1993) of permanent conflict and total insecurity. As the state's capacity to protect its citizenry declines, the legitimacy of the state among the population decreases as well.

Brazil's crisis can thus be characterized as a paralysis of the implementation process—a serious crisis of authority whose manifestation is the lack of state resources, autonomy, legitimacy, and political clout needed to implement policy decisions. Weakened institutions are easily penetrated by corruption, and social conflicts turn to violence when perpetrators are convinced of their impunity. This severe crisis of governability led to concerns about a possible sudden reversal of democracy through a military coup. Others foresaw a "slow death" for democracy because of "a progressive reduction of existing spaces for the exercise of civilian power and for the effectiveness of the classic guarantees of liberal constitutionalism" (O'Donnell, 1992: 19). A third, nonauthoritarian possibility would be that of a "nonfatal chronic illness," which would entail a repetitive process of systemic ungovernability—an entropic force that regularly cancels previous advances toward market stabilization and democratic consolidation.[11] Accordingly, after the traumatic experience of Collor's impeachment followed by a far-reaching corruption scandal involving the House Budget Committee, the system recovered, and constitutional order was preserved— albeit with reduced state capacity to implement policy. Prior to considering that process, however, I will look into the factors that contributed to the repeated failures of stabilization efforts in Brazil.

Making Profits from Inflation

From the time President José Sarney took office in 1985 until the 1994 initiation of the Real Plan, Brazil experienced nine failed stabilization attempts. Each plan succeeded only temporarily. Soon, inflation crawled back; interest rates increased, producing a sharp escalation in the country's internal debt payments; and public deficits continued to rise despite government promises to keep them under control. Of the major shock treatments applied to the economy during this period, the Collor Plan of March 1990 was the most radical and also one of the least successful. The Collor Plan directly attacked the money supply, allowing the government to confiscate all corporate and private savings exceeding an established amount (approximately U.S.$2,000 for individuals) for a period of one year—a total of 70 percent of all financial assets. The aim of the program was to cut drastically what was considered excess purchasing power in the economy.

Although opinions on the potential effectiveness of this measure differ, the fact is that it could not be implemented. Firms, banks, and wealthy individuals successfully devised ways to escape the new regulations. Within three months, an estimated 85 percent of the confiscated purchasing power had been recuperated and reinjected back into the system (Flynn, 1993: 350). The failure of the Collor Plan had become evident by the end of 1990 when the monthly rate of inflation reached almost 20 percent. This development marked the definitive demise of Collor's "heterodox shock treatment" and led to the May 1991 resignation of Collor's finance minister. The new finance minister, named amid impeachment proceedings against the president, had few options other than to try to prevent the system from spiraling into hyperinflation. Real interest rates increased to 40 percent annually, and the economy was driven into recession.

Collor's successor, Itamar Franco, took more than a year and four finance ministers to announce a plan to stabilize the economy, the Real Plan. Franco's finance minister, Cardoso, implemented the plan in stages, beginning with the introduction of new financial parameters to relieve pressure on prices and culminating with the most spectacular stage—the July 1, 1994, introduction of a new currency, the real, whose value was fixed to the U.S. dollar (at the rate of R$1 = U.S.$1). In the two years following the introduction of the real, inflation averaged around 2 percent per month (less than 1 percent during the first three quarters of 1996). The reasons for the apparent success of the Real Plan are considered in the next section.

Since owners of financial capital and net creditors generally suffer from high inflation, one would think an irresistible coalition of interests would have forced economic stabilization to the top of the government's agenda. The Brazilian economy largely escapes this simple logic, however; in fact, the strongest coalition has long been the one composed of those sectors that thrive on high inflation. When faced with chronic inflation, the efforts of economic agents to protect their relative share of income led to an indexation of prices and wages to some measure of past inflation. This system of indexation has insulated some privileged social groups from the effects of inflation, whereas the real income of the vast majority of the population has fallen under the weight of the inflation tax. Brazilian banks also made inflation work for them because of the particularities of Brazilian financial regulation. Armijo (1996) presents five ways in which Brazilian banks have benefited from inflation: (1) Financial institutions have gained from citizens holding funds as non-interest bearing deposits; (2) banks have profited from the "float" while a check cleared—that is the time between the dates the money is withdrawn from one account and deposited to another; (3) society's need to cope with inflation has bid up the value of the financial sector's consulting services; (4) rapidly changing prices disguise high service charges and spreads from customers; and finally, (5) owners of financial capital have gained from the willingness of government to pay high real interest rates to induce banks and the public to hold the domestic public debt.

Generalized indexation and many other peculiarities of Brazilian financial regulations thereby enabled owners of financial capital (bankers and corporate and individual investors) to reap large profits under high and escalating inflation. Financial regulations also operated as an important, autonomous source of inflation. To encourage financial savings despite high inflation, the government permitted indexation to generate positive real interest rates on financial assets. Indexation, however, interacted with expectations and further fueled inflation as economic agents made the rational assumption that this month's inflation would equal last month's plus something additional (Armijo, 1996). Industry, labor, and holders of financial assets thereby incorporated a margin of "inflation protection" into their bargaining with one another and with the government. This added margin of indexation sped up price increases while perpetuating those sectors' immunity to the costs of inflation.

Through indexation, most wage earners were reasonably well protected against inflation, as was Brazil's "new" middle class. Rapid growth during the 1970s and early 1980s had created a new class of middle-income earners. Some were found in industry, but most were situated in the service sector and in public administration. Defended by large, powerful unions, this group was one of the major beneficiaries of indexation (bureaucrats also benefited from the permanent job stability guaranteed by the constitution). Despite the protection from inflation afforded to Brazil's middle class through indexation, by 1985 the fiscal crisis had begun to erode its acquisitive power and self-assertive image. As the group's lifestyle and expectations came under threat, its members cohered in opposition to any stabilization program that offered less than full protection of their purchasing power. The middle class thus offered unconditional support for the first stabilization attempts of the 1980s.

When the Cruzado Plan was introduced in 1986, thousands of volunteers rampaged through the streets to check prices and publicly denounce any unwarranted price increase. The logic behind this behavior was simple to understand. Once the program was imposed, it was in the interest of the middle class (whose wages were frozen by the plan) to ensure that the real distributional costs of stabilization would not fall disproportionately on its members. The failure of this plan and a series of ensuing stabilization programs to deliver price stability, however, produced a population cynical of the government's capacity to defeat inflation and thereby undermined popular support for stabilization efforts.

The sector that suffered the most from inflation and that was thus most likely to support government stabilization efforts had little policy influence. The majority of the Brazilian population—the underemployed and the poor, whose incomes were unprotected from the ravages of inflation—lacked both the organization and the access to the political system needed to make itself heard. The majority, therefore, could not provide sufficient political support to ensure successful stabilization.

The extreme market instability produced by the government's inability to stabilize the economy effectively immobilized economic policymaking. Struggling to prevent a market collapse, the government was unable to implement much-needed fiscal reform and, in fact, its entire reform agenda (with the exception of trade liberalization, which was introduced in 1990) because of the urgency created by economic instability. With annual inflation above 1,000 percent and peaks of up to 80 percent a month, economic policy addressed little except the urgent need to ease the extreme distortions in resource allocation.

Economic Stability Restored: Putting a Check on Rent Seeking

The outlook for Brazil changed significantly with the election of President Cardoso. Inflation declined dramatically, and billions of investment dollars flowed into the São Paulo stock exchange. The successful 1994 stabilization program was the most important factor in changing the economic situation. Economic stability translated into a restored government capacity to build stable coalitions, which provided the political capacity to implement policy and thereby garner legitimacy and support from the electorate. Before we consider the manifestations of expanded governability, however, we need to look at the nature and causes of this change. Explanations focusing on timing, luck, or personalities are not convincing; rather, this considerable and radical shift is explained by the sources of ungovernability identified in the first section of this chapter. I argue that the new government consciously adopted measures that addressed the central causes of ungovernability and thereby built public support and restored a part of the state's lost capacity to act.

Successful economic stabilization requires courage, administrative determination, and political capacity. A common view ascribes these qualities to authoritarian regimes and established democracies (Bresser Pereira, in Bresser Pereira, Maravall, and Przeworski, 1993: 55). The argument holds that when democratic institutions are weak, as in a period of democratic consolidation, sufficient political support is unlikely to be mobilized to implement reform without threatening the survival of the government. The Brazilian and Argentine cases, however, have shown that a democratic way to stabilization does exist. In each country, political leaders (Carlos Menem as president in Argentina and Cardoso as finance minister in Brazil) exploited their political strengths to garner support for the adoption of strong reform initiatives (see Chapters 7 and 8). The democratic road to economic stabilization thus lies with a leader's ability to design a reform program that fits the nature and quantity of available political support.

The successful implementation of the Real Plan benefited from the institutional crisis surrounding the impeachment of Collor and the deterioration of the economic situation, which weakened the proinflation coalition and popular opposition to a new stabilization effort. Nevertheless, Cardoso still needed to structure the plan to overcome fears that remained in Brazilian society about the distribution of the costs associated with yet another stabilization program; he did so through the gradual and negotiated introduction of the Real Plan.

Rational choice theory explains that stabilization measures are often politically difficult to adopt because costs tend to be immediate and concentrated whereas benefits are more diffuse and are obtained only in the long run. In this situation, state officials will rationally attempt to maximize their material and political utility by responding to the rent-seeking efforts of those who will be hurt by stabilization (Schamis, 1995: 170). This leads to the conclusion that market stability will be restored when the economic costs of instability outweigh the costs of stabilization for the majority of citizens.

In Brazil, market instability during the last months of Collor's government and the first months of Franco's administration (during which prices increased at a rate of 20 to 80 percent per month) exceeded the protection provided by indexation for most actors. A lag always exists in the application of wage indexation—increases are corrected only for the previous month's inflation and thereby allow the current month's inflation to erode income. The costs to Brazilian society in lost purchasing power thus tended to increase as the rate of inflation picked up, leading to a growing demand for stabilization. The unprecedented sense of popular urgency about the need to halt price inflation, produced by declining living standards, moved economic stabilization to the top of the political agenda.[12] Also, the exposure of numerous corruption scandals involving major corporations and the disclosure of huge profits realized by the financial sector despite high inflation undercut the influence of powerful actors who had opposed stabilization and strengthened the government's determination to maintain a consistent course of action. Finally, Argentina's successful stabilization program, begun in 1991, inspired the Brazilian plan and demonstrated the possibility for its success.

It is not enough for economic agents to realize that they are losing because of inflation, however. If they believe the costs of stabilization will be higher than the losses from inflation, they will hesitate to join the anti-inflationary battle. The resounding failures of previous stabilization programs, including the negative impact of the Collor Plan on middle-class savings, had taught Brazilians that the medicine can be worse than the disease. That experience forced the government to adopt a radically different approach to implementing stabilization. The success of the Real Plan thus should be attributed not only to the opportunity created by hyperinflation and the discredit suffered by financial and business elites in the wake of the corruption scandals; it was also the result of the way the costs and uncertainties of stabilization were managed through the design of the program, as well as the timing and manner in which it was implemented.

The implementation strategy of the Real Plan was simple: gradualism replaced shock treatment. Starting in early 1994, and after repeated public statements of its intentions, the economic team created new financial indicators and implemented limited monetary reform designed to lower inflationary expectations. Only after expectations had been lowered did the government target the large inertial component of inflation through the July 1 introduction of a new currency—the real—whose value was fixed relative to the U.S. dollar and was backed by substantial reserves (nearly U.S.$40 billion) held by the Central Bank. Price controls and indexation were rapidly relaxed to allow for more flexible, market-induced adjustments in relative prices, and interest rates fell. Finally, the government tightened controls on the deficit and simultaneously entered into negotiations with the states to limit their deficit spending and address the huge debts accumulated by the state banks.

The timing of the plan was also key to its successful implementation. The program was implemented progressively during the buildup to the 1994 presidential election. With the monthly inflation rate above 50 percent, government opponents saw an opportunity to blame the outgoing administration for this economic disaster and thereby gain politically. At the same time, however, if this plan were successful, open opposition could prove politically costly. This election season dilemma convinced much of the opposition to hedge its bets and remain silent. The political class thus refrained from denouncing Cardoso's stabilization program, with the significant exception of the Workers' Party. As the Real Plan began to work and opinion polls registered its resulting political payoff, however, it was too late for the silent opposition to take credit for the program's success, and the fate of the Workers' Party presidential candidate was sealed.

Political Conditions to
Sustain and Implement Reforms

Thanks largely to the success of his stabilization program, President Cardoso enjoyed an uncommon eighteen-month honeymoon. The Congress approved two significant constitutional changes during that period, open corruption was checked, and human rights violations were placed squarely on the agenda with some important cases brought to court. These limited advances raise a central question: Are they sufficient to claim that governance has been restored? Will the conjunctural increase in governability produced by price stability, renewed economic growth, and the consequent high approval ratings of the administration actually expand the long-term capacity of the state to implement its policies?

Much has not changed on the political front. The highly fragmented character of political representation has weakened Cardoso's majority in Congress and led to the defeat, amending, or withdrawal (for lack of sufficient support) of major pieces of legislation (see Chapter 6). Clientelism is still a powerful force in Brazilian politics, and, notwithstanding Cardoso's ability to play the clientelistic rules to his advantage, this practice can be a significant obstacle to efforts to reduce the budget deficit, especially with regard to the state governors. Restoring state capacity to deliver services in a context of fiscal restraint will thus face opposition from the numerous groups that stand to lose access and power. Cardoso's adept construction of coalitions through clientelistic networks and his free use of provisional measures, however, provide room for cautious optimism. In addition, advances in addressing and controlling institutionalized violence, increasing authorities' determination to restore respect for the law, and setting a new agenda for building a renewed social contract are also hopeful signs. Finally, Cardoso's "reform of the state" initiative is designed specifically to restore state authority and autonomy.

From Electoral Coalition to Fragile Government Majority

Cardoso's electoral strategy was clear from the outset of his presidential campaign. His main opponent, Lula da Silva of the Workers' Party (who had received 48 percent of the vote in the second round of the 1989 election against Collor), enjoyed a substantial head start. He benefited from the unconditional support of the organized urban workers in manufacturing, services, and the public sector and from a hyperinflationary environment through June 1995. Realizing that only limited gains could be made on the left, Cardoso reached to the right to form a broad, centrist coalition. As the candidate of the Social Democrat Party of Brazil (PSDB), Cardoso aligned himself with the conservative Liberal Front Party (PFL) and the Brazilian Labor Party (PTB).

This electoral strategy, combined with the stunning success of the Real Plan (inflation was only 1.5 percent for the month preceding the election) and the reticence much of the electorate felt toward the PT candidate, helped Cardoso to win a clear majority of 54.2 percent of the October 1 vote. The new president now faced the challenge of converting his electoral coalition into a working majority in the Congress without undermining his own political agenda. That strategic task was made easier by the fact that prominent members of Cardoso's electoral coalition had ridden his coattails to victory, including the new governor of the country's most important state. Finally, the popularity of the president, linked closely with the success of the Real Plan, undoubtedly played a pivotal role in enticing the political elite to cooperate, which helped the new president consolidate his electoral coalition into an unprecedented, regionally diversified political alliance. But the situation also suggested that if the economic situation were to deteriorate, the government's congressional majority would quickly evaporate.

Although Cardoso's party occupied only sixty-two seats in the Legislative Assembly and ten in the Senate, his broader alliance (including the PFL, the PTB, and two minor parties, the Popular Party and the Liberal Party) accounted for 45.2 percent of the votes in the legislature. With the added but unstable support of some sectors of the Progressive Reform Party and the Party of the Brazilian Democratic Movement (PMDB), Cardoso could count on the votes of nearly 68 percent of Brazilian legislators during his first year in office. This broad centrist coalition provided enough votes to pass the constitutional amendments (which required a three-fifths majority) that were part of Cardoso's political agenda.

Given that interest group representation in Brazil cuts across party lines,[13] maintaining the large coalition would be costly. Within six months of the October 1994 elections, twenty-nine deputies and three senators had switched their party loyalties, mostly in favor of the PSDB and the PFL. Cardoso was thus forced to resort to clientelistic practices in an effort to sustain his congressional majority. Trading votes for patronage resources, however, can be expensive for the treasury. To gain the support of the institution representing the interests of large landowners, for example, in June 1995 the government agreed to provide a subsidized rate for a large accumulated debt at an estimated cost of U.S.$3.5 billion. Despite the cost, this clientelistic strategy worked for eighteen months with only a single setback, and Cardoso was thus able to get most of his legislative agenda approved by both the Legislative Assembly and the Senate. In short, the government was successful because rather than trying to change the established rules of the political game, it was willing to play by those rules and to generate the greatest possible advantage from favorable circumstances.

Nevertheless, difficulties were to be expected. First, by 1996 a lack of serious reform of the tax system threatened economic stability. Unable to raise the revenues needed to reduce the budget deficit, the government relied on a tight money supply and an overvalued exchange rate to keep inflation down. The persistent budget deficit also reflected government assistance to failing banks and the need to issue large numbers of government bonds to control the flow of foreign funds attracted by high interest rates (around 28 percent above inflation) (*Economist,* May 4, 1996). The result was an economic slowdown, a wave of bankruptcies, and a sharp rise in unemployment. As the middle class began to feel the pinch of higher costs of education, health, and housing (because of reduced government subsidies) and workers grew disappointed with the government's refusal to raise the minimum wage, Cardoso's approval ratings fell. From his 54 percent electoral majority in late 1994, the president's approval rating fell to 38 percent in March 1996 and to 25 percent in May of that year (*Economist,* June 1, 1996).

The government also had limited success with its privatization program, which revealed the state's lack of institutional capacity. Despite a constitutional amendment in May 1995 that ended the monopoly of Petrobrás, Brazil's state-owned petroleum company, over a year later private firms still lacked access to the country's oil reserves. The much awaited privatization of the large public mining conglomerate Companhia Vale do Rio Doce was postponed several times. And the privatization of the electrical power company did not occur until eighteen months after the new government had taken office. This failure was the consequence of the state's lack of autonomy relative to distributional coalitions and other rent-seeking interest groups in the Brazilian polity, and it risked weakening the credibility of the government's commitment to economic reform among investors, both foreign and domestic.

The source of this limitation of the government's policymaking autonomy became strikingly evident as the November 1996 municipal elections—the first electoral test of Cardoso's government—neared. Within the government's legislative coalition, dissent among the member parties increased as each tried to expand its electoral advantage in key municipalities. The result was growing conflict between the executive and Congress. During this period, a constitutional amendment designed to reform the national pension system was so severely weakened by the legislature that the government decided to kill its own project; in June 1996, the government announced that it would instead rely on provisional measures to implement reform. It also took measures to shore up its support in Congress: former finance minister Francisco Dornelles, congressional leader of the opposition Brazilian Progressive Party, was named minister of industry and trade, and Luiz Carlos Santos of the PMDB was named to the politically strategic post of minister of parliamentary affairs.

The Reform of the State Initiative

Concurrent with its economic reform efforts, the Brazilian government embarked on an ambitious reform of the state apparatus. The government's project was designed to both make the bureaucracy more efficient and recuperate state capacity to implement government initiatives and deliver services to the population. The 1988 constitution, however, stood in the way of such reform. That constitution resulted from the fragmented political representation, lack of party discipline, and absence of a coherent and stable legislative majority that made it so difficult for Cardoso to preserve his legislative coalition during his first two years in office. During the writing of the constitution, coalitions and instant majorities formed on the basis of tradeoffs among members of Congress or between them and powerful lobbies. One such tradeoff integrated the rights and benefits of civil servants into the constitution. Any reform of the public administration in Brazil thus requires a reform of the 1988 constitution and the requisite three-fifths majority support in the legislature.

A program for reforming the structure of the state was published in November 1995; it proposed a thorough program review, a significant change in management practices and style within public administration, and the passage of constitutional amendments required to carry out needed reforms (Presidency, 1995). Implementation of this proposed reform of the state faces a number of obstacles. If successful, reform will challenge the deeply rooted clientelistic political culture and the flourishing rent-seeking activity characteristic of the Brazilian bureaucracy. The proposed privatization of "nonexclusive services" (such as universities, hospitals, research centers, and museums), for example, will delegate managerial authority to outside agencies, thus limiting the patronage resources available to politicians. Since all political parties stand to lose from this and similar proposals, implementation of the reform as proposed by the Cardoso government is unlikely.

Further resistance can be expected from both within the bureaucracy and among its clients. Streamlining bureaucratic procedures and increasing bureaucratic efficiency will eliminate the need for the middlemen who handle the petty corruption required to "ease" the delivery of public services. The delegation of authority will also include management contracts specifically designed to curb the corporatist privileges enjoyed by the bureaucrats who populate agencies within the state structure. Finally, the reform intends to undermine the established relationship between the public bureaucracy and private interests. Special interest groups have established direct and "privileged" relations with sectors of the public administration that go well beyond conventional lobbying. The resulting deterioration of clientelism into generalized and pervasive corruption intended to capture state resources by private interests has seriously blurred the boundaries between "public" and "private" (Martins, 1993: 18) and has also ensured that any reform of the state apparatus would threaten established clientelistic networks by attempting to restore the social scrutiny and political intermediation of bureaucratic operations.

Transforming the Brazilian bureaucracy into a professional public administration thus faces serious obstacles that demand a cautious, incremental approach to reform and will likely require more than one electoral mandate to achieve. Nevertheless, there is reason to believe the outcome of the Cardoso project might be successful. The level of popular support enjoyed by the project and its proposed strategy for implementation suggest that the Cardoso government will be able to take advantage of a conjunctural increase in governability to rebuild long-term governability in Brazil. Four factors support this contention that Cardoso's reform of the state is a manifestation of restored governance: (1) The idea of "reinventing the state" has gained acceptance in administrative and political circles, as have changing views about the "model of development" Brazil should adopt; (2) the erosion of public administration and its limited capacity to deliver services have convinced governors and mayors to support reform; (3) the incremental approach chosen for implementation and limited personnel cuts at the federal level could help to dispel opposition among civil servants; and (4) citizens' right to demand and receive high-quality, efficient services and the eradication of corruption are popular political issues.

First, as in the case of economic restructuring, a consensus has emerged in Brazil about the need to rehabilitate the state, improve the delivery of public services and the management of public resources, and eradicate corruption (Martins, 1993: i). The reinventing of the state initiatives, like studies produced by major multilateral institutions such as the World Bank (Frischtak, 1994) and the Organization for Economic Cooperation and Development (OECD, 1995), reflect this growing concern about the need to modernize state structures and public administration. Successful reforms implemented in Brazilian towns such as Curitiba, Fortaleza, and, more recently, Porto Alegre have set precedents that have further popularized the issue among top bureaucrats and some sectors of the political elite.

Second, the urgent need for reform is evident at all levels of government. Because of clientelistic concessions, corporatist lobbies, and legislative loopholes, administrations at the federal, regional, and local levels have been paralyzed by an army of expensive bureaucrats. As a result of the limits imposed on inflationary financing of government spending, state governors and mayors have rallied behind reform of the state. To cut costs, they have been attracted by proposed flexibilization in bureaucrats' job security and in contracting procedures. Out of necessity rather than ideology, a pragmatic consensus is emerging.

Third, although unions are not convinced, reform apparently does not include a massive reduction of the bureaucracy, at least at the federal level. In fact, the project claims the requisite reduction has already occurred. From 1988 to 1994, the number of civil servants at the federal level declined 17 percent (from 1,442,657 to 1,197,460) (Presidency, 1995: 33). Brazil's public administration is inefficient, but that is not a function of its size. Ratios in relation to total population and to the labor force are very low compared with those of European countries.[14] Union opposition can also be attenuated through public pressure and the decisions of individual civil servants; at the state and municipal levels, for example, the government has offered generous retirement packages.

Fourth, reform plans to make administrative and political accountability in the management of public funds a concrete component of citizenship. The plan envisions steps to inform citizens of their rights when dealing with the bureaucracy, which should, to the extent that it encourages citizens to air their grievances, help to make traditional populist intermediation less common. Complaints and suggestions from end users, as intended in "project citizen" (Presidency, 1995: 81), can be used to build support for administrative reform and thereby counteract resistance from civil servants.

Restoring State Authority

Beyond the reform of the state, limited advances on the corruption and human rights fronts are also cause for an optimistic assessment of Cardoso's chances for enhancing the legitimacy and, thus, the capabilities of the state. The fight against impunity was at first an economic necessity. At the height of the economic crisis in the early 1990s, fiscal evasion became chic. Brazil's economic elite openly defied fiscal authorities, and entrepreneurs announced their right to resist exploitation by an abusive and corrupt state. Following Collor's ouster, strong public support for the fight against corruption radically changed the situation. Instead of announcing the fiscal amnesty tax evaders had expected, the federal government applied the law. In 1993, revenues soared by 26.5 percent over the previous year, and fines increased by more than 30 percent.[15]

On the issue of human rights, dos Santos (1996) stresses the importance of the Cardoso administration's effort to break with the past. The government has recognized that the state has not only failed to implement its own laws but that it has also committed serious criminal acts. No human rights issue is more sensitive than the repression that occurred under the military. Although the Cardoso government has respected the amnesty law issued by President João Baptista Figueiredo to enable the transition to civilian rule, it created a commission to identify those who had disappeared. The commission produced a list of more than 300 victims and offered compensation to their families (Law 9.140/95). The measure leaves unaddressed continuing demands for the punishment of those responsible for the crimes, but it is nevertheless a major step toward eliminating citizens' fear of arbitrary state behavior. In May 1996 the government also presented a new human rights program. Three years in the making, the program committed the government to eliminate police impunity, make torture a crime, make human rights abuses federal offenses, and force police officers accused of crimes to be judged in civilian courts. In light of the daily human rights abuses in Brazil, it is tempting to dismiss these reforms as insignificant. But they can also be seen as a courageous demonstration of political will in a violent, authoritarian culture.

Finally, the Cardoso administration has intervened in conflicts between large landowners and smallholders and peasants. The government has made it clear that it plans to put an end to the abuses committed by large landowners under the eyes of security forces and to the immunity from prosecution they have traditionally enjoyed. Again, little has changed in the rural areas, where conflicts occur daily. Nevertheless, the government has repeatedly dissociated itself from the actions of landowners and has refused to legitimize their claims for self-justice.[16] The equality of all citizens within the law can only be achieved in the long term, but Cardoso's demonstrated intention to break the "perverse pact between the private landed elite and the state" is both clear and historic (dos Santos, 1996: 7).

These advances against institutionalized violence are signals to those who denounce the abuse of state power. The administration will listen to them, support them, and protect them from retaliation by those who feel threatened by their actions. To succeed on the human rights front, however, the Cardoso government must undertake a difficult balancing act. An unrestricted settlement of past violations would risk political instability, yet significant advances must be made in the name of justice. Challenging the impunity of the security forces and punishing those convicted of human rights violations are essential steps in restoring the legitimacy of public authority and, thus, of governability in Brazil.

Conclusion

I have focused here on the concept of governance in Brazil. The broad scope of the term *governance,* however, can lead to some ambiguity in its meaning. In thinking about political regimes, particularly about democratic ones, this analytic imprecision can be mitigated by distilling the subject of governance into a single question: What makes democracy work? Camou (1995: 17) has helped to answer this question by identifying three basic components of governance: legitimacy, stability, and efficiency. To this triad I believe it is necessary to add respect for the rule of law. The capacity of any regime, democratic or otherwise, to implement policies that advance the goals of its leaders can thus be measured along those four dimensions. Since the dimensions touch on so many factors, however, it was necessary to narrow the focus of the present study considerably to keep the analytic task manageable; hence my decision to concentrate on the policymaking process and a selected group of policies that are crucial to the issue of governance.

In this chapter I have linked recent changes in Brazil's political and economic situation with the issue of governance in a democratic setting. I attempted to illuminate the changes in democratic governance evident under the Cardoso administration and to consider whether those changes mark a significant break from the repeated failures to implement policy effectively in the past and, if so, why? This analysis of the Cardoso administration thus extends beyond the conjunctural. I argue that in the years leading up to the Cardoso government, Brazil suffered a situation of systemic ungovernability that manifested itself in a weakening of the state and in a decline in its capacity to implement policy. The sources of that ungovernability included elite fragmentation, a crisis of the state apparatus, increased corruption and institutionalized violence, and the striking inability of the government to stabilize a chaotic economic situation.

The external shock produced by Collor's impeachment gave Brazilian governments the opportunity to begin to reestablish governability. The exposure of widespread corruption coupled with hyperinflation helped to weaken opposition to the transitional costs of stabilization and thereby laid the groundwork for a successful assault on inflation. Price stability achieved in the context of growth allowed the newly elected Cardoso government to address, albeit with mixed results, the more structural sources of ungovernability. These circumstances have significantly increased the Brazilian government's capacity to transform its preferred policies into political reality. The successful implementation of the Real Plan followed by Cardoso's election victory showed that a new coalition of actors favoring economic stability had finally replaced the old proinflation coalition. Equally significant, the collapse of popular support for the moderate-left candidate of the Workers' Party offered further evidence of the shift in electorate preferences, which translated into increased legitimacy for the Cardoso government.

This dramatic expansion of government legitimacy and of the resulting capacity to implement policy, however, has not been accompanied by an equally dramatic transformation of public policy. Reform of both the economy and the state during the Cardoso administration has been painfully slow. I have shown here that Cardoso's incremental approach to reform reflects political reality: policies are only as good as the political support that enables their implementation. In the case of economic reform, Brazil was not only a latecomer to the "Washington consensus" but has also been slow to implement basic reforms such as trade liberalization and privatization. The effectiveness of Brazil's state-led development model during most of its existence has created a pool of powerful interests that have resisted reform. Equally, as memories of the economic nightmare of the past decade fade and the costs of sustaining price stability through needed budget cuts continue to be felt, popular dissatisfaction with reform is bound to increase.

Without an alternative development model to the new market-based approach, Brazil will inevitably move forward with reform, but the need to sustain the minimum political consensus to ensure effective implementation in a democratic setting suggests that the pace of economic reform will remain slow. The Cardoso government's incremental strategy for reform of the state and its step-by-step approach to crucial human rights issues also reflect the conflicting pressures the government must balance to make policy advances. This slow pace of reform inevitably raises the concern that the Cardoso government might squander the opportunity for change afforded by the unique circumstances surrounding the defeat of hyperinflation. Yet, it is difficult to envision how Cardoso could otherwise preserve popular support for reform. As democratization increases the autonomous representation of societal interests and the structure of Brazilian politics continues to erect legislative obstacles, incrementalism seems the most appropriate pace for producing real, long-lasting reform.

Notes

This chapter is a completely revised version of a paper initially entitled "Repeated Failures and Ungovernability: What Is Wrong with Brazil?" presented at the Thirteenth Congress of the Latin American Studies Association in Atlanta in March 1994. Generous and insightful comments were provided by Leslie Elliott Armijo, André Blais, Graciela Ducatenzeiler, and Jorge Schvarzer. Marie Whelan contributed to the bibliographical research. This version owes a lot to comments from the faculty of the Department of Estudios Políticos of Centro de Investigación y Docencía Económicas (CIDE) Mexico, from Blanca Heredia, and from Philip Oxhorn and Pamela K. Starr, the editors of this volume.

1. Delegative democracy applies when democracy is neither consolidated nor representative. Whoever is duly elected is entitled to govern with full authority, surpassing all other domestic powers, in a highly individualistic fashion to fulfill the nation's high expectations for a resolution of the crisis inherited from the authoritarian regime.

2. After five years of near stagnation and two years of zero growth, economic activity increased an average of 4.8 percent between 1993 and 1995. Inflation, which had reached 2,670 percent in 1994, was down to 22 percent in 1995 and 9 percent in 1996.

3. Based on a review of the literature (Crozier, Huntington, and Watanuki, 1975; Malloy, 1991; Frischtak, 1994; Diamond, 1993; Leftwich, 1994), governance can be understood as the degree to which power holders manage to make decisions, have them accepted by (or imposed on) all actors concerned, and implement them through established routines. This definition is inspired by the one coined by Coppedge (1993): "Governance is the degree to which relations among strategic actors obey stable and mutually acceptable formulas."

4. Brazilian political parties are poorly organized on a national scale, meaning national party leaders have limited say over who will run under the party banner. An elected member of Congress can thus change his or her party affiliation or vote against the party leadership without much sanction. See Chapter 6.

5. The process of "gradual political liberalization" began in 1975 and produced its first civilian president in 1985, a new constitution adopted in 1988, and the first free election of a president in 1990.

6. From September 1988 through the third month of Cardoso's term, 954 provisory measures were issued (Diniz, 1995b: 2).

7. Electoral legislation also limits legislators' accountability to their constituents. Citizens vote for a party list of candidates and cannot identify their elected representative. Parties also have little control over the composition of the list; legislators in office are automatically placed on their party's list.

8. The ideological diversity of most Brazilian parties, whether in the opposition or allied with the government, is extremely wide. The only notable exceptions are the parties of the Left—the Communist Party of Brazil and the Workers' Party (Lamounier and de Souza, 1995: 45).

9. The investigation into these corruption charges revealed that between March 1990 and June 1992, the Collor government signed 2,540 contracts for public works, from which an estimated $1.7 billion was paid as bribes to Collor's entourage (*O Estado de São Paulo,* November 7, 1993). A preliminary report issued by the congressional investigation on fraud perpetrated by members of the House Budget Committee showed that 36 percent of the overall expenditures on public works were earmarked for companies and legislators involved in public works (*Folha de São Paulo,* December 2, 1993, reported in Martins, 1993).

10. Weffort (1991: 10) calls this the "dynamic of disorder," which leads to "anomic situations," defined as the absence of social norms.

11. The idea of entropy to characterize Latin America's politics is borrowed from Richard Morse, quoted in Weffort (1991).

12. I owe this observation to Jorge Schvarzer. See also Weyland, 1996.

13. Groups of legislators representing special interests in the legislature operate independent of party affiliation. The main group is the *bancada ruralista* with ninety-nine members who defend the interests of large landowners. Other economic sectors are also represented, such as construction (sixty-two members), communications (forty-six), and banks (twenty-one). Religious groups are also represented; the most notorious group is the evangelists with twenty-one members (*Veja* [São Paulo], February 1, 1995: 26–28).

14. Brazil has 9.0 civil servants per thousand inhabitants compared with 91.4 for England, 65.0 for Italy, and 46.4 for France. Civil servants represent 2.0 percent of the Brazilian labor force, 18.9 percent in England, 16.1 percent in Italy, and 17.0 percent in France (Martins, 1993: 30).

15. Political and administrative determination apparently makes a difference. That same year, fiscal revenues in the state of São Paulo increased only 6 percent, whereas in the state of Rio de Janeiro they declined by almost 7 percent (*Veja,* January 26, 1994).

16. Since 1979, more than 200 peasants have been killed by police or by hired guns in land conflicts, and rarely has anyone been prosecuted for those crimes. On April 17, 1996, in Eldorado de Carajás in the Brazilian Amazonia, a violent clash between 1,500 peasants and the military police ended with nineteen demonstrators dead and forty others wounded. Pushed to move quickly on the issue, Cardoso announced that he would create a separate Ministry of Land Reform. His justice minister pushed forward congressional debate on bills to make it more difficult for farm owners to evict peasants squatting on their land and to speed government expropriation of unused private land. Cardoso also urged the Senate to speed approval of a bill that would give civilian courts jurisdiction over crimes committed by the military police (*New York Times,* May 6, 1996: 17).

Part 3

Political Constraints to Neoliberal Reform

6

Constitutional Reform and Macroeconomic Stability: Implications for Democratic Consolidation in Brazil

Peter R. Kingstone

In the late 1980s and the 1990s, Latin American nations embraced the challenge of radically altering their economic growth strategies while simultaneously trying to consolidate new democracies. The specific character of the new economic strategy, neoliberalism, made the challenge even harder. Neoliberalism required that Latin American states strip domestic interest groups of a wide array of protections and benefits. Rapidly implemented reform policies generally provoked increased unemployment and concentration of wealth as they limited the state's capacity to address distributive or redistributive concerns. The experiences of countries such as Argentina, Mexico, and Peru in the mid-1990s illustrated the tensions between democratic consolidation and neoliberal reform.

Brazil's experience illustrated a potentially different relationship between the two processes. Brazil's large internal market and highly adaptive domestic industry meant neoliberal reform implied a more equal redistribution of wealth. In some ways, especially through successful price stabilization, neoliberal reform in Brazil actually acted as a complement to democratic consolidation. Both competitive adaptations and continuing price stability, however, depended on reforms to the 1988 constitution. In fact, the challenge to Brazilian democracy in the early 1990s was not the impact of reform itself but the slow pace of reforms crucial to consolidating the neoliberal package.

In Brazil, reforms began in earnest in 1990, but even then they occurred at a much slower and more erratic pace than in most other large Latin American nations. Neoliberal reform produced several positive effects, such as a dramatic decrease in poverty following the successful 1994 stabilization plan,[1] the Real Plan, and it enjoyed relatively wide but shallow support among diverse groups such as urban poor workers and business. Even organized labor groups, such as the Central Unica Trablahista (CUT), cooperated in some respects in facilitating reform.[2]

The repeated failures of successive Brazilian governments to pass constitutional reforms of the tax system, civil service, and the pension system, however, weakened government efforts to control the fiscal deficit and provoked sharp increases in the public debt. Although Fernando Henrique Cardoso's Real Plan successfully stabilized prices after July 1994, the rising fiscal deficit and public debt continued to threaten the plan on its second-year anniversary. In turn, the failure to contain the fiscal deficit forced the government to rely on a range of mechanisms to contain inflation that imposed high costs on a wide range of social groups and, consequently, threatened continued support for the program. Domestic business suffered through high real interest rates and an overvalued exchange rate that undermined the capacity to adjust to new competition. Organized labor suffered through rising unemployment, as did the middle class. Urban and rural poor workers who had benefited from price stabilization stood to lose badly if inflation returned. Finally, the political system suffered through increasing discontent with the Cardoso government and the Real Plan, as well as growing contempt for the political system in general (poll conducted by ISTOÉ/Brasmarket, *ISTOÉ* [São Paulo], June 19, 1996: 22).

Why did successive Brazilian governments fail to pass these crucial reforms? As noted earlier, reforms did not lag because well-organized social groups resisted neoliberalism. Reforms lagged because Brazil's electoral and party systems combined to give disproportionate influence to narrow, distributional coalitions within the legislature, such as retiree associations, civil service employee unions, and farmers. In each of the three critical areas—taxes, civil service, and pensions—well-organized lobbies could count on sufficient political force to prevent any meaningful changes to the constitution. While this quality is not unique to Brazil, Brazil's dependence on foreign capital, its vulnerability to high inflation, and the need to muster two-thirds votes to change the constitution of 1988 make its patronage politics particularly challenging to democratic consolidation.

Fiscal Crisis, Neoliberalism, and Democracy

As of 1998, Brazil had made only very limited progress in confronting its fiscal crisis. The fiscal crisis represented an exhaustion of sources of financing and of state credibility that arose out of the final breakdown of import-substituting industrialization (ISI) and the debt crisis. The crisis helped to push even the most reluctant states toward neoliberalism as a solution to rising debt, spiraling inflation in some cases, and stagnant growth rates in most cases.

For most Latin American states, ISI had run its course by the 1960s. In many cases, ISI found continued support in well-organized social groups and military governments committed to developing the internal market. The 1973 oil shock and the recycling of petrodollars offered the opportunity for almost all Latin American states to replace declining or unreliable sources of domestic financing with foreign debt. When the second oil shock hit in 1979, however, a bad situation turned completely untenable. The debt crisis and its accompanying fiscal crisis officially began in 1982 with the Mexican default and the resulting suspension of foreign lending to Latin America, even to creditworthy nations.

For the most part, responses to the crisis fell into two categories: a turn to neoliberal restructuring (gradual or rapid) or a turn to neoliberal restructuring following a failed populist experiment. In either event, the staggering impact of the fiscal crisis on virtually all Latin American societies led to much greater tolerance for neoliberalism's often draconian measures. Business communities bought into the antistatist rhetoric inherent in neoliberalism's critique of import substitution and populism. The poor seemed to support the antielite rhetoric of neoliberalism and often seemed willing to support austerity in exchange for a real reduction of inflation. Labor groups seemed battered into silent acquiescence. In almost all Latin American nations, technocratic elites set to work to dismantle the institutional foundations of import substitution, populism, and patronage politics.

In general, the restructuring worked. Countries on the brink of collapse benefited from the crisis to forge new coalitions behind restructuring. The effects of the fiscal crisis led to political pacts in Bolivia that permitted legislative passage of reforms; in Chile, successful restructuring under Augusto Pinochet shaped the political arena in ways that limited antineoliberal options; in Argentina, Carlos Menem cemented his hold over the traditionally unruly Partido Justicialista with popular support from a society worn out by inflation; in Peru, high levels of popular support allowed Alberto Fujimori to close the Congress as an obstacle to reform.

In fact, most Latin American nations performed relatively well in reducing budget deficits, improving tax collection, liberalizing trade and finances, and privatizing state industries. Although neoliberalism proved to be an incomplete blueprint, it was not because Latin American nations failed to gain control of their financial situations. For most of these nations, neoliberalism revealed its weakness by not leading to renewed growth or by promoting growth with relatively narrow distributions of the benefits. In that context, some neoliberal coalitions collapsed or faced mounting pressures through the 1990s.

Brazil's experience with its fiscal crisis and the resulting implications for neoliberal reform differed in several crucial ways. Unlike many Latin American nations, Brazil was unable to form a stable coalition to support reforms that would address the fiscal crisis. On the contrary, in the midst of the fiscal crisis, Brazilian legislators produced the 1988 constitution, which enshrined a number of key articles that deepened the fiscal crisis rather than resolving it. As a result, as of 1996, Brazil stood virtually alone as a nation that had not yet fully addressed its fiscal crisis, primarily because of those parts enshrined in the constitution. Whereas Brazil's party system made it extremely difficult for any president to address the fiscal crisis, several other economic factors played a role in delaying efforts to control that crisis.

First, ISI worked better and longer in Brazil than anywhere else in Latin America. As a result, it took longer to convince key actors of the need for reforms. State technocrats resisted embracing neoliberalism well into the 1980s. Similarly, business groups expressed hostility to statism under the military but, like Brazilian technocrats, were slow to shift from a specific critique of the military to a general critique of the model. Second, Brazil's sophisticated indexation mechanism protected key social groups from the effects of inflation. Thus, even into the 1990s, business, organized labor unions, bankers, farmers, and the middle class in general were willing to tolerate inflation. Even after Fernando Collor began his reform efforts in 1990, many of those key actors could imagine a return to an inflationary economy without concern.

Finally, Brazil has probably been the only country in Latin America (and among the very few in the developing world) that has been inherently attractive to foreign investors. As a result, the international financial community has at times been very tolerant of Brazil's policy setbacks and incoherence. For example, the International Monetary Fund (IMF) has been willing to negotiate favorable terms or approve standby loans even in the face of questionable accounting practices or apparent policy chaos. Thus, Brazil and Brazilians have enjoyed some insulation from the worst effects of the fiscal crisis. For most Latin American nations, fiscal responsibility was crucial to attracting new investment flows. Some worked hard to create well-insulated central banks or even currency boards, as in Argentina. Brazil, however, managed to attract significant foreign investment with bankrupt state banks that still issued credit and a Central Bank that displayed virtually no independence. Thus, Brazil faced far weaker external constraints on its policymaking.

Ironically, this very quality made Brazil a better candidate for success under neoliberalism. For many other nations, the problem with neoliberalism was the implicit assumption that once those nations got the prices right, investment and exports would follow. There is no reason, however, why poor states like Bolivia would attract great amounts of investment. As a result, not even larger nations such as Mexico grew fast enough or equitably enough to address the brutal levels of poverty in the region.

Brazil was in an entirely different position. Neoliberal reforms offered tremendous growth potential for multinationals interested in the domestic market; thus, a stable macroeconomic environment promised substantial growth in investment, employment, and real wages. Brazil's lingering problem was its failure to secure the fiscal crisis, which limited the entrance of vast numbers of foreign direct investors interested in the country. Thus, when Collor finally began Brazil's slow road to reform, a large number of groups stood to gain—if Brazil could solve its fiscal problems and begin to grow. At that point, Brazil had to confront the weaknesses of an electoral system that gave great weight to narrow groups with vested interests in the elements of the constitution that preserved the fiscal crisis and, conversely, muted the voices of those who stood to gain.

The Slow March to Neoliberalism

Neoliberalism emerged in Brazil in response to the obvious failings of the older, state-led model. When the Brazilian military voluntarily ended its rule in 1985, it left a legacy of significant economic disarray. The military had pursued a statist strategy that relied on import substitution with heavy state subsidization and spending until the early 1980s, when the debt crisis finally made it untenable. In that context, the military shifted its strategy to orthodox stabilization. By 1985, the military had achieved some success in reducing state spending and improving the balance of payments but without any progress on inflation.

The New Republic began with deepening poverty, worsening inflation, and growing hostility toward the presence of the state in the economy within the middle and business classes.[3] Unfortunately, the republic's first president, José Sarney, faced staggering limits to his political capacity. Sarney's political problems included, among others, a weak party system that fragmented significantly during his term, a surge in distributive and redistributive demands, and the need to write a new constitution. By the end of Sarney's term, Brazil had hyperinflation, five different (and equally unsuccessful) stabilization plans, much worse poverty, and a constitution so poorly written that its framers included a clause calling for a constitutional review in 1993. Although Sarney's term accomplished little in terms of reforms, it opened Brazil's population to alternative solutions to the country's clearly worsening problems.

Ultimately, the 1989 presidential election came down to a choice between Luís Inácio "Lula" da Silva, who offered a statist solution, and

Collor, who offered neoliberalism. Collor's victory in December 1989 marked Brazil's turn to neoliberalism. Observers have noted that Collor's coalition did not necessarily vote for his neoliberal strategy. Poor voters, who made up the bulk of Collor's electorate, probably supported his right-wing populism, particularly his attacks on corruption and privilege. Business supporters opted for Collor as the only alternative to the leftist Lula da Silva.

It is important to note several points: First, in terms of both policy and rhetoric, Collor's neoliberalism was entirely consistent with his populist attacks on privilege. Second, although many business voters chose Collor over Lula da Silva, their preferred candidates offered more moderate variations (meaning, in particular, no attacks on elites) of the same policy themes (Kingstone, 1994: chapter 3). Finally, it is crucial to note that no politician, including Collor, promoted anything but a moderate, gradual version of neoliberalism. Thus, whereas the vote for Collor was not an explicit endorsement of neoliberalism, it reflected an openness to a moderate neoliberal approach. This was the key to both Brazil's initial turn to and continuing support for neoliberalism through 1998.

This potential support for neoliberalism rested on two critical groups: poor workers and business. For poor members of society—possibly 50 percent of the voting population—the benefits of neoliberal reform lay in stabilization. Brazil's sophisticated indexation system protected all contracts from the effects of inflation, thus creating a large constituency that was relatively indifferent to inflation.[4] Poor workers (in both the rural and urban informal sectors), however, felt its full brunt. As a result, eliminating inflation promised to raise millions of people out of poverty and to allow poor families to plan, save, and consume much more. In fact, the data from the two years of the Real Plan reveal staggering increases in the consumption of meat, poultry, consumer electronics, fast food, building materials, and white-line goods—driven significantly by a large influx of new consumers.

For business, support for neoliberalism emerged as a result of the increasingly chaotic presence of the state in the economy. A range of problems—from the uncertainty produced by frequent and wild swings in policy to the inability to contain the public deficit to the increasingly negative impact of chronic inflation—all contributed to a profound sense that something had to change. The business community identified the state in particular as a source of problems and, as a result, supported neoliberalism with its emphasis on reducing the size of the state. In addition, most businesses felt they could compete in an open economy if they had a fair chance to adjust. The size of Brazil's internal market and the sophistication of its industrial economy made that truer for Brazilian business than for any other country in the region.[5]

It is unlikely, however, that either group would have strongly supported a drastic "shock" neoliberal policy program. The program introduced by Collor pursued a careful privatization program that emphasized improving the quality of firms' performance, as opposed to being simply a mechanism for raising funds for the state. Furthermore, commercial liberalization proceeded at a gradual, measured pace negotiated by business and government officials. Later, under Cardoso, the government repeatedly passed measures to create jobs, provide further assistance to sectors in difficulty, and increase spending on social services. Thus, both Collor and, later, Cardoso pursued policy programs that limited the degree of dislocation experienced by key groups in society.

Although Collor's impeachment in December 1992 has tended to color the impression of his presidency, it is important not to let that event cloud his real accomplishments or the assessment of his real failures. His most important achievement was to shift Brazil's developmental course decisively through initiating privatization, commercial liberalization, and substantial deregulation of the economy. His key failure was his inability to stabilize the economy.

Ultimately, Collor's stabilization program, which began with a truly shocking heterodox shock (freezing 80 percent of the nation's savings), depended on reforms to the constitution, especially in the areas of civil service, the tax system, and the pension system. To pass those reforms, Collor had to push them through a powerful array of interests committed to maintaining patronage benefits linked to those systems (Kingstone, 1994: chapter 7). Collor's strategies for dealing with the legislature ranged from trying to forge social pacts to authoritarian use of executive decrees to more traditional patronage politics. None of these strategies, however, successfully brought about constitutional reform.

Collor's most serious bid to reform the constitution came in late 1991 through a giant reform project at a time when he was already losing popular support. The *emendão* (literally, the "giant amendment") lumped all of the necessary changes into one package, which Collor tried to get through Congress by forging a deal with the nation's influential governors to use their considerable influence in the Congress to back the *emendão* in exchange for favorable terms on rolling over state-level debt. Members of Congress, however, many of whom anticipated running in the October municipal elections, forced the governors to back off their commitment. Those prospective mayoral candidates were particularly concerned with protecting the tax system's transfer to municipalities, as well as with the patronage opportunities in the pension system and the civil service. In compensation to the governors, the Congress forced Collor to give in on state debt and roll it over on favorable terms anyway while permanently tabling constitutional reform legislation.

Collor may have made strategic errors in the way he tried to push through reforms, and his behavior certainly justified his critics' labels of rash, arrogant, and ultimately dishonest. He also had to contend, however, with one of the least coherent and poorest functioning party systems in Latin America. During Collor's presidency, nineteen parties held seats in the Chamber of Deputies, and seventeen held seats in the Senate. Of those parties, only the opposition Workers' Party (PT) had any voting discipline. Collor's own party, the National Renovation Party (PRN), was a last-minute creation for his presidential election and held a small fraction of the seats in Congress.

By December 1992, the Congress had first suspended and then impeached Collor. The interim president, former vice president Itamar Franco, had no credibility, no support, and no particular inclination to push policy in any direction, neoliberal or otherwise. Although scheduled privatizations and the tariff reduction process continued, no new policy emerged. Inflation raced back toward hyperinflationary levels, and businesses held off new investments in a climate of tremendous uncertainty.

Franco's most important contribution was to appoint Cardoso as finance minister in 1993 and then to relinquish virtually all control over government policy. Cardoso's performance as finance minister was outstanding. Although he only succeeded in getting the Congress to pass a single reform (and a temporary one at that) during the 1993 scheduled constitutional review, he did implement the Real Plan, the most successful stabilization plan in modern Brazilian history.

The Real Plan differed from previous heterodox plans in several crucial ways. First, the plan avoided shocks by changing the currency in a gradual, measured, predictable, and highly transparent way. The real replaced the cruzeiro only after a transition period in which a unit of reference, called the Unit of Real Value (URV), allowed economic actors to adjust their contracts gradually and carefully. Second, as part of the plan, Cardoso carried out fiscal adjustment by using hardball politics to force Congress to pass a reform of the constitution that temporarily transferred revenues from the states and municipalities back to the federal government. Finally, the Real Plan benefited from beginning at the end of the tariff reduction process so that import competition prevented businesses from raising prices.[6]

By the October 1994 presidential election, inflation had dropped to below 2 percent per month. Not surprisingly, Cardoso won handily in the first round of voting. With inflation down and Cardoso at the helm, Brazil appeared ready for rapid expansion. Cardoso had vanquished the problems in the political system that Collor had claimed made the country ungovernable. Two years later, inflation remained low, and investment poured in as a response to business expectations of future policy stability and potentially significant gains in Brazil. Yet, the assessment of the risks in the country grew substantially in the first half of 1996, as Cardoso celebrated the second anniversary of the Real Plan. The reason was simple: despite great expectations, Cardoso had failed to pass virtually any of the key reforms of the constitution in spite of several notable and dismally unsuccessful efforts. As with Collor, Cardoso may have made strategic errors, but he also had to contend with a political system that severely complicated his task.

Political Parties and
the Logic of Patronage in Brazil

The party system and electoral laws powerfully shape individual legislators' incentives and policymaking dynamics in several crucial ways. Those crucial aspects include the number and ideological character of parties, the amount of control parties exert over their individual members, and the relation of the party to its base. They also include more general traits of the electoral system, such as proportional representation (PR) versus first past the post, the size of electoral districts, open versus closed party lists (candidate selection), and campaign finance laws.

Together, these variables affect how autonomous legislators are from their parties, the logic of their election and reelection, and the ease or difficulty of constructing stable, programmatic coalitions in the legislature. By shaping legislators' incentives, they also affect an executive's capacity to build legislative support for policies of collective importance.

Brazil's particular set of parties and electoral laws worked to make legislative coalition building extremely difficult. Brazil's combination of PR, open candidate lists, and large electoral districts promoted a significant proliferation of weak parties.[7] When Cardoso took office, eighteen parties had representatives in Brazil's Congress, with most members valuing patronage over any ideological position. Individual members were not dependent on parties for financing or career advancement and, as a result, displayed high levels of individual autonomy. Not surprisingly, most of these parties had very weak bases of support in society.

Analysts have identified a wide range of problems that weaken Brazil's political system,[8] but perhaps the most serious are the absence of party discipline and the statewide districts members of Congress represent. Brazilian parties do not finance their candidates and have little, if any, control over the nominating process. As a consequence, party leaders have almost no way to ensure that members vote on party lines or support an agreement backed by the leadership. Members of Congress also tend to focus on their own particular interests because few parties in Brazil have any strong ideological identity. During the life of the New Republic, the PT has been the only ideologically consistent major party and, not surprisingly, the only one to show a significant degree of party-line voting. Under

Cardoso, the Liberal Front Party (PFL) improved its performance by threatening to dock the pay of noncompliant members, but that threat had only limited effects.

Running for office in statewide districts compounded the discipline problem. To win in a statewide PR district, candidates had to bring either great name recognition or a strong regional or functional base. This situation had three critical consequences. First, it created very strong incentives for members of Congress to focus heavily on delivering patronage benefits, whether developing public works projects or defending sectoral interests such as the pension system or farm loans. The absence of ideological commitments meant legislative support was available for most projects and programs but at a potentially high price and without reliability, particularly if it threatened access to those same benefits. Second, it meant parties needed candidates more than candidates needed parties, which sharply limited the influence a party could wield over its members. In fact, Brazilian candidates switched parties frequently since they brought their own voting bases and could use them to further their own career aims. Finally, the weak ties between members and parties generated two other, more powerful ties: one to the bloc (or blocs) that shared members' interests and the other to the member's state or municipality. The typical politician used Congress as a platform to pursue higher ambitions, such as mayoralties and governorships, which tended to create strong ties among governors, mayors, and state caucuses in Congress.

All told, this nonexhaustive list points to powerful structural features of the political system that shaped individual legislators' incentives and made them focus on individual patronage payments. They tended to diminish any value legislators might have placed on collective goods such as low inflation or avoidance of fiscal deficits and balance-of-payments difficulties. Without a clear attachment to a party voters could reward or punish based on its economic management, individual legislators derived little benefit from such collective goods; in fact, in an election year they derived some benefit from denying those goods to a president. The features of the system tended to give legislators very short time horizons, especially given the large number of legislators who used the Congress as a launching pad for loftier political aspirations. In sum, there were powerful structural reasons to believe that in the Congress Brazilian presidents faced a nearly insurmountable obstacle to building coalitions behind fiscal caution.

One consequence of this system is that it blunted the influence of groups such as big business that had not found a successful means of influencing Congress on broad policy issues and issues of collective concern. Representatives of big business, multinational corporations (MNCs), foreign investors, international lending institutions such as the IMF, and foreign governments can visit Brasília on a regular basis to lobby the government. Lobbying Congress is much more difficult because of the weakness of Brazil's numerous parties and the extent to which individual members owe their loyalties to well-defined constituencies, whether regional or functional. Specific lobbies such as hospital owners and construction firms may help to finance candidates and therefore wield influence on very narrow sectoral concerns. Unfortunately, business as a community strongly supported the full range of measures to promote fiscal responsibility, without success. In fact, throughout the New Republic the Congress repeatedly demonstrated that it could ignore the positions of the most powerful economic actors when they clashed with access to patronage or political responsiveness to large voting blocs.

That insulation from the influence of economically powerful groups affected Cardoso's capacity to use public support to help push his agenda of constitutional reforms. Those reforms addressed a series of institutions established in the 1988 constitution that actively promoted fiscal instability; they also provided and protected legislators' access to patronage. In fact, several key reforms, such as reform of social security, the tax law, and civil service regulations, challenged crucial elements of legislators' access to patronage.

These problem areas also help to reveal the limited influence of powerful economic actors, primarily when they are pushing issues of collective concern.[9] Business groups organized in 1987–1988 to oppose many of the measures targeted by Cardoso's agenda, and they supported Collor's efforts to pass a package of constitutional amendments in 1991. They organized again to support the constitutional review process in 1993[10] and yet again to support social security reform under Cardoso's new government. At the heart of their support was a concern for fiscal stability and for a resolution of the state's fiscal crisis. Despite continual improvements in their organizational efforts, business groups' scorecard was dismal—it showed virtually complete failure to change the outcome of debates in Congress in 1988 and complete failures in 1991, 1993, and under Cardoso (Kingstone, 1994; Payne, 1994; Weyland, 1992; and Aragão, 1995).

This lack of influence of big business on broad policy issues was unfortunate for Cardoso. Given his priority to protect the stability of the real and keep inflation low, Cardoso could have used more help from economically powerful groups, particularly because a stable currency and low inflation did not reflect the triumph of foreign investors' or creditors' concerns. Cardoso observed that such groups were linchpins for his broader social democratic agenda.

Cardoso's Reform Agenda

Cardoso entered office in January 1995 with an ambitious program of constitutional reforms that included reform of the social security system

(*Previdencia*), which was rapidly approaching insolvency; fiscal reform; administrative reform; and constitutional reforms that would end or limit state monopolies and restrictions on foreign capital. All of these issues had been present on the policy agenda at least since Collor's term of 1990–1992. Analysts widely agreed that those specific issues were important elements that were preventing the resolution of Brazil's long-standing fiscal crisis. Cardoso's social democratic inclinations, as well as the long-term success of his stabilization plan, depended on his ability to pass them.

In principle, most of the reforms presented difficult political challenges. Social security represented a major source of patronage for both state and federal politicians.[11] Thus, important political players within the Congress, governors, and well-organized groups—especially public service unions—opposed significant changes to the system, regardless of its fragile financial situation.

Fiscal reform in Brazil was vital to restore efficiency and fairness to the tax system, as well as to correct an imbalance in the division of revenues and spending obligations between the federal government and lower levels. In the 1980s and 1990s Brazil's tax burden fell primarily on two groups: salaried workers, who could not prevent tax withholding, and businesses in the formal economy, which faced a significant number of indirect taxes—especially larger companies that could not easily evade taxation. As it existed, the tax system was substantially regressive and damaging to industrial competitiveness. Not surprisingly, the unfairness of the system provoked high levels of evasion.

Perhaps even more serious was the constitution's protection of transfers of federal revenues to the state without accompanying spending obligations. The practice stemmed from the writing of the new constitution in 1987–1988, as members of Congress sought to protect the states from abusive behavior by the federal government. The end result was the deepening of the federal government's fiscal deficit and the provision of patronage funds to states that they could and did use to finance a massive increase in state government employment. In some states, payrolls accounted for over 100 percent of state revenues, and in most they came close. Accompanying this problem of revenue transfers was the practice of state banks, such as Banespa (São Paulo) and Banerj (Rio de Janeiro), of issuing credit and then covering their deficits by borrowing from the Central Bank. Together, these two practices generated state-level debt in excess of $70 billion. The strong link between federal members of Congress and the state and municipal governments, however, provided a formidable alliance against limiting the states' ability to accumulate more debt and maintain their revenue transfers.

Administrative reform presented another profoundly difficult political problem that was intimately linked to the previous two. The 1988 constitution guaranteed civil service employment and permitted retirement based on years of service rather than age. Together, those guarantees maintained badly bloated state-level payrolls and contributed to the extraordinary increase in pension payments to retired civil servants. Once again, a formidable array of political forces stood together to prevent reform in this area—including federal members of Congress, governors, and mayors who used civil service jobs as patronage rewards, as well as public-sector employees, the PT, and the CUT (the country's largest labor central).

Of Cardoso's most important constitutional reforms, privatizing state monopolies and easing restrictions on foreign capital faced the least resistance. During the 1980s the continually worsening fiscal crisis manifested itself in the public sector through several financial problems, including late payment or nonpayment of bills, poor competitive performance, accumulation of debt, and so on. Perhaps more important, the worsening financial situation in the public sector meant less and less investment in infrastructure. One result of this condition has been the erosion over time of the potential political constituency to protect state ownership, specifically among private-sector firms. Furthermore, although publicly owned companies provide some patronage possibilities, they are less vital to politicians than the institutions noted earlier. As a result, the only real opposition to privatization has come from the Left.

Cardoso and the Congress: Evaluating the First Two Years

When Cardoso took office as president in January 1995, the press reported (with great satisfaction) that he had assembled an impressive supporting coalition in the legislature, which was vital given Cardoso's need to pass his reform agenda through the Congress. The alliance among the Social Democratic Party, the PFL, the Party of the Brazilian Democratic Movement (PMDB), the Brazilian Labor Party (PTB), the Progressive Reform Party, and the Progressive Party (PP) assured him of a legislative majority for his reform package. The 1994 legislative elections occurred at the same time as the presidential election for the first time since 1950. Observers expected this change in electoral scheduling to have a positive impact on the composition of the Congress by tying the congressional electoral agenda to the presidential one. The change in the election timing did have an effect on the composition of the Congress, but that did not mean the optimistic view had solid evidence to support it. Collor entered office with similar expectations about his success in stitching together a legislative coalition.

The optimistic view reasoned that the problem in executive-legislative relations resulted in part from legislative elections that turned on local patronage issues, whereas the presidential election turned on national issues. Tying the two elections together (or marrying them, in the Portuguese) would link the electoral logics, permitting the presidential program, it was hoped, to influence the dynamics of legislative support. Interestingly, the 1994 legislative election did have the effect of reducing the number of parties with representation and producing a higher concentration of representatives among a smaller number of major parties.

The shift in the number of parties and the higher concentration of representatives from the major parties constituted good news. At the least, to the extent that legislative coalition building is something of a coordination problem, a smaller number of players makes it easier to achieve a solution. This is particularly true given the Brazilian presidential practice of exchanging cabinet positions for legislative support. The fewer parties the president needs to secure a legislative majority, the easier it is to purchase support with cabinet posts.

Nevertheless, Cardoso still had to work within one of the least coherent and effective political systems in Latin America. Observers from journalism, academia, business, and politics routinely called for political reforms that would address the system's flaws, but powerful political forces remained opposed to any changes that would alter its character. The most important reason for that opposition was that the system protected the most salient feature of Brazilian politics—clientelism. The same political forces that supported the clientelistic features of Brazilian politics worked against fiscal austerity in general and constitutional reform in particular.

Nevertheless, despite the political challenges of passing the constitutional reforms noted previously, the early prognosis for Cardoso was fairly positive. Several factors contributed to that impression. First, Cardoso had already tamed inflation through his well-crafted and well-implemented heterodox plan, the Real Plan. Second, as a result, he brought tremendous popular support and credibility through the election to the inauguration. Third, Cardoso was renowned as an excellent legislative coalition builder who had a strong record in the complex art of legislative compromise. Fourth, unlike his three predecessors in the New Republic, he began his term with a well-respected, highly qualified cabinet. Fifth, with the peso crisis well under way, current events were conspiring with Cardoso to underscore the importance of constitutional reform.

Finally, Cardoso began his term facing a new Congress formed from the first married elections since 1950. That Congress had a higher concentration of seats among a smaller number of large parties, some of which had openly campaigned on the same reform platform Cardoso sought to implement. Cardoso quickly forged a legislative majority that stemmed in part from the electoral alliance of center-right parties that had formed behind him as the only candidate who could beat the PT's Lula da Silva.

Although embedded in his cabinet was some conflict about the priorities and direction of policies (particularly between Finance Minister Pedro Malan and Planning Minister José Serra), Cardoso had used the appointment process well to cement his legislative alliance. His doling out of cabinet and important legislative posts promised him support from 60 percent of the Congress.

At this point, a skeptic might have noted that Collor could have claimed many of the same advantages going into his inauguration. Although Collor faced hyperinflation and caution (even antipathy) among elites, he successfully forged a legislative majority before his inauguration and brought tremendous popular support. Collor's tendency to use his popular support as a blunt weapon against the Congress (among other tactics) led to widespread charges of incompetence. Cardoso offered the counterfactual experiment in January 1995: Could a competent president willing to bargain accomplish more than a bullying president trying to cow the Congress into submission?

The early answer appeared to be no. Within weeks of his inauguration, Cardoso faced his first confrontation with the clientelistic Congress when it voted overwhelmingly to significantly increase the minimum wage (from 70 reals to 100 reals) over Cardoso's objections and threatened veto. Much of Brazil's economy is indexed to the minimum wage, including all payments in the financially strapped social security system (such as pensions). As a result, the Congress's action represented a very real threat to the fiscal stability of Cardoso's Real Plan.

Despite Cardoso's objections, the Congress did not back down. What particularly hurt Cardoso was his willingness to veto the increase in the minimum wage but not the 100 percent pay increase the Congress had simultaneously granted itself and, by extension, him. Thus, Cardoso publicly appeared willing to deny increased wages to the working class while accepting increased pay for himself. Cardoso ultimately backed down in the face of significant congressional resistance while insisting that those who had granted the increase now had a moral responsibility to back reform, especially that of the social security system.

Cardoso's first month contained other early clues that working with the Congress would not be easy. In early January, the Senate blocked the confirmation of Cardoso's choice for president of the Central Bank, Persio Arida, using the well-established technique of simply not appearing for the vote so that barely a third of the Senate even bothered to vote. The protest was launched because the Senate hoped to pressure the lower house into granting amnesty to former Senate president Humberto Lacena, who had recently been convicted on corruption charges. Lacena was eventually granted amnesty.

In February 1995, the newly elected Congress sat for the first time. If any analysts thought the new Congress, the result of the simultaneous election, would behave differently than the previous one, they quickly revised that view. In March, Cardoso suffered an early defeat of one of his highest priorities—social security reform. The *Previdencia,* which combines social security and pensions, represents one of the key points for restoring Brazil's fiscal health. The Cardoso administration had sought several constitutional reforms to the system: replacing retirement for years of service with retirement at a set age; introducing a contributive principle, that is, linking payments to contributions; cutting the link between pensions and the minimum wage; and preventing retirees from collecting more than one pension. The upshot of the government's reform was a proposal that Brazilians work longer for smaller pensions.

Not surprisingly, the proposal was unpopular. The PT and the Democratic Workers' Party, largely silent since Lula da Silva's defeat in October 1994, roared back to life and led large protests against Cardoso's proposal. All three labor centrals (the CUT, the General Workers' Confederation [CGT], and the Union Force [FS]), a social movement umbrella organization, and the pensioners' association joined in vocal and visible protest. Federal politicians, although publicly supporting the need for reform, faced both the threat of political unpopularity and the loss of patronage resources.

Several potential bargains surfaced in the deliberations, including Cardoso's offer to exclude military and civil service workers from the reform. He also offered to increase the minimum wage in exchange for cuts in pensions. In essence, Cardoso's administration was willing to forgo sweeping reform in exchange for limited changes that preserved the viability of the *Previdencia* in the short term and gave the government room for future reform under ordinary law. In mid-March, the Committee on the Constitution and Justice of the Chamber of Deputies (in which the fate of reform lay) divided up the reform bill against Cardoso's wishes. This tactic allowed the Congress to pass elements that were less controversial or non-controversial while protecting the more popular—yet more urgent—elements such as the link between pensions and the minimum wage.

The most damaging part of this vote was that the decision to divide the proposal depended on defections from virtually every party in Cardoso's coalition. Eight progovernment deputies in the fifty-one-member committee defected, including representatives of the PFL, the PP, the PMDB, and the Liberal Party (PL). Clearly, the electoral alliance that had brought the right-wing parties together to support Cardoso against Lula da Silva did not protect Cardoso from the resurgence of patronage and clientelistic congressional politics. Facing certain defeat on reform of the *Previdencia,* the government tabled its own proposal for a later date.

In general, Cardoso's performance in the first few months of his term seemed poor. In addition to his visible struggles with his own coalition, both in Congress and within his cabinet, several factors suggested that the government was flailing. On the economic side, lower inflation had fueled a consumption boom as stable prices, low tariff barriers, and an overvalued currency made imports very attractive. The resulting consumption boom began to drain capital reserves dramatically exactly at a time when the "tequila effect" had led to capital outflows as foreign investors left the market. From a position of great strength, new estimates repeatedly lowered the period during which reserves could finance imports. At the same time, prominent economists, such as André Lara Resende (a former Cardoso official) and Antonio Barros de Castro, pronounced the end of the Real Plan. To add to the pessimism, the government surprised and disappointed members of Congress by introducing an exchange rate band after repeatedly saying it would not do so. The move allowed the real to float to a more realistic exchange rate, but it angered politicians such as Antonio Delfim Neto, the architect of the "Brazilian miracle," who publicly hammered the Central Bank for its poor handling of the matter. The adjustment of tariff rates in the auto sector added to the sense that the government was operating without a clear strategy. The government moved to slow consumption in March 1995 by raising tariff rates to 70 percent on 109 products in the automotive and domestic electronics sectors. The initial criticism that the rate increase was too high grew when the government lowered the rates on twenty-three of those 109 products within a few weeks of raising them.

On the political front, Cardoso's losses in the Congress increased visibly when the strongest voting bloc, the agricultural bloc, voted to exempt farmers' loans from monetary correction (indexation to the official inflation rate). The vote, which passed 431 to 88 in April 1995, affected R$16 billion in loans to 400,000 farmers. On other fronts, Senate President Sarney warned Cardoso that his reform agenda was provoking gridlock in Congress. As a critical player in the Congress because of his ability to affect the legislative agenda of the Senate, Sarney's request-demand that Cardoso slow down the process was not trivial. In other political news, Cardoso's social agenda was losing credibility. Although he had declared it one of his primary priorities at his inauguration, by April a majority of Brazilians (54 percent) believed he had not kept his promise (Brasmarket poll, cited in *Lagniappe Letter* [Washington, D.C.], April 14, 1995). Finally, even as Cardoso worked to preserve a fiscal balance, spending on personnel rose by 49 percent in the first trimester of 1995, whereas revenues increased only 19 percent (*Veja* [São Paulo], May 3, 1995: 35).

Despite these problems, the news was not all bleak. Most important, Brazil was less affected than either Mexico or Argentina by the tequila crisis. On the political front, survey results showed that clear majorities in the Congress favored much of Cardoso's reform agenda. Issues such as privatization, the breaking of state monopolies, and reform of the tax system, the administrative system, the political system, and even much of the

Previdencia all had potential majority coalitions in Congress. The polls suggested that if Cardoso played his patronage politics carefully, there was probably room for reform—although perhaps more limited than the reform he would have found ideal. In essence, room for muddling through existed, even if a glorious revolution was unlikely.

In addition to the apparent room for negotiation in Congress, the bloated state bureaucracies and state bank failures placed financial constraints on the nation's governors that opened them to negotiation. In fact, by October 1995 almost no state government could afford to pay the thirteenth salary portion (a bonus equivalent to one month's salary for all salaried workers dating back to Getulio Vargas); some could not even afford the twelfth. This situation opened the possibility of trading relief for the governors in exchange for support for difficult reforms, especially administrative reform that would permit governors to reduce their payroll.

Using these strengths, Cardoso went on the offensive beginning in May 1995. Ironically, Cardoso was reversing Collor's pattern. Whereas Collor started off playing hardball and softened as he lost political force, Cardoso began playing compromise politics and hardened as he lost ground to patronage politics. He openly attacked critics of the Real Plan and pessimists who disparaged his chances for carrying out reform. He encouraged cabinet members to speak out openly against critics; even the normally taciturn Malan publicly denounced critics as "the gravediggers of the Real Plan." By September, Cardoso was openly attacking groups and individuals who complained about recession, even saying those pessimists should shut up. The widely read journal *Veja* noted the change in style with the headline "The Government Goes on the Attack" (*Veja,* May 3, 1995).

Perhaps the most important evidence of Cardoso's new hard line came with a strike by the militant oil workers' union in May and June 1995. In the wake of the resurrection of the Left on the issue of the *Previdencia,* the union, a leading union within the CUT, went on strike against the privatization of Petrobrás—one of the country's largest and most successful parastatals and an important symbol of the country's statist development model. Cardoso refused to back down on the issue. Publicly, Cardoso blasted public-sector unions for their defense of corporatism and later (in July) attacked the Left in general, accusing it of "stupidity." Finally, on May 24, after the strike had been ruled illegal by a labor court, Cardoso called on the military to break it up.

Cardoso's stand shifted the political terrain in a crucial way. As the strike led to shortages of gas for automobiles, cooking, and heating, it became extremely unpopular with the public. As a result, Cardoso's resolve increased his standing and badly weakened the political strength of the Left—an important source of resistance to his program.

In the wake of the strike, Cardoso began to register much greater success on the policy front. Building on his success in liberalizing several public-sector services not guaranteed by the constitution, Cardoso turned to the more difficult task of opening the petroleum and telecommunications sectors. By the end of August 1995, Cardoso had successfully removed the constitutional obstacle to privatization of and foreign participation in telecommunications. Petroleum presented more of a problem, as its historically symbolic importance provoked more nationalist resistance than did telecommunications. Nevertheless, Cardoso successfully outflanked his opponents by modifying his proposal from privatizing to "flexibilizing" the sector. The more limited proposal easily gained enough support to pass through the Congress.

In September, Cardoso began negotiations on his next major constitutional proposal—administrative reform. The proposal appeared doomed to defeat in the Committee on Constitution and Justice (CCJ) almost from the outset. As with reform of the *Previdencia,* public-sector employees and politicians committed to protect civil service employment mobilized significant resistance. Negotiations were difficult, with progovernment parties indicating they were likely to defect again. The CCJ seemed willing to back most of the reform proposal but not the most crucial aspect—the end of employment stability.

Finally, two key factors salvaged the proposal from defeat in committee, which would have been disastrous for the government. First, Cardoso's aggressive new style worked well as he actively threatened government allies with the loss of posts in the event of defections. He repeatedly stated in public that the only legitimate reason for voting against the proposal was technical but that, in fact, there was no technical justification for voting against it. Second, a compromise finally emerged that established a ceiling for payroll spending at 60 percent of state revenues; beyond that threshold, state governments could dismiss workers. The more moderate proposal won out, securing a narrow margin of victory for Cardoso by the end of October 1995. In fact, Cardoso received support for all of his administrative reform proposals except for the one that would have permitted the government to privatize a sector without congressional approval. The Congress rejected that plank on the grounds that it violated congressional jurisdiction.

Cardoso's success was short-lived, however, as negotiations on other crucial measures forced him to suspend his efforts at administrative reform. One measure in particular was the renewal of the Social Emergency Fund (FSE), a legal trick established by Cardoso as finance minster in 1994 that appropriated a share of state and municipality revenues for the government to use to cover its deficit. In 1995, the FSE equaled roughly U.S.$10 billion. Negotiations to extend it proved difficult. The government offered to roll over state government debt for thirty years in exchange for the governors' support on extending the FSE. Ultimately, the Congress approved an extension of the fund for an additional eighteen months but at the price of the government's retreat on administrative reform. With the gap between government payroll expenses and revenues growing, it was a costly concession.

Thus, as Cardoso headed into 1996, he had succeeded in opening sectors that had previously been closed to foreign and private capital, and he had maintained some control over the fiscal deficit; however, he had not passed a single reform linked to long-term fiscal responsibility. As a consequence, the stability of the Real Plan continued to depend on high interest rates and an overvalued exchange rate. These policies held inflation in check, but the cost was a significant recession with a record number of bankruptcies and rising unemployment.[12] Furthermore, if the government failed to maintain fiscal control, rising public debt threatened the future of the plan in the medium term.

With the 1996 municipal elections promising to dominate the second half of the year, the government openly conceded that it had to pass its agenda by June or give up on reform. Thus, when the new session opened in February, Cardoso, congressional leaders, and labor groups began difficult negotiations over social security reform. When negotiations began to break down, the president of the lower house, Luis Eduardo Magalhães, gambled with a call for a vote before the full chamber.

Cardoso's position took a turn for the worse the day before the scheduled March 6 vote when he delivered a speech to Mexico's legislature denouncing the Congress's emphasis on private interests and patronage. Both opponents and supporters received his speech poorly and delivered a stinging defeat by failing to approve Cardoso's reform package and setting up a Parliamentary Commission of Inquiry to look into the handling of the banking crisis. Although Cardoso was able to reverse both defeats, they ushered in a difficult period of negotiations.

In particular, Cardoso faced a new round of political jockeying as key figures like José Sarney and Paulo Maluf positioned themselves for a 1998 presidential run. At the same time, Cardoso faced court challenges over his reintroduction of social security reform and a significant increase in patronage demands from government allies nervous about public outrage over the banking scandal. As a consequence, Cardoso had no choice but to resort to *fisiologismo*—the traditional practice of purchasing congressional support. By mid-1996, Cardoso faced a deluge of demands for public support, leading to expenditures of at least 840 million more reals on public projects than in 1995 (*Latin American Weekly Report* [*LAWR*], August 8, 1996: 352). Cardoso also faced a public outcry that the government was using the budget selectively to reward allies and punish the opposition.

Unfortunately for Cardoso, the resort to *fisiologismo* did not deliver the hoped-for results. As of July 1996, he had not passed reforms of social security, the civil service, or the tax system. A badly watered-down reform had passed the lower house at the end of June 1996 but had not yet reached the Senate. That reform spared all public employees (the principal source of the state's problem) and shifted the costs of reform to workers in the private sector.

Public opinion and economic indicators turned against the government. Although inflation continued to drop to an anticipated 12 percent for the year (the lowest rate since 1950), other indicators proved worrisome. Public domestic debt had increased sharply to over 200 billion reals (more than doubling since the start of the plan), and the fiscal balance had declined from a surplus of over 1 percent of gross domestic product (GDP) in 1994 to a 5 percent deficit in 1995, with continued loss of control in 1996. The government's difficulty in limiting the fiscal deficit was largely caused by debt servicing and constitutionally protected payments such as social security, which alone reported an anticipated deficit of 5 billion reals for 1996 (*LAWR,* August 29, 1996: 386). The government also reported a commercial balance deficit of over 200 million reals for the month of June, with concerns that the deficit could reach 2 billion reals by year's end. GDP growth seemed likely to hit 2.5 percent, which was positive yet below or equal to the rate of population growth and thus not particularly encouraging, especially with the nearly continuous rise in unemployment. Although Brazil was not in a situation similar to that of Mexico before the peso crisis, even cautious observers noted that the government's window of opportunity was narrowing for passing reforms and saving the Real Plan.

Cardoso's travails with Congress had begun to hurt him politically. Although public opinion continued to hold him in high regard, approval ratings of his government had declined. In June 1996, nearly 40 percent of those surveyed rated his government as bad or terrible (17 percent and 22 percent, respectively); only 17 percent viewed it as good or excellent (15 percent and 2 percent, respectively) (ISTOÉ/Brasmarket poll, cited in *ISTOÉ,* June 19, 1996: 22). Moreover, large majorities held that Cardoso had not kept his campaign promises. Cardoso had built his campaign around the powerful image of holding up his hand with fingers spread and committing himself to five priorities: employment, agriculture, security, health, and education. With the exception of education, where 50 percent of citizens polled thought he had not met his commitment and 43 percent thought he had in part, a substantial majority thought he had not kept his promises (ISTOÉ poll, June 19, 1996).

Social groups had begun to display other signs of discontent. Business, led by the National Confederation of Industry and the Federation of Industry of the State of São Paulo, called on unions to join them in a symbolic strike. In May, over 2,000 businesspeople descended en masse on Brasília to press Congress to pass reforms and to recognize that government policy was making competitive adjustments untenable. In June 1996, Brazil's three labor centrals—the CUT, the CGT, and the FS—called a one-day general strike. The strike proved unsuccessful for a variety of reasons, but its general goal of protesting government policy received considerable sympathy, even from business. Urban crime had risen substantially, and the rural landless movement continued to use land invasions and occupations to provoke violent responses. Finally, individual sectoral associations had begun to press sharply for relief from competition.

Cardoso's policy agenda shifted in response to growing public pressure over health care, land invasions, unemployment, and bankruptcies. To placate public concern and protest, Cardoso shifted course and reintroduced an unpopular tax on financial transactions to finance health care, introduced a controversial land reform proposal, promised 90 billion reals in new social spending, and proposed and introduced a host of measures to alleviate business problems. Those measures included granting export incentives, lowering taxes on exports, raising tariff and nontariff barriers, and lowering interest rates for consumers, export financing, and capital equipment purchases. Most important, Cardoso offered to use the National Bank for Social and Economic Development as an instrument for substantially increased lending and export promotion for domestic business.

Although Cardoso's policy responses effectively appeased domestic opposition in the short term, they also created at least four new sources of tension for him and his program. First, the policy changes renewed conflicts within his cabinet that had been present from the beginning. The conflicts primarily pitted proponents of greater protectionism and the use of industrial policy—such as the newly appointed minister of industry and commerce, Francisco Dornelles, and minister of planning, Antonio Kandir—against proponents of free trade such as the minister of finance, Pedro Malan, and the minister of the foreign office, Itaramaty. The changes also produced new conflicts between those ministers and the highly regarded health minister, Adib Jatene (who began to emerge as a rival presidential candidate in August 1996), over the introduction of the unpopular tax on financial transactions. Similarly, Brazil's turn toward greater reliance on protectionist measures produced some tension with key trade partners, particularly its Mercosur partners and Japan. A third source of tension emerged as Cardoso became more dependent on purchasing support for his program. By June 1996, public bickering over who was receiving money for support had reached significant levels. The Revenue Service publicly complained that it was swamped with demands to appoint favorites of government allies, and the PTB left the government in anger because it had received insufficient support. The last source of tension emerged as the business community increasingly pressured the government to promote growth, ease consumer credit, provide protection from imports, and weaken the only true mechanisms maintaining the Real Plan—namely, high interest rates and an overvalued exchange rate.

In short, Cardoso had overseen some tremendous gains in reducing inflation and poverty in Brazil. He had successfully pushed constitutional changes allowing for the privatization of key sectors, such as energy and oil (and, in August 1996, telecommunications). He had not, however, succeeded any more than his predecessors in passing reforms in the key areas of social security, civil service, and the tax system. As a result, the government's fiscal deficit continued to defy efforts to contain it, and the stability of the real continued to depend on measures that limited growth and imposed high costs on key social groups such as business and labor.

Conclusion

The second anniversary of the Real Plan marked an important point for Brazil. With inflation projected at less than 10 percent for 1997, the country seemed poised for significant gains: firms announced over 600 investment projects totaling more than $16 billion, average Brazilians continued to consume at record levels, and democracy seemed to have significant support at both the elite and mass levels. Nevertheless, troubles remained that posed risks for economic restructuring and democratic consolidation.

As noted earlier, a range of factors undermined efforts to maintain fiscal discipline. Those factors included the tremendous cost of maintaining solvency in the banking system, particularly because of the state bank crisis; the patronage cost of maintaining fragile government support; the policy cost of purchasing societal support; the cost of servicing the rapidly growing public debt; and the continued drain the 1988 constitution placed on the country's finances. Ultimately, many of the problems listed in this chapter hinged on constitutional reform.

Politically, the most damaging consequences of not passing the reforms were the undermining of social support for economic restructuring and the weakening of public support for democracy. Business groups and leaders had complained throughout the 1990s that competitive adjustments depended on the government reducing the "Brazil cost," which meant reducing the tax burden on production, renewing public (or private) investment in infrastructure, lowering real interest rates, and setting a more realistic exchange rate. In the absence of these reforms, more domestic business groups charged that the government was de facto destroying national industry in favor of MNCs that felt the Brazil cost less sharply (in particular because of their access to international loans and their ability to shift to importing when domestic production lost its attraction). Both government and MNC representatives dismissed those claims, responding that domestic business-people were "cartorialists"[13] and protectionists. Nevertheless, several sectors showed signs of (and serious negative consequences from) rapid increases in import consumption.[14] MNCs planned over 600 investments but had undertaken only sixty as of July 1996 (*Latin American Special Reports* [*LASR*], August 1996: 5). Thus, as domestic businesses actively suffered from the Brazil cost, MNCs were also hedging their bets.

Publicly, business representatives strongly supported democracy. For example, in both public statements and private interviews, FIESP (Federation of Industries of São Paulo) officials pointed to the unprecedented trip of 2,000 individual businesspeople to Brasília as an example of their commitment to the democratic process. Private interviews suggested more mixed views, however. Most important, whereas some businesspeople strongly defended democracy in private, others either endorsed a *Fujimorização* (closed Congress) or suggested that resistance to it would be limited. In fact, the mixed views in the business community mirrored society's mixed views: a poll conducted by Brasmarket in conjunction with the magazine *ISTOÉ* found that 30 percent of respondents believed democracy was the right path for Brazil's development; however, 33 percent either believed the Congress should be a *Fujimorização* or that the military should return to rule (ISTOÉ/Brasmarket poll, cited in *ISTOÉ,* June 19, 1996: 22).

Thus, on the second anniversary of the Real Plan, Brazil's prospects remained unclear. One thing that was clear was that two key groups in the twin processes of neoliberal restructuring and democratic consolidation stood to lose a great deal from the ongoing failure to pass constitutional reforms. Yet, they had little capacity to influence the process. The millions of poor Brazilians who benefited from the Real Plan's success in taming inflation lacked organization, any link to a political party, or any real impact on congressional elections. Unfortunately, they had little understanding of the relationship between constitutional reforms and their benefits.[15] Business groups could lobby the executive and the bureaucracy as individual firms or sectors; as noted earlier, however, they had virtually no success lobbying Congress on issues of collective concern.

The consequence was that key reforms remained in the hands of members of Congress who had weak incentive to pass them. Powerful public-sector unions, teachers, the military, and parliamentarians themselves all benefited from the pension system and the civil service system as they stood. The states and municipalities and parliamentarians anticipating running for offices at those levels all benefited from the tax system as it was.

Reforms appeared possible largely because of Cardoso's political skill and enduring personal credibility and because one of the Congress's largest parties, the PFL, remained relatively united and, at least rhetorically, committed to the reform process. Furthermore, the absence of ideological opposition meant the Cardoso government could continue to purchase support. Thus, Brazil generally and Cardoso specifically had room for muddling through that might not have been available otherwise.

Although room existed, both economic indicators and political events were narrowing that space. By June 1996, commentators had begun to raise warning signals: in June, noted economist Rudiger Dornbusch sounded an alarm (that was sharply criticized), which was followed by more modest criticisms from some of Brazil's leading economists, including the developers of the Real Plan. Dornbusch warned that Brazil's exchange rate was overvalued by roughly 40 percent and that the country could be heading for its own peso crisis. Dornbusch's comments provoked widespread criticism from Wall Street and from within Brazil, but economists such as Celso Martone and Real Plan creators Edmar Bacha and Andre Lara Resende, among many others, raised warnings that echoed Dornbusch. Politically, the reform process faced new threats as Cardoso presented a virtually constant stream of new measures funded by the state to appease growing social resistance. Cardoso also faced new pressure in anticipation of the October 1996 mayoral elections and as the maneuvering for the 1998 presidential elections began. Not surprisingly, several potential candidates built their budding candidacies on sharp attacks on the Real Plan and offers to return to more protectionist policies.

If Cardoso succeeds, Brazil's economic restructuring may actually play the most important role in consolidating democracy.[16] The medium- to long-term benefits real stabilization held out for Brazil's urban and rural poor informal-sector workers (estimated at roughly 50 percent of the workforce) and the possibility for a significant growth and investment boom should work to develop a true stake in democracy for the two groups with perhaps the weakest commitment. If Cardoso fails, it is not clear that powerful segments of Brazilian society would want the military to return or that the military would return if asked. The quality of democracy and, therefore, democratic consolidation would definitely suffer. As long as narrow distributional coalitions hold enough sway in Congress to maintain their benefits at the expense of large, less organized groups, real stabilization will probably elude Brazil. As long as stabilization rests on high interest rates, an overvalued exchange rate, and huge foreign capital inflows, the rates of bankruptcies, insolvencies, urban crime, rural violence, and unemployment will likely rise. Brazil may not return to military rule, but the quality of its democracy may significantly suffer.

Notes

1. Institute for Applied Economic Research researcher Sônia Rocha published a study that revealed that the number of people living below the poverty line (a figure that varies from region to region but that equals roughly two-thirds of the minimum wage) in six capitals declined from over 16 million to just over 11 million from 1994 to 1996. Reported in *O Estado de São Paulo,* June 12, 1996.

2. In particular, the CUT actively negotiated flexible labor contracts, which were illegal. Labor and firms saw them, however, as an important step in simultaneously permitting competitive restructuring and maintaining employment. Reported in *Latin American Research Review (LARR), Brazil,* March 21, 1995: 7.

3. See Kingstone (1994: chapter 3) for a discussion of the rise of business support for neoliberalism.

4. Armijo (1996) focuses particularly on the way the banking community was shielded from the effects of inflation—and, in fact, profited from it.

5. Evidence of business support for neoliberalism and business confidence in its ability to adjust is found in Kingstone (1994). Another source on business confidence is Oilveira (1991).

6. Insightful discussions of the Real Plan can be found in Oliveira and Toledo (1995) and Sachs and Zini (1995). A clear summation of the plan is in Baer (1995: 377–379).

7. Mainwaring (1991, 1992, and 1995) has written extensively about the perverse incentives Brazil's set of electoral features produces.

8. Haggard and Kaufman (1995) focus particularly on fragmentation of the party system. Power (1991) has discussed the frequency of elections in Brazil and the resulting "civic fatigue" that has weakened voter interest in the electoral process. Mainwaring (1991, 1992, and 1995) has probably come the closest to exhaustively cataloging the problems inherent in Brazil's electoral rules and institutions.

9. For a discussion of the sources of business difficulties in organizing collective action, see Weyland (1992, forthcoming).

10. Business efforts to support the constitutional reform process are discussed in Payne (1994); Kingstone (1994); and Aragão (1995).

11. The repeated efforts to reform social security are discussed in Weyland (1995).

12. Data on bankruptcies, consumer credit problems, and rising unemployment can be found in *LARR, Brazil* (February 5: 8; June 6: 6; and July 11: 2), as well as *Latin American Weekly Report (LAWR)* (February 5: 185), and the *Gazeta Mercantil* (São Paulo), Internet version (July 4 and July 17, 1996).

13. The word refers to the network of ties among firms, banks, and specific government agencies, *cartorios,* through which government resources flowed and around which the government protected and promoted its favorites. The dynamics of *cartorialismo* are discussed in Nylen (1992).

14. See data from Abinee (National Association for Electro-Electronics), Abimaq (Brazilian Association of the Machine Tool and Equipment Industry), and Sindipeças (National Syndicate for Auto-Parts), as well as newspaper accounts of dumping in several sectors, particularly textiles.

15. CNI polling cited in private interview, June 1996.

16. Cardoso benefited from the Asian crisis in October 1997. Within days, Brazil lost U.S.$8 billion from its reserves, and the country's key stock markets declined by over 20 percent. Cardoso successfully managed this minicrisis with an

emergency austerity package that sharply increased taxes and cut state spending. The crisis also pushed legislators to pass long-stalled civil service reforms. As of July 1998, however, Cardoso remained vulnerable. First, the Congress continued to resist tax and social security reforms, as well as additional civil service changes; moreover, civil service reform had been watered down substantially. Second, the impact of the austerity package fell heavily on middle-class and lower-income voters. Polls and pundits pointed increasingly to a difficult reelection for Cardoso. Finally, the president's successful containment of the crisis did not resolve the key underlying problems. Brazil still faced the threat of a real attack on its currency. Despite limited progress, the reform process remained as fragile as ever.

7

Balance Sheet or Ballot Box? Incentives to Privatize in Emerging Democracies

Leslie Elliott Armijo

When do policymakers decide to privatize?[1] The sale of state production to private buyers in the 1980s and early 1990s was the newest patent medicine in the kit bag of would-be doctors of national economies as diverse as slow growth advanced industrial countries of the capitalist West (such as Great Britain), heavily indebted developing countries emerging from a decade of depression only to face hyperinflation (Argentina, Peru, and Brazil), newly liberated nonhard currency countries of Eastern Europe (Poland and Czechoslovakia), and protected, state-dominated mixed economies in very poor countries (India). Economic advisers to governments usually assumed or hoped that the demonstration of an objective "need" to reduce the state sector would result in the implementation of a privatization policy. But politicians often had other concerns.

In this chapter I argue the obvious yet frequently neglected point that a supportive political environment for privatization is at least as important, and probably even more crucial, to democratic politicians confronting the difficult decision to shrink the government's directly productive role as are compelling economic reasons to privatize. As contrasted with politicians in advanced industrial countries, democratic leaders in new, fragile, or emerging democracies in relatively poor countries may find privatization a harder sell to their populations, whose expectations of access to a long delayed political voice are likely to be coupled tightly to anticipation of improvements in short-term economic circumstances. Several possible immediate consequences of privatization—including job losses for previously protected employees, foreign ownership, and higher prices for goods and services previously supplied by the state-owned enterprise—may be unpopular with voters. As compared again with politicians from wealthy capitalist democracies, however, leaders in developing countries are also typically under relatively greater political pressure from abroad to pursue privatization and other economic liberalization measures. For both of these reasons—the political fragility of many developing democracies and their vulnerability to international pressures and blandishments—the presence or absence of an objective economic need to privatize is seldom a good predictor of actual public policy choices in emerging democracies.

I examine actual progress on privatization while assessing the comparative strength of both economic and political incentives for elected chief executives in the three Latin American countries with the largest, most industrialized economies: Brazil, Mexico, and Argentina. To illustrate that the argument is general rather than culture or region specific, the comparison also includes India for a total of nine administrations in four country cases during the years from the early 1980s through the end of 1992. I conclude with a return to the link between politicians' incentives to privatize and the larger issues of the interaction of democratization and economic reform.

Case Selection and Incentives to Privatize

The main criterion for choosing Argentina, Mexico, Brazil, and India as the four country cases was the absolute size of the industrial sector, which was comparable in each. In 1988, roughly midway through the period studied, Brazil's industrial gross domestic product (GDP) was $139 billion, India's was $71 billion, Mexico's was $62 billion, and Argentina's was $35 billion.[2] The ratio of overall gross national product (GNP), likewise, was a maximum of about four to one within the group, with 1988 figures ranging from Brazil's $324 billion to Argentina's $79 billion.

The economic role of the state in each country also had important similarities. The best quantitative indicator of the size of the state sector is the public sector's share of gross fixed capital formation—roughly speaking, the state's direct contribution to productive investment. In 1980, that measure ranged from a low of just under 20 percent in Argentina to 29 percent in Mexico to a high of 34 percent in both Brazil (in 1979) and India.[3] The qualitative aspects of overall state economic regulation varied widely among the four countries but appeared to yield approximately the same ordinal ranking from least to most state involvement: Argentina, then Mexico, followed closely by Brazil, and finally India. The greater role of Brazilian and Indian, as contrasted with Argentine and Mexican, public enterprises in manufacturing was closely related to the larger share of heavy versus light industry (irrespective of ownership) in the first two countries (see Encarnation, 1989; Ramamurti, 1987; Trebat, 1983). The

1987 ratios of producer to consumer goods were 81 percent for Argentina and 72 percent for Mexico—but 132 percent for Brazil and 152 percent for India. The state regulated agricultural production and pricing and owned some distribution networks in all four countries, with least to most direct ownership and limits to free private competition in Argentina, Brazil, Mexico, and—with by far the largest state involvement—India.

Curiously, differences in national political rhetoric often made outsiders conclude that the directly productive role of the state differed more than it actually did. All four countries had mixed economies with a large role in the industrial sector for both state and private capital, including foreign capital, although the space for foreign-owned production in India was significantly smaller than in the three Latin American countries. In Brazil and Argentina in the 1970s and early 1980s, policymakers professed their commitment to free markets, yet they managed and even expanded weighty state-owned enterprise (SOE) sectors. Conversely, to hear Mexican and Indian politicians describe themselves, the listener might imagine Mexico as a peasant and workers' state and India as a socialist mecca dedicated to the redistribution of income and inherited wealth. At best, those visions of Mexico and India were only occasionally true.

The nine administrations in the study are those of President Raul Alfonsín (1983–1989) of Argentina, President Carlos Menem (inaugurated 1989) of Argentina, President Miguel de la Madrid (1982–1988) of Mexico, President Carlos Salinas (inaugurated 1988) of Mexico, President José Sarney (1985–1990) of Brazil, President Fernando Collor de Mello (1990–1992) of Brazil, Prime Minister Rajiv Gandhi (1984–1989) of India, the combined terms of Prime Ministers V. P. Singh (1990) and Chandra Shekhar (1990–1991), and Prime Minister Narasimha Rao (inaugurated 1991) of India. The study ends at the close of 1992, although Menem, Salinas, and Rao were still in office.

Why does one administration decide to pursue thoroughgoing privatization while another balks? In any government, many people participate in such decisions. All of the usual caveats about the limits of assuming that multiperson national governments are unitary rational actors apply to my discussion (Allison, 1971). I assume that the chief executive wields the ultimate authority over economic policy decisions that come to be defined as "important" and that privatization in all four countries was sufficiently contentious to be politically important. The discussion of probable benefits from privatization, that is, always assumes the viewpoint of the president or prime minister (as advised by senior technocrats). Possible benefits include both the self-regarding (as in maintaining oneself in power regardless of substantive public policy achievements) and the altruistic (as in governing well) types.

Policymakers thus face four kinds of incentives when considering privatization: (1) intrinsic economic, (2) pragmatic economic, (3) domestic political, and (4) international political. I will next detail a reasonably replicable set of indicators of each of these four composite incentives for each of the administrations examined. The great virtue of the parallel case study method of inquiry, however, is that the researcher is able to incorporate his or her detailed knowledge of the specific cases into the design. That is, I have suggested cookbook lists of factors that should be considered for each of the cases but have also tried to ensure that the coded outcomes have been consistent with descriptions of each administration arrived at by those using more intuitive assessment methods.

1. Intrinsic economic incentives to privatize turn on the assertion that the unit or sector to be privatized will be directly benefited by either more efficient management or improved access to resources. The presence of intrinsic reasons to privatize implies the expectation of improved performance within the sector, firm, or organizational task. For example, sales to private owners can maximize competitive efficiency by increasing the power of the profit motive for firm managers and decreasing the temptation for public-sector bureaucrats to treat their employment as a sinecure or to engage in corrupt practices, such as exacting bribes from customers for services to which they are legally entitled. Privatization can also permit entry into previously closed arenas, thus exerting competitive pressure on the SOE (or former SOE) and improving efficiency in the sector.[4] An intrinsic disincentive to privatize exists if policymakers judge that specific policies of privatization will result in private monopolies in the sector and, thus, in less competition or that it will be more difficult to regulate the new private firm(s) than it was to police the old public firm or sector.

A related intrinsic economic argument embodies the hope that privatization will improve access to resources, usually of capital and technology, to a fundamentally sound but undercapitalized state productive activity. Policymakers do not necessarily need to be convinced that the state has been a poor manager of the sector, firm, or organizational task in the past; the sole salient point implied is that private owners are richer and, thus, more able to invest. Particularly if they are foreign, private investors may also have access to new technology. The most significant intrinsic reasons *not* to privatize in this category occur when policymakers fear the new private owners plan restructuring that may be more efficient in generating profits but less effective in providing the good or service policymakers believe society "needs."

One would like to measure the expected efficiency gains from privatization by comparing factor productivity between private and public firms in similar sectors over time, then aggregating the results by administration and country. The data are unavailable. I therefore use a composite indicator.

The most important component is the general reputation of the SOE sector for efficiency, as measured by a qualitative synthesis of reports of SOE performance. Also relevant to assessing SOE performance is growth of the GNP because, in each of these countries, the explicit role of state firms was to operate at the "commanding heights" of the economy, thus ensuring high levels of growth and industrialization in the private as well as the public sector. GNP growth performance was assessed comparatively, with allowance for regional downturns. When available, I also considered information on the productivity of investment. The second indicator is trends in public investment; when this indicator is very low or has fallen sharply, SOEs' future performance prospects have probably been compromised. The third component is a qualitative assessment of the degree to which those local actors favoring privatization stressed access to new technology as the crucial issue. When all three elements (SOE reputation, public investment, and SOE technological neediness) indicate a strong reason to privatize, the administration has "high" intrinsic economic incentives to do so. The presence of two elements indicates "moderate" intrinsic incentives, and one or none suggests "low" intrinsic incentives. Table 7.1 summarizes the indicators in each of these composite variables for each administration examined.

Table 7.1   Intrinsic Economic Incentives[a] to Privatize

Chief Executive	Poor SOE Reputation	Low or Falling Public Investment	Acute Need for New Technology	Score[b]
Alfonsín	Yes	Yes	Yes	High
Menem	Yes	Yes	Yes	High
De la Madrid	No	No	No	Low
Salinas	No	Yes	No	Low
Sarney	No	Yes	No	Low
Collor	No	Yes	No	Low
Gandhi	Yes	No	Yes	Moderate
Singh/Shekhar	Yes	No	Yes	Moderate
Rao	Yes	No	Yes	Moderate

Notes: a. Assessment of incentives was done on a comparative basis within the group of four countries rather than on an absolute scale.

b. Scoring: High = 3 "yes" answers to questions about the presence of intrinsic economic incentives, moderate = 2, low = 1 or none.

2. Pragmatic economic incentives to sell or otherwise open hitherto state-owned production rights to private owners exist when policymakers value privatization for its contribution to other economic goals of the administration, goals not directly related to improved performance in the

units privatized. The crucial point is that these other goals can have more immediate political payoffs for political incumbents than does a successfully completed privatization that, over the medium term, raises productivity in the firm or sector privatized. One such reason to sell SOEs is the belief that sales will help government finances. Clearly, no chief executive can be effective if the government treasury is empty. The sale of valuable state assets can bring revenue to a depleted treasury, even if the new private owners are not better managers. Conversely, a reason not to privatize by firm is that once assets are sold, governments will no longer have access to that revenue stream. In addition, if the primary reason for the sale of state assets is to raise revenue, it is impractical to proceed enthusiastically in a depressed market.

Another pragmatic economic incentive to privatization is to aid the balance of payments. External payments crises can bring on politically damaging outcomes, ranging from devaluations to the inability to import to heightened foreign pressures from creditors to make unwelcome and domestically unpopular "reforms." Privatization that includes debt-equity swaps can directly reduce foreign debt. Alternatively, privatization by sector can attract new net inflows of foreign capital. Reasons not to privatize by sector include several of the classic objections to foreign direct investment. For example, once the initial investment has been made, the foreign company may become a net foreign exchange drain because of profit and dividend repatriation and a high propensity to import. Similarly, if the subcontractor is a foreign firm, privatization by organizational task may lead to increased imports of good and services.

I assume that most types of privatization can have positive revenue implications, at least in the short term. Even privatization by sector may be a logical precursor to, for example, pushing SOEs to feel the need to compete by raising funds from private investors through sales of minority equity, thus reducing the demands for budgetary transfers from the center.[5] To gauge the strength of pragmatic economic incentives to privatize, I use a composite of indicators of macroeconomic hardship or looming crisis: central government budget balance, difficulty financing budget deficits, size of the foreign debt relative to GDP, the trade balance, and inflation. In each case, the quantitative indicators are measured as they stand when the incoming chief executive assumes office.

If the central government budget shows a balance of −8.0 percent or less of GNP (that is, a deficit of 8 percent or more), privatization looks attractive.[6] If institutional arrangements are such that government deficits cannot be financed without generating inflation or huge increases in future deficits (as in all three of the Latin American countries but not in India through 1992), that is a second incentive to privatize. An accumulated foreign debt of more than 30 percent of GDP provides a third incentive.[7]

Finally, a trade balance of –$3 billion indicates that the country will have difficulty financing foreign debt payments, possibly even if the total debt is small.

Inflation is assessed only in terms of whether, in the context of the country concerned, hyperinflation is present or imminent. The relationship between privatization and inflation reduction, which probably exists in most high-inflation countries, is far less direct than that between asset sales and government deficit-debt reduction. Comparing absolute levels of inflation in Latin America and South Asia makes little empirical sense because of the very different financial structures and reigning economic ideas. Annual consumer price inflation of 15 percent provokes food riots in India; 30 percent inflation might incite a revolution. In contrast, between 1980 and the close of 1992, Brazilians would have felt great relief if policymakers had achieved stable annual inflation of 30 or even 40 percent. In both Argentina and Brazil in 1989, inflation reached a four-digit annual level. At that level, policymakers were under great pressure to try radical economic policy changes, including drastic privatization, even when their direct link to lowering the price level was tenuous.

An incoming administration encountering three or more of these five difficult circumstances has high pragmatic incentives to privatize, whereas two indicate moderate and one or none low incentives. Table 7.2 summarizes the indicators in each of the composite variables for each administration examined.[8]

Table 7.2   Pragmatic Economic Incentives[a] to Privatize

Chief Executive	Government Budget Balance of –8 Percent of GNP or Worse at Inauguration	Inflationary Deficit Finance Institutions	Foreign Debt More Than 30 Percent of GDP at Inauguration	Trade Deficit of $3 Billion or More at Inauguration	Hyper-inflation Looms	Score[b]
Alfonsín	Yes	Yes	Yes	No	No	High
Menem	No	Yes	Yes	No	Yes	High
De la Madrid	Yes	Yes	Yes	No	No	High
Salinas	Yes	Yes	Yes	No	No	High
Sarney	Yes	Yes	Yes	No	No	High
Collor	Yes	Yes	No	No	Yes	High
Gandhi	No	No	No	Yes	No	Low
Singh/Shekhar	No	No	No	Yes	No	Low
Rao	No	No	Yes	Yes	No	Moderate

Notes: a. Assessment of incentives was done on a comparative basis within the group of four countries rather than on an absolute scale.

b. Scoring: High = 3 or more "yes" answers to questions about the presence of pragmatic economic incentives, moderate = 2, low = 1 or none.

3. Domestic political incentives come into play when policymakers privatize to attract or reward crucial domestic constituencies or punish political opponents. One goal may be to appeal to a mass electorate. Under certain circumstances, as in Eastern Europe after the dramatic fall of the Communist state, transferring production from the state to private owners may have wide positive political appeal to voters. Another common domestic political reason to privatize is to woo the business community. To the extent that businesspersons, domestic and foreign, rightly or wrongly associate privatization with generic good economic management, central government privatization policies can signal seriousness about economic reform to skittish investors. In particular, if the government has a credibility problem because of a past record of interrupted or reversed austerity policies, privatization can broadcast a willingness to burn bridges (since renationalization will always be more costly than merely retaining a firm in the state sector). On the other hand, businesses may feel threatened by some types of privatization, as of infrastructure or large SOEs with which they have had long and cosy relationships as preferred suppliers.

A third domestic political motive to privatize is to shore up the incumbent's political coalition or position within that coalition. For example, political incumbents engaged in a power struggle within a single party that has long dominated the machinery of government may find selective privatization is a convenient way to weaken the rank-and-file supporters of rival national leaders whose base lies in the civil service or in one branch of it. On the other hand, leaders elected by leftist or working-class parties typically have a disincentive to privatize. Furthermore, if military officers hold prestigious (and lucrative) positions as directors of state industrial firms, privatization may be a dangerous strategy for the political incumbent. Disincentives to privatize (that is, high expected domestic political costs) also figure into policymakers' calculations. Thus, for example, a weakening of public-sector unions as a result of some unrelated factor (such as a structural change in manufacturing away from heavy industry in which historically unions have been strong) can make privatization more attractive than before, all other things being equal, by lowering its probable costs. The single score for domestic political incentives to privatize assigned to each administration is a product of inevitably subjective aggregation by the researcher.

4. International political incentives also confront national politicians. Because developing countries are at most middle powers in the interstate system, policymakers in those countries usually experience larger potential benefits (and costs) from foreign pressures and opportunities than do leaders of advanced industrial countries. Policymakers may feel pressure from abroad to respond to international political pressures falling equally on all developing countries. In the late, as compared with the early, 1980s, givers

of foreign aid were significantly more likely to insist on privatization as a necessary condition for assistance. A comprehensive list of typical World Bank policy recommendations as of 1981 omits privatization, as does a similar catalog of International Monetary Fund (IMF) recommendations for the early 1980s (Feinberg, 1988: 551; Walton, 1985: 10). But a list of IMF policies from 1986 includes privatization, and the 1986 report of a standard-setting international conference on Latin American development taps privatization and state enterprise reform as one of three core policies needed (the others are outward orientation and an increase in domestic savings) (Feinberg, 1988: 551; Belassa, 1986: 24).

In the late 1980s, the U.S. Labor Department sent at least one economist to Latin America to explain to governments and the business community ways to pitch privatization to public-sector unions; that economist went to India on the same mission in the early 1990s (Accolla, 1989). In 1990, John Williamson, senior fellow of the Institute for International Economics, referred to the existence of a rough but potent consensus in the Washington, D.C., policy community on ten policy reforms needed in most developing countries, including privatization (Williamson, 1990b: 9). The degree of compliance with the Washington consensus had consequences, as a country's access to aid and investment flows depended largely on Washington's image of that country's policy soundness.[9]

Leaders also respond to specific international linkage attempts directed at them. For example, a wealthy country may make bilateral aid, trade access, or other benefits conditional on its firms gaining access to investment opportunities in profitable but previously off-limits sectors in a developing country. An evaluation of the strength of such pressures depends on whether international actors have strong preferences about privatization in developing countries, as well as on structural or conjunctural factors that make the developing country more vulnerable under some conditions than under others.[10] As with domestic political incentives, the assignment of a single score for international political incentives is necessarily subjective.

Thus far, I have described how I intend to measure my independent variable: through politicians' motives to privatize. Before proceeding, four research design caveats are in order. First, I use a neoclassical definition of "intrinsic economic" reasons to privatize: low microeconomic productivity and lack of allocative efficiency are taken as evidence of an objective need to divest. There are perfectly legitimate developmental and social reasons for the creation of SOEs and for economically "inefficient" degrees of state regulation. Nonetheless, evaluating the performance of the state productive sector on purely economic grounds provides a necessary baseline for thinking about its costs and benefits. Second, the research design brackets the actual thought and decision processes of politicians in the proverbial black box. The investigation simply compares the presence or absense of probable benefits to the incumbent (as assessed by the researcher) from privatization in a given situation to privatization outcomes. Conclusions thus can shed light on apparent motives to privatize but cannot claim to have examined the actual reasons policymakers believed they pursued certain policies. Third, I explicitly assume that the actual extent of privatization reflects the strength of chief executives' preferences. Shrinking the state was on the political agenda in each of these semi-industrial countries by the early 1980s. Had any of these national leaders been willing to spend political capital for that purpose, significant privatization could have occurred. Fourth, there is no control for length of administration, except that two extremely short tenures—those of Indian prime ministers Singh and Shekhar—have been joined into one observation. In three of the four countries, the later years of the last administration have been ignored; the comparison ends in late 1992. Given that the later administrations, although shorter, tended to privatize more, the inequality of time periods seems comparatively unimportant.

Defining and Measuring Privatization

I define privatization to include all types and increments of transfer of ownership, partial or complete, from the government to the private sector.[11] Privatization also occurs when previously excluded persons or groups, such as foreigners or limited liability corporate entities, are recategorized as eligible "private" owners.

The usual practice is to understand privatization to mean the sale of state firms to new owners in the private sector. That definition implies that "ownership" is a dichotomous variable: either the government holds 51 percent of a firm's equity, or private persons do. The drawback is that we then have no way to conceptualize other changes in the percentages of public and private ownership. For example, a shift from 100 percent public ownership to 75 percent public ownership can be very significant in reducing the direct productive role of the state. Politically, the divestment of 25 percent of equity may signal a new era of opportunity for private entrepreneurs. The purely economic impact may be even more substantial. Let us suppose the goal of allowing 25 percent private ownership is to increase economic efficiency within the SOE. The requirement of maintaining the value of a bloc of shares freely traded in the country's capital markets can easily be a form of competitive pressure on the firm, even if management and majority ownership remain with the state.

Privatization might more usefully be thought of as a continuum of policies that share the characteristic of transferring ownership of production of goods and services from the state to the private sector. The continuum begins with nearly total government ownership of the firm and of the sector within which it operates. Defense industries or electricity generation and distribution are typical examples of state monopoly sectors, even in many advanced capitalist societies. Not only is the firm itself government owned; all of its competitors and potential competitors are state owned as well. The midpoint on the continuum shows a wholly owned public-sector firm competing with private firms; entry to the sector is free (that is, privatized), but the firm itself is entirely public. The ownership continuum's far end shows minority state equity participation in one or more firms within a sector that also contains large, dynamic private firms. If the shares held by private owners are dispersed, a firm with state equity holdings of as little as 30 percent may operate under effective government management. On the other hand, if more than 30 percent of the 70 percent of equity in private hands is closely held by one entrepreneur or group, the government's same 30 percent holdings may not yield de facto state managerial control.

A strong functional similarity exists among three activities, each of which constitutes privatization in terms of my definition. The activities are: (1) liberalization of the right of entry into an economic sector previously reserved for state production only, (2) sale of equity in a state-owned and managed firm, and (3) subcontracting out an organizational task previously performed by state employees, either within a state-owned enterprise or by a government administrative agency. In each case, production of goods or services previously owned and controlled by the government passes to the profit-seeking private sector. Privatization of the sector or organizational task implies the possibility of increased competition from potential new suppliers. Full or partial sale of equity in a state firm implies an enhanced role for transparent, market-based judgments about the unit's true profitability. When either increased competition or transparency occurs, enterprise managers should be pressured into becoming more efficient. That is, the economic efficiency argument in favor of privatization is equally valid for opening up the space for private ownership in the sector, firm, or organizational task.

In fact, variations in cross-national use of the language of privatization reinforce the intuition that these processes are similar. In the early 1990s, Indian policymakers talked of "privatizing" the steel sector: what they meant was for the first time permitting private entrepreneurs to open steel mills to compete with mills owned by the government. Argentine president Menem, meanwhile, boasted of his intention to "privatize" bill collection for urban utilities—that is, to contract out an organizational task. Interestingly, understanding the functional similarities of private entry into sector, enterprise, and organizational task allows us to recognize privatization even when governments have political reasons for preferring that their transfer of production to the private sector go unheralded.

Privatization has another dimension that may also go unnoticed. A nation's understanding of "private" owners is often continuous rather than dichotomous. A country's corpus of business law, in fact, usually distinguishes among three categories of enterprise owners: the state, nationals resident in the country, and other private persons. For example, from the 1950s through the 1970s, Brazilian governments developed the public relations of managing the public-private and, simultaneously, the national-foreign ownership dichotomies into an art form with their famous "four-thirds" formula. The Brazilian government's contribution to equity investment was announced as both "public" and "national." Similarly, the multinational investor's contribution was dubbed both "private" and "foreign." Thus, the ideal-typical new heavy manufacturing plant in which the investment was a third foreign, a third state, and a third private local capital could be sold as promoting both Brazilian control of industry (two-thirds Brazilian) and private ownership (two-thirds private).

Countries may also discriminate among private owners on the basis of ethnicity. For example, countries such as Ireland, India, and Taiwan extend an intermediate category of privileges to expatriate nationals, former nationals, and their descendants, giving them access to certain kinds of property rights forbidden to ordinary foreigners. Israel offers citizenship and, thus, ownership privileges on the basis of religion. Finally, the familiar distinction made in every advanced industrial society (but not yet in every developing economy) between individuals as owners of firms (subject to unlimited liability for potential losses) and corporate entities as owners of firms (in which case the individual owners are subject only to limited liability) also illustrates the multiple rather than dichotomous nature of private ownership. Table 7.3 illustrates these continua.

Logically, then, one ought to acknowledge as privatization all changes in national regulations that expand the allowable participation of private citizens in the ownership of production of goods and services—including those policy changes prescribing movement from a more to a less restrictive definition of who is a legally admissible private investor. By the same logic, allowing previously forbidden institutional forms for private participation in a sector (or firm or organizational task) also qualifies as privatization. The economic efficiency rationale for favoring privatization operates identically in all of the examples just discussed. Extending the option of participating in entrepreneurship or minority shareholding to a previously excluded category of private citizens increases potential competition by enlarging the pool of potential entrants.

Unfortunately, my suggested definition of the term *privatization*

Table 7.3   Varieties of Privatization

What Is to Be Privatized?	Who Fits Within the Definition of Allowable Private Owners?[a]
The Sector Private entrants are allowed into a sector previously reserved to the state. (Note: A variant is to permit nonresident nationals or foreigners to own or produce in a sector previously reserved for citizen residents.)	**Rough Continuum** Minority participation of citizens, residents only. Minority participation of citizens, plus nonresident nationals and descandants. Majority participation of citizens (resident and nonresident).
The Firm The government sells state-owned enterprises, in whole or in part, to private buyers.	Minority participation of anyone (including foreigners). Majority participation of anyone (including foreigners).
The Organizational Task A functional task (for example, a utility's billing, a raw materials' firm's research and development) or geographic subunit is delinked and given to a private subcontractor.(Note: Governments may choose not to call this privatization.)	

Note: a. Illustrated by framing possible answers to the question, Who can purchase shares in an SOE undergoing privatization?

presents one thorny terminological problem. Suppose entry into a given economic sector, such as commercial banking, has previously been permitted to one level of government (perhaps the central government) but forbidden to other levels (such as individual states or cities). What do we call liberalization of the rules of entry into a sector by novel levels of the government itself? That is, the definition of who is a "public-sector" owner may also not be dichotomous. Furthermore, competition among different public-sector owners probably has some of the same economic characteristics as competition among private owners. For the present discussion, I ignore the possibility of such privatization within the state.

Despite its occasional potential for terminological awkwardness, the suggested definition has two important virtues. First, it highlights the similarities in terms of competitive pressures that should result from an expansion of ownership opportunities in all of the ways listed. Second, the broadened definition proposed here is more helpful for comparative analyses of complex empirical cases, which may begin with differing degrees of state ownership of production, than is the simple dichotomy of "state" versus "private" typically employed. The usefulness of a flexible definition should become apparent in the empirical discussion later in the chapter.

In one respect, however, I argue for a narrow definition of privatization. It has become fashionable to speak of "privatization of management" in countries or industries in which greater efficiency in enterprise operation is desired but actual transfer or liberalization of ownership is shunned, usually because of political considerations. For example, the literature on privatization in China and, until recently, in Eastern Europe contains ample discussion of privatization of management. I will discuss only privatization of ownership. The empirical status of the rules governing who is legally permitted to be a private owner and who actually is an owner at any given point in time is relatively straightforward to measure. That is, the concepts are unambiguous, although the data may not be readily available. On the other hand, managerial autonomy is probably more difficult both to specify conceptually and to measure empirically. In addition, granting managerial autonomy to state enterprise managers is at least as problematic in its effects of increasing competitive pressures on the firm as is full or partial sale to private owners. The sale of an SOE to its main private-sector competitor does not increase competitive pressures and probably does nothing to inspire managerial efficiency. Similarly, granting decisionmaking autonomy to managers who have no stockholders to please and who are difficult or impossible to fire is unlikely to enhance competitive pressures.

Finally, what of other measures of economic liberalization (and enhanced competition) that do not involve expanding the actual or the legally permissible amount of private ownership in a sector, firm, or organizational task? One might be tempted to include privatization as defined here in the same category as, for example, trade liberalization or liberalized rules for floating corporate bonds in national or international markets. I submit that private ownership per se is important enough in the realms of both politics and economics that it deserves to be investigated separately.

I define privatization as having four possible values. Little or no privatization has occurred when there has been very little change during the administration in either the broad regulatory framework governing public versus private activity or the amount of production in state hands. Minor, symbolic privatization indicates that the regime has gone on record as intending to implement SOE sales or significant regulatory changes but that, thus far, actual implementation of those policies has been limited. There is reason to believe the chief executive supports privatization, although he or she may have been unwilling to expend much political capital on pushing the policy through. In the three Latin American cases, the preexisting framework of state ownership of production meant that typically privatization would involve majority sales of state-owned enterprises. For economies of the size studied here, total sales should net, say, more than $100 million but less than $500 or $600 million. For India and other economies with extensive barriers to private entry into sectors exclusively reserved for either SOEs or limited categories of private entrepreneurs, the changes indicated by this category would be significant enough to cause political controversy but would not be large enough to alter, say, the future investment calculations of most private businesspeople.

Moderate privatization represents a serious move to reduce the comprehensiveness of reserved productive arenas and the quantity of state assets. If SOE sales are involved, they should encompass at least one or more historically state-owned firms; the dollar value of privatizations should exceed $500 million. Privatization by sector or organizational task should alter the rules in a fashion immediately apparent to the country's most dynamic entrepreneurs.

Finally, vigorous privatization means a real change in the nature of the domestic economy has taken place during the incumbent's administration. For economies of the size discussed here, asset sales above, say, $5 billion might be seen as a very rough cutoff point. When privatization by sector or organizational task or minority sales of SOEs are the principal reforms, the degree of regulatory change has long-range and probably irrevocable consequences for national industrial organization.

Argentina

I code privatization in the nine administrations as follows. In 1983, the state sector in Argentina included urban utilities (water, sewerage, electricity, the postal service), transportation facilities and companies (railroads, ports, highways, airports, and airlines), communications (telephones, television), the state petroleum monopoly (Yacimientos Carboníferos Fiscales, or YPF), development and some commercial banks, and a complex of manufacturing firms (including steel and defense production) in a holding company, Fabricaciones Militares, run by the military.[12] Most sectors were open to both foreign and local private capital.

Under Alfonsín there was little or no privatization. Through 1987, only four state firms were sold, for a total of $32 million (Ramamurti, 1992: 5). The state opened some organizational tasks to private contractors, the most important of which was to allow foreign oil companies to explore unused YPF oil fields. Although Alfonsín's government announced significant privatizations of the telephone company and four historically state-owned firms in steel and petrochemicals in 1985–1986, these plans were not carried out.

Menem, however, privatized vigorously. Sales of state-owned enterprises during the period 1990–1992 raised $9 billion in cash plus $12 billion in foreign debt reduction through debt-equity conversions (World Bank, 1993: 3). Foreign buyers were welcome. Major privatizations included the national telephone company, Entel; eight petrochemical firms managed by the military; the airline Aerolíneas Argentinas; 3,000 kilometers of railroad track; power plants; two television stations; road networks around major cities; first secondary, then primary oil fields of YPF;[13] coal mines; the merchant marine; the postal service; the port authority; the Buenos Aires subway system; and storage facilities of the national grain board. Related liberalizing moves allowed foreign banks and international financial operators to participate directly on the Argentine stock exchange. Private firms bid for the contracts for crucial organizational tasks, such as bill collection for urban public utilities and highway maintenance for many interurban routes. Regarding privatization by sector, the president went so far as to announce that government procurement would be opened for bidding to multinational firms.

Mexico

In late 1982, the Mexican state controlled the same economic sectors as the Argentine government plus all commercial banks.[14] State development banks had unintentionally acquired title to numerous small and medium-sized commercial and manufacturing enterprises as their former owners defaulted. Most of agriculture was in private hands, but the state owned large agribusinesses. Furthermore, the *ejido* (large, communally owned but individually farmed estates formed in the 1930s) sector, covering half of the nation's arable land, was characterized by limited private property rights. Farmers had use and inheritance rights but could not sell or otherwise transfer their plots. Mexico limited the percentage of foreign ownership in manufacturing firms to less than 49 percent in most sectors and disallowed entry to foreign banks but permitted foreign portfolio investment in government securities.

De la Madrid was a moderate privatizer. Sales reached around $1 billion during his administration; $612 million of that figure, however, represents firms sold in the last six months of 1988, some finalized after de la Madrid left office in early September of that year. With the prominent exception of one large, historically state-owned firm—the airline Aeroméxico, which sold for $330 million—the great majority of the more than 120 firms sold represented reprivatizations of small, nonstrategic commercial and industrial firms that had come to be owned by the state because of defaults on debts owed to public-sector development banks (Schneider, 1990).

Through 1992, Salinas accomplished vigorous privatization. Funds raised totaled $21 billion (Bazdresch and Elizondo, 1993: 52). Firms sold included a second airline, Aerolíneas Mexicanas; the copper mining firm, Cananea; Telmex, the telephone company (in which the government sold a controlling, although minority, interest for $1.76 billion plus $8 billion in promised investment); seven commercial banks (including Banamex, the country's largest, for $2.3 billion); several large steel plants; and much of the state's interests in food processing and distribution, including sugar refineries worth $700 million. Privatizations of organizational tasks included the exploration and development of oil fields owned by Petróleos Mexicanos (PEMEX), the state petroleum monopoly, and highway maintenance concessions. The Federal Electricity Commission (CFE) contracted with foreign manufacturers to build or renovate factories in Mexico to produce generators that CFE would then lease back. For the first time since the Mexican Revolution, foreign investors were welcome as joint private owners (up to 25 percent of total equity) in the banking sector. In early 1992, Salinas moved to permit a market in land on the *ejidos*. Mexican peasants had fought the bloody Mexican Revolution (1911–1917) over land, much of which large Mexican and North American landowner-investors had stolen during the nineteenth century. To privatize *ejidal* land was a deliberate effort to retire an important symbol of the twentieth-century Mexican political economy.

Brazil

As of 1985, Brazil's state sector looked like Mexico's except that television and most airlines were private, as was about half of the financial system and over half of petroleum distribution.[15] The larger overall state presence in Brazil resulted mainly from its role in heavy manufacturing in sectors such as steel, petrochemicals, aircraft, and armaments. In 1980, the top fifty SOEs, compared with the 500 largest private, nationally owned firms, generated the equivalent of 43 percent of the country's sales and 44 percent of profits, held 151 percent of its assets, and owed 145 percent of its corporate debt (*Exame: Melhores e Maiores* [São Paulo], April 1993: 120–121). As in Argentina and Mexico, the largest single public firm was the state petroleum company, Petrobrás. Brazilian agriculture and agribusiness were largely in private hands, with the exception of state trading enterprises in a few very important traditional commodities, notably coffee and sugar. State firms, including commercial banks, routinely raised capital from the private sector through minority share and debenture issues; many entered into joint ventures with multinationals. Foreign investors encountered relatively heavy taxation on repatriation of profits and dividends but were free to enter most sectors. Legislation disallowed most direct foreign participation in local capital markets.

Sarney presided over minor, symbolic privatization. His administration raised $475 million through reprivatization of six manufacturing firms acquired by the Banco Nacional de Desenvolvimento Económico e Social (BNDES), Brazil's industrial development bank (Schneider, 1990: 328).

There were also three noteworthy liberalizations of entry. From 1986, multinationals could lease exploration and development contracts for oil fields from Petrobrás. From 1987, foreign owned and operated country funds could trade corporate securities directly in Brazilian capital markets. The Sarney administration also opened the computer, or "informatics," sector to new foreign direct investment.

Collor accomplished moderate privatization. By late 1992, the government had sold industrial firms to the private sector for $3.9 billion (World Bank, 1993: 9). The largest sale was that of Usiminas, a historically state-owned steel mill, which raised $1.5 billion. Other large firms included three additional steel mills, Cosinor, Piratini, and Tubarão; a shipping firm, SNBP; the fertilizer and petrochemical installations INDAG, Petroflex, Copesul, and Alcalis; and the heavy equipment manufacturers Celma and Mafersa. Planned privatizations to end in 1993 amounted to an additional $13 billion (Baer and Villela, 1992: 16). Collor was impeached for corruption in December 1992; his successor, Vice President Itamar Franco, suspended most privatizations through 1993.

India

As of 1984, the Indian government dominated the sectors as its Latin American counterparts plus virtually all of the financial sector, including insurance.[16] It played a large role in manufacturing, from machine tools to heavy electrical equipment to armaments. For example, India was the only country of the four discussed here with a large presence in the capital goods sector. Furthermore, the Indian government, unlike Latin American authorities, reserved many sectors exclusively for state production. Since the 1950s, its concept of planning had not only encompassed allocating resources to desired uses and geographic regions but had also implied preventing the "waste" of scarce capital on "unnecessary" projects. Thus, even most productive activities dominated by private ownership lacked free entry for new entrepreneurs, even if they were resident citizens of India. Instead, would-be producers had to obtain multiple licenses to set up any factories and even for comparatively trivial expansion or diversification of existing production facilities.[17] Many labor-intensive and traditional cottage industry sectors, such as cotton textiles and furniture, were protected from competition by larger firms. In fact, larger firms and even medium-sized companies with a dominant market share had to petition the government's Monopoly Commission for permission for virtually all strategic business decisions. Foreign investors could own no more than 40 percent of companies. Yet, from the late 1970s, the Indian government had begun to rely on foreign capital inflows arising from new kinds of portfolio investments from South Asians resident abroad managed by commercial banks in

India. Thus, there came to be two principal categories of foreign investors, with different rights and duties—the ordinary outsider and the nonresident Indian (NRI). Noncitizens, including NRIs, were barred from direct participation in local stock markets.

Rajiv Gandhi oversaw minor but symbolic privatization. His government greatly expanded the number of manufacturing sectors open to entry for most domestic entrepreneurs under the so-called open general license. The licensing regime began the switch to a much streamlined negative list of reserved sectors, with all sectors not explicitly prohibited to new domestic entrants, in principle, permitted. His government raised the lower size limit for firms subject to regulation by the Monopolies Commission. Country funds directed at NRIs were allowed to invest in Indian equities. Perhaps the most important privatization achievement of Gandhi's administration was making open advocacy of economic liberalization respectable within the dominant Congress Party at the national political level, a not inconsiderable feat.

The short-lived administrations of minority coalition leaders Singh and Shekhar[18] engineered little or no actual privatization, although in March 1991 Shekhar's finance minister announced future plans to divest 20 percent of the equity of selected state firms. Two large public-sector industrial development banks, the Industrial Development Bank of India and the Industrial Credit and Investment Corporation of India, received unprecedented permission to raise new capital by share issues to be directly subscribed by the general public.

In the subsequent year and a half, to late 1992, Shekhar's successor, Narasimha Rao, privatized moderately. Under Rao, there was further significant liberalization in the licensing regime, the scope for foreign direct investment, and the rules governing SOEs' access to private financing. The government freed investment and production by Indian firms in the steel sector and also made such investment attractive by loosening price controls.[19] Privatizations of organizational tasks included opening competitive bidding contracts for the modernization, development, and management of ports, oil, and natural gas fields; concessions and station amenities for Indian Railways, the largest employer in the country; and urban cellular phone systems. The system of licensing imports was greatly simplified and reduced. Breaking with almost two decades of politically symbolic tradition, Rao's minority government pushed through amendments to the Foreign Exchange Regulation Act of 1973 that permitted multinational investors, previously limited to a minority position, to hold 51 percent of equity in most sectors and up to over 75 percent in sectors deemed strategic for future industrialization—notably those involving sophisticated technology, high export potential, or both. By early summer 1992, about $1.1 billion had been raised through divestment of up to 20 percent of the equity of thirty-one state-owned enterprises (public-sector units, or PSUs in Indian parlance). The government announced plans to liberalize entry into commercial banking, to allow foreign institutional investors direct access to Indian capital markets, and to fully privatize such traditionally state-owned sectors as power generation.

Incentives to Privatize, from Alfonsín to Rao

What explains politicians' diverse records of privatization? In this section I review the evidence on the economic and political logics of the possible policy choice of privatization for each administration. Tables 7.2, 7.3, and 7.4 summarize the information on each administration.

Table 7.4   Privatization and Incentives to Privatize in Four Countries

Country/Chief Executive	Privatization[a]	Intrinsic Economic	Pragmatic Economic	Domestic Political	International Political
Argentina					
Alfonsín	Little	High	High	Low	Low
Menem	Vigorous	High	High	High	Moderate
Mexico					
De la Madrid	Moderate	Low	High	Low	Moderate
Salinas	Vigorous	Low	High	Moderate	High
Brazil					
Sarney	Minor	Low	High	Low	Low
Collor	Moderate	Low	High	Moderate	Low
India					
Gandhi	Minor	Moderate	Low	Low	Low
Singh/Shekhar	Little	Moderate	Low	Low	Moderate
Rao	Moderate	Moderate	Moderate	Low	Moderate

Note: a. Privatization is scored as little, minor, moderate, or vigorous. Each of the four incentives to privatize is scored as low, moderate, or high.

Argentina

Argentina had one government that barely privatized at all and a second that vigorously reduced the state sector. Under President Raul Alfonsín (1983–1989), intrinsic economic incentives to privatize were high: most observers concluded that the majority of SOEs were both inefficient and corrupt. In 1980, for example, Fabricaciones Militares alone had losses estimated at $600 million (Lewis, 1990: 454). The SOE sector's deficit averaged 5.6 percent of GDP in the early 1980s. Moreover, the state's general management of the economy had been abysmal for some decades. Argentina's GNP grew only 2.5 percent annually in the 1970s, compared with the Latin American average of 5.5 percent, and, on average, it fell by 2 percent annually from 1980 to 1984. Frieden (1991: 80) constructed an "investment efficiency index" for Latin America for the 1970s and early 1980s in which higher numbers indicate greater efficiency. The regional mean is 22.0, but Argentina received a dismal –1.5 percent. The public sector's ability to invest was also eroding. In the 1970s, public investment as a share of GDP was 8.7 percent; in the early 1980s, it was only 7.1 percent. Furthermore, chronic problems in urban infrastructure such as telephones indicated both a lack of funds and an acute need for new technology.

Alfonsín's pragmatic economic incentives were also high. The government budget balance in 1983 was –13.9 percent of GNP. The government's maladroit attempt to finance itself through "nationalizing deposits" (instituting 100 percent reserve requirements) in the early 1980s could not be sustained against the opposition of banks and their erstwhile borrowers (Bekerman, 1986). Other options implied either immediate inflation or very high interest rates, thus worsening the deficit over the medium term. As of 1980, the ratio of external debt to GDP was already 35 percent; by 1985 it had risen to 57 percent. The trade (in goods plus nonfinancial services) balance was slightly positive, however, in transition from –$3.2 billion in 1980 to $4.7 billion in 1985.

Domestic political incentives to privatize were low. Alfonsín faced the difficult task of restoring government credibility after years of repressive, bloody military rule (1976–1983). As the leader of the confusingly named Radical Party, heading a centrist coalition of business, the urban middle class, and economic nationalists, Alfonsín confronted a splintered but powerful Peronist movement—ranging from populist, agrarian economic nationalists to militant industrial workers to leftist intellectuals—loosely arrayed to his left. The business community, which favored privatization, generally supported Alfonsín in preference to the Peronist alternative, but he needed to tread gingerly with the country's potentially volatile industrial workers, the best organized of which worked for the state. During his term Alfonsín faced several military rebellions and coup attempts (Pion-Berlin, 1992; Huser, 1994). He was aided by the triply discredited condition of the military, vilified by much of the public as abusers of human rights, losers in battle, and failures at economic management. Still, an additional reason to avoid rapid privatization was the fact that many senior officers retained lucrative sinecures in the government oil monopoly and throughout the public productive sector.

Finally, external political pressures were low. Given the economic and political disasters of the final years of military rule, policymakers in the advanced industrial democracies and the international financial organizations they dominated were willing to support any democratically elected Argentine government. In fact, those international actors were delighted to be dealing with other than a Peronist president. Thus, Alfonsín was able to pursue a comparatively confrontational international debt negotiation strategy culminating in a partial moratorium in 1988, which helped him consolidate domestic political support. Although creditor country governments and international agencies such as the IMF were increasingly critical of Argentine state firms, they were reluctant to pressure Alfonsín too strongly.

Carlos Saúl Menem (inaugurated 1989) also had high intrinsic economic incentives to privatize. In the late 1980s, SOEs were no more efficient and only slightly less deficitary than they had been when Alfonsín came to the presidency. Telephone service and other essential urban infrastructure continued to deteriorate, although there was a problem finding potential buyers. The major bidders for Argentina's public utilities were either oligopolistic private competitors or foreign SOEs including the Spanish and Italian telephone companies, neither of which had impressive service records in its home market. Economic growth, at the debt crisis level of –2.1 percent in the early 1980s, had recovered to only –0.4 percent in the late 1980s. Public investment fell dramatically, to only 4.9 percent in the late 1980s. Politicians claimed to be driven by the objectively urgent need for new technology. The administration's decision to accept bids from foreign parastatals with mediocre service records casts doubt, however, on how much importance policymakers actually placed on solving this problem (Manzetti, 1992).

Menem's pragmatic economic incentives were high. Alfonsín's administration had adjusted economically, although the president had not dared to challenge the powerful interests tied to the large SOEs. The government balance for 1989 was only –0.5 percent of GNP, the best result of the nine administrations surveyed. The institutional arrangements for financing even this low deficit were poor, however. The trade balance was positive, reaching $7.8 billion by 1990. The foreign debt was drifting down and would reach "only" 44 percent of GDP in 1990. The economic outlook overall was hardly rosy. Menem had assumed office four months early because the economy and political confidence in Alfonsín were deteriorating rapidly: the country was entering hyperinflation. Given the acute economic crisis, the new government was under great pressure to do something dramatic to wrench the economy back on track.

Domestic political incentives were also high. Menem won the 1989 election as the representative of the working- and middle-class Justicialist (Peronist) Party. Voters did not expect him to privatize. What happened? Despite several coup attempts, democracy had survived two presidential elections. Menem could probably count on controlling the military as long as he retained the support of the business community and the urban middle class.[20] But in the Radical Party, Menem faced a credible alternative multiclass political coalition located, on the whole, somewhat to his right, or at least seen as less threatening by both Argentine businesspeople and foreign investors. To compete politically, Menem moved right, in policy choice if not immediately in rhetoric. He appointed as a senior economic adviser Alvaro Alsogaray, a widely known and economically liberal former army officer and minister. Menem's later elevation of Domingo Cavallo to be economy minister was an appointment in the same vein. Winning over the business community remained a challenge. Capital flight had long been a problem in Argentina. The quadruple-digit annual inflation of 1988 and 1989 was unprecedented and frightening. Privatization had the political advantage of signaling seriousness to the capitalist class (Pinheiro and Schneider, 1993; Bazdresch and Elizondo, 1993). Historically, Argentina's middle classes, many of whom held government jobs, also had not been supporters of a small state. Their gradual, reluctant shift on this issue followed more than a decade of bad economic news.

Even if Menem's move toward neoliberal economics brought him the support of capitalists, we must also explain why Menem felt comfortable abandoning his own party's historical constituency: public-sector unions. As a Peronist, Menem did not have intraorganizational incentives within his own committed support group for moving to the right on economic issues.[21] By August 1990, just over a year into Menem's term, a total of 900,000 workers were on strike to protest wage restraint and privatization, many from public-sector unions in telecommunications, oil fields, and state mortgage and investment banks (the real purchasing power of wages had fallen between 30 and 64 percent over the previous six months) (*Latin American Weekly Report* [*LAWR*], August 9, 1990). Although workers cursed Menem, they had few political alternatives. The military's "dirty war" against subversives in the 1970s and early 1980s had decimated Argentina's non-Peronist leftists. Overall, Argentine workers were unlikely to secure a better deal by following any politician or political party that had a viable chance of coming to power; thus, the political costs to Menem of disregarding worker preferences were not great. As a rational politician seeking to broaden and strengthen his support, Menem therefore faced strong domestic political incentives to privatize.

Finally, Menem's international political incentives to privatize had increased to the moderate level. International pressures increased on all four of the countries in this study as privatization became an important symbol of economic sincerity to both the Bush administration and the IMF. Moreover, Argentina was less shielded from normal foreign political pressures in the very late 1980s, when the maintanence of democracy per se appeared assured, than it had been in the early and mid-1980s. In January 1989, the World Bank had suspended its loan program because of Argentina's failure to meet agreed-upon economic targets. Argentina needed the approval of both the IMF and the United States on a variety of international economic issues, most importantly debt relief and trade.

Mexico

The first Mexican administration studied oversaw moderate privatization; the second was a vigorous privatizer. President Miguel de la Madrid (1982–1988) had comparatively low intrinsic economic incentives to privatize. The most visible symbol of public-sector production, PEMEX, the state petroleum conglomerate, remained a credible symbol of state control of the "commanding heights" of the economy. Furthermore, under state leadership Mexico's economy had done well: GDP growth in the 1970s had averaged 6.3 percent annually. Frieden (1991) awards Mexico in the 1970s a score of 23 on his investment efficiency index. The financial problems of the SOE sector as a whole were relatively serious; SOE deficits were high, at just under 6 percent of GDP in 1980 and over 9 percent in 1981 (Pinheiro and Schneider, 1993: 13). Nonetheless, public investment as a share of GDP, uniquely among the six Latin American administrations profiled, was rising as de la Madrid took office. That share had averaged 7.6 percent through the 1970s but rose to 9.3 percent in the early 1980s, suggesting that it had not yet become a serious problem. In fact, many observers saw the problems of Mexico's large, historically public-sector firms as ones of liquidity and international prices for PEMEX's oil rather than of fundamental incompetence. There was no urgent need for access to new technology; much had been imported during the flush 1970s, and close ties to the United States ensured Mexico of relatively easy future access as well.

De la Madrid encountered high pragmatic economic incentives to divest. The central government's 1982 balance was –16.0 percent of GNP, and financing that deficit would be problematic, particularly given the traditional ease of capital flight northward. The situation forced the Mexican government to issue bonds that had high interest rates and, worse yet, were often denominated in dollars. The debt to GDP ratio for 1982 was 49 percent. Still, the trade balance had just become positive, passing from –$4.3 in 1980 to $7.8 billion in 1985.

Domestic political incentives to privatize were also low. In contrast to Alfonsín and Sarney, de la Madrid did not have to worry about keeping the military in line or, so it appeared through the 1980s, about regional rebellions, as did Rajiv Gandhi. De la Madrid belonged to the Institutional Revolutionary Party (PRI), which had reigned over Mexico's soft authoritarian political system since the 1920s. His predecessor, Lopez Portillo, was an economic expansionist who in the last days of his term suddenly nationalized all commercial banks and their associated empires, blaming them for the foreign debt crisis. Many victims of bank nationalization, however, had long been important, albeit surreptitious, financial backers of the PRI, a party whose rhetoric exalted industrial workers and the peasantry but that, in practice, was on cosy terms with the business community.

Consequently, a major challenge for the new president was to reinforce the PRI's informal links with big business, especially entrepreneurs located in northern Mexico. Immediately after assuming office, de la Madrid moved to woo big business by reprivatizing the nonbank businesses that had belonged to the conglomerates headed by the now nationalized banks. In 1986, Mexico joined the General Agreement on Tariffs and Trade, a step that implied the phased dismantling of a long-established structure of industrial protections and was popular with internationally oriented business. In addition, in the 1980s many middle-class voters and small and medium-sized businesspeople producing for the domestic market began to gravitate to the National Action Party (PAN), a conservative, proclerical, and private-sector party that did surprisingly well in local elections in 1983. The needs to solidify ties to big business and to manage attrition losses to the PAN were forces pulling de la Madrid's policies to the right.

At the same time, de la Madrid also had to watch his left. The PRI's traditional corporatist organization into peasant, labor, and "popular" sectors (the latter a catchall category dominated by white-collar public-sector unions, such as teachers) no longer reflected true power realities. Structural changes in the economy since the 1960s had made both industrial labor and especially peasants less and less important economically and thus increasingly less likely to be considered by the central government power brokers. Furthermore, post-1982 economic austerity meant the central government had significantly fewer resources to distribute, thereby weakening regional party bosses' ability to dispense patronage to their clients (Heredia, 1994: 279–283). Those constituencies plus disaffected urban intellectuals opposed economic liberalization and had coalesced around the PRI faction led by Cuauhtemoc Cárdenas, the son of one of Mexico's best-loved presidents. De la Madrid therefore wooed workers, farmers, and the urban middle sectors by reaffirming the sacred nature of state monopolies in petroleum, mining, telecommunications, and the new task of commercial banking. Reprivatization of hotels and such was one thing, but threats to PEMEX were not to be tolerated.

International political pressures were moderate. Pressures from abroad intensified after 1985, when the United States began pressing Mexico to sign on to its Baker Plan for modest creditor concessions on debt rescheduling in exchange for market-oriented domestic economic reforms. The Reagan administration was pleased with Mexico's economic adjustment in the form of gradual trade liberalization and massive wage compression. Nonetheless, the tremendous economic leverage the United States had over Mexico meant that as privatization became popular in Washington policy circles, Mexico would be among the first to be proselytized.

Six years later, President Carlos Salinas (inaugurated 1988) inherited intrinsic incentives to privatize that remained low. The reputation of the large, historically state-owed firms was still sound, at least in comparative terms. Although the debt crisis and subsequent stringent adjustment reduced GNP growth to 0.9 percent annually in the early 1980s, it recovered to 2.1 percent from 1985 to 1989. Public investment, however, plummeted from an average of 9.3 percent for the period 1980–1984 to only 5.4 percent for the period 1985–1989. Still, foreign investment had begun to flood in, and access to technology was also not a major problem. Nonetheless, by the end of the period covered here, attitudes were slowly changing. In 1992, a *Financial Times* reporter interviewed Francisco Rojas, head of PEMEX, which was undergoing restructuring as a way to head off demands from some quarters for outright privatization. Rojas admitted that formerly "There was no maximization of profits, there was no business criteria [*sic*] in the activities of Pemex. What they demanded of Pemex was that it supply effectively all the hydrocarbon needs of the nation and there is no doubt it did it" (*Financial Times,* October 8, 1992). This level of official honesty was novel.

Pragmatic economic incentives to privatize, however, were high and rising when Salinas took office. He inherited a central government budget balance of –10.8 percent of GNP in 1985. The institutional basis for financing government deficits remained fragile, although possibilities for financing showed promise of short-term improvement as Mexico's liberalizing reforms began to make the country attractive to foreign investors. The foreign debt was 59 percent of GDP in 1988, down from its 1986 high of 76 percent. There was a trade surplus in 1988, although it had become a huge gap of –$18.3 billion by 1992 because of rapid trade liberalization.

Domestic political incentives, meanwhile, had increased to become moderate. It was more important than ever for Salinas to retain the support of large, internationally oriented Mexican business. Despite widely believed charges of ballot stuffing, predictably the PRI candidate, Carlos Salinas de Gortari, had won Mexico's 1988 presidential contest, defeating challenger Cárdenas, who broke with the PRI late in de la Madrid's term. Cárdenas's leftist coalition was greatly weakened by factional fighting after the election, whereas the rightist PAN won three state governorships—two so overwhelmingly that the government party could not, as it had tried to do, disguise the results through fraud. By privatizing, Salinas took advantage of the postelection political weakness of the Left and moved to meet the challenge from the PAN. Reduced opportunities for patronage-based access to SOE manufacturing jobs also undercut the power of traditional political bosses (the so-called dinosaurs) within the PRI and thereby strengthened the mostly foreign-trained technocratic modernizers (literally, the "philosophers" but closer in meaning to "scientific managers") in the Harvard-trained president's camp. Privatization therefore allowed Salinas to strengthen his own influence and that of like-minded young reformers within the long-ruling political party (Langston, 1990).

Finally, Salinas's international political incentives to sell SOEs were high. Just as international pressure to privatize increased for all developing countries, there was an additional shift in Mexico's international vulnerability. Canada and the United States negotiated and, in 1989, signed a historic agreement for a Free Trade Area. Suddenly, Mexico was in danger of being permanently cut out. To bring Mexico into the renamed North American Free Trade Agreement (NAFTA), Salinas had to woo the new Bush administration, the U.S. border states, and the U.S. Congress—all of which expected very specific changes in Mexican domestic economic policy, ranging from liberalization and privatization to tough new environmental safeguards (see inter alia *New York Times,* December 15, 1991; *Financial Times,* September 16, 1992). Salinas's decision to pursue NAFTA vigorously brought him still closer to the business constituency in northern Mexico and further from the PRI's historical base among the small, marginal farmers and workers of the economically depressed South. As Salinas burned his bridges to the still powerful Mexican constituency for statist, inward-looking economic policies, his political need for the strong affirmation of U.S. acceptance in NAFTA became intense.

Brazil

Meanwhile, in Brazil in the 1980s and early 1990s, one administration engaged in minor, symbolic privatization and the next was a moderate privatizer. President José Sarney (1985–1990) faced low intrinsic economic incentives to privatize because historically the performance of the SOE sector had been quite good.[22] Senior government economists questioned the competitiveness rationale for selling off state firms in oligopolized sectors. Private businesspeople reluctantly credited the state with having shepherded the country's impressive postwar industrial growth. Even prominent economic conservatives seldom directly criticized the performance of large SOEs, instead emphasizing the need for staffing cuts in the civil service and central government ministries. The deficit of the SOE sector averaged a comparatively low 2.8 percent of GDP in the early 1980s. GDP growth in the 1970s had been an impressive 8.1 percent annually, but the early 1980s, with first a local recession and then the regionwide debt crisis, experienced growth of only 0.4 percent. Frieden (1991) awarded Brazil a 32, against the regional average of 22, in investment efficiency through the early 1980s.

Nonetheless, public-sector investment had dropped from an average of 8.3 percent through the 1970s to only 6.8 percent in the early 1980s. Some economists suggested that the central government budget was being augmented by the deliberate squeezing of the SOE sector, whose controlled prices lagged substantially behind inflation and whose capital investment budget fell (Afonso and Dain, 1987). There was no pressing need for access to foreign technology, particularly since SOEs had long been encouraged to form joint ventures with multinationals.

Pragmatic economic incentives were high. The government budget balance for 1985 was −11.40 percent. Financing the deficit would prove to be one of the Sarney government's greatest long-run failures. By 1984, the accumulated public debt was already over 13 percent of GDP (Dias Carneiro, 1987: 227). The cost of financing the debt rose as interest rates increased to extraordinary levels. Real monthly interest rates on bank certificates of deposit were about 1.50 percent in 1985; by 1989 they averaged 7.23 percent (Economist Intelligence Unit, 1993). Foreign debt to GDP was high at 39 percent, although that figure was down from 63 percent in 1980. A trade surplus of $10.8 billion in 1985 made the foreign debt far less threatening than the domestic one.

Sarney had low domestic political reasons to privatize. Like Alfonsín, he first had to focus on navigating the transition to civilian rule after twenty years of military authoritarianism (1964–1985). Brazil's redemocratization was made more difficult by the fact that Sarney, trusted neither by his new allies, the moderate reformers, nor by his old friends in the military's tame political party, inherited the top position suddenly and unexpectedly when the popular president-elect died. Maintaining regime stability meant minimizing direct economic threats to those social groups that had supported the authoritarian regime, including the military officer corps and the urban middle class, which had benefited from three decades of expansion of state employment. Domestic business and even some multinationals had grown accustomed to generous indirect subsidies in the form of cheap goods and services from state-owned enterprises, subsidies that would have to cease if private owners took over. Large-scale privatization could also potentially produce threats of strikes or mass action from the Left, provoking a reaction from the Right. The new democratic government, unlike military rulers, had to avoid the use of repressive methods to prevent strikes, which could easily occur if workers in the large SOEs felt threatened. Moreover— unlike Menem—Sarney, a historical conservative, did not need to move right to reassure a nervous business community; further, he had a motive to privatize to try to consolidate his position within his own party, like Salinas. Finally, capital flight had been less of a problem in Brazil than in either Argentina or Mexico through the mid-1980s; consequently, there was less need to entice home Brazilian funds invested abroad through "responsible" policies such as privatization.

International political incentives were low, but they became stronger during the later years of Sarney's term. The United States used its "super 301" threat of bilateral trade sanctions to privatize foreign entry into Brazil's computer manufacturing sector. Brazil's greater distance from the United States compared with Mexico's, however, and the superior diversity of both its trading partners and its multinational bank creditors gave Brazilian policymakers more bargaining freedom. Furthermore, Brazil's ability to transform its 1970s trade deficit into a surplus after 1981 was another source of bargaining strength. Throughout the 1980s, Brazil repeatedly failed to live up to its restructuring commitments with the IMF, but the country escaped serious sanctions.

When President Fernando Collor de Mello (1990–1992) assumed office, intrinisic economic incentives to reduce the state's directly productive role remained low, although they were slowly increasing. State-sector performance remained generally strong (Ribeiro, 1992) and Brazilian elites continued to believe SOE production in such sectors as petroleum, energy, and telecommunications was essential.[23] Access to foreign technology was a need, perhaps, but not a pressing one. In fact, by some measures the overall economy was astonishingly resilient: GNP growth of 0.4 percent during the period 1980–1984 rose to 2.1 percent for the period 1985–1989, which was fairly reasonable for the region in the context of the debt crisis. GNP growth in 1990, however, was –4.7 percent. In the late 1980s, compared with the early years of the decade, total public investment was down from 6.8 to 6.0 percent of GDP, in itself a comparatively small drop but a worryingly low absolute figure. Baer and Villela (1992: 6) disaggregated SOE investment, which averaged 4 percent of GDP in the early 1980s but only 2 percent in the late 1980s. One problem was that redemocratization in 1985 had encouraged leaders to reallocate state investment spending to visible projects such as new school buildings and other public works.

Collor encountered high pragmatic economic reasons to privatize. The central government balance was approaching meltdown, at –16.6 percent of GNP in 1992. Inflationary finance was still in place, although Brazil's means for accomplishing financing were unusually convoluted (see Armijo, 1996). Even worse, Brazil's central government did most of its domestic borrowing not from captive financial institutions—as was the case in India and, to a lesser extent, in Argentina during the early 1980s—but in the market. Real monthly interest rates on bank CDs fell during Collor's first year in office but only to 4.1 percent. Slightly more comforting was the fact that in 1990 the foreign debt, which at $116 billion in absolute terms was still the largest among developing countries (followed by Mexico with $97 billion and India with $70 billion), was only 24 percent of GDP. The external trade balance the year Collor took office stood at a comfortable $9.5 billion. In fact, the arrangements for the privatizations that occurred under

Collor clearly show that the domestic debt was a much bigger problem than the foreign debt. Although the government allowed swaps of foreign debt as one of the "privatization currencies," the debt was discounted 25 percent. Virtually all buyers preferred paying by means of domestic debt instruments, including treasury securities and bonds that had been issued by various state-owned enterprises and were exchangeable at face value. Inflation reached four digits in 1989, indicating severe macroeconomic problems although not necessarily ones privatization could fix. Although Brazilian policymakers steadfastly maintained that Brazil, unlike its neighbor to the south, was not entering hyperinflation but rather a vaguely defined but less worrisome "superinflation," these numbers forced the administration to take drastic action.

Collor's domestic political pressures to privatize were moderate.[24] Despite having won Brazil's first direct presidential contest in nearly thirty years, Collor's authority was weakened by an extremely rambunctious legislature that was fractured among almost thirty mostly novice political parties and in which the president's party held less than 5 percent of the seats. Collor was unpopular with both the working-class Left and with most of the São Paulo business community, which had supported him in the runoff election mainly to prevent a win by the Workers' Party (PT) candidate, Luís Inácio da Silva, known as Lula. Collor needed to strengthen his political base. Meanwhile, Brazil's worsening economic crisis put pressure on the chief executive to do something. Many Brazilians were prepared to support dramatic economic "shock" programs, a tradition begun under Sarney.[25] Collor first tried a macroeconomic shock that froze over 70 percent of the public's assets in the banking system for eighteen months. Structural reforms were also planned, including the sale of large profitable state firms. Middle-class state employees tended to work in white-collar bureaucratic jobs or in service industry monopolies such as the post office and the big state banks, all of which were overstaffed by any efficiency standard. The major privatizations scheduled in Brazil—unlike those in Argentina and, in part, Mexico—were in the state manufacturing sector. Those firms largely employed blue-collar workers, most of whom had voted for left parties like the PT and not for Collor.

International political incentives continued to suggest privatization but only at a low level. Although the advanced industrial countries were more positive about privatization than they had been when Sarney took office, Brazil under Collor was less dependent on their goodwill than it had been earlier, largely because of the country's at least partial success in managing the balance of payments. By the early 1990s, despite inflation and half-hearted privatization, large SOEs like Petrobrás, as well as private banks and firms, could again borrow in the Euromarkets.

India

The final country considered here is India. If we find Indian incentives to policymakers to privatize, as well as privatization outcomes, to be similar to those in the larger, more industrialized new democracies in Latin America, that is a good indicator that any observable patterns are not, for example, culture or region specific. Halfway around the globe but during the same years as those studied for the Latin American countries, three Indian administrations privatized, first, in a minor but symbolic way, then hardly at all, and then, surprisingly, moderately. Prime Minister Rajiv Gandhi (1984–1989) had moderate intrinsic economic incentives to privatize. A core group of influential economists had argued for over a decade that India's slow GDP growth had resulted from the government's stifling of the economy through overregulation through the so-called permit-license raj (regime). Several scholars suggested a strong relationship between the growth of bureaucratic power and corruption in the distribution of public resources (see Ahluwalia, 1985; Bardhan, 1984; Jalan, 1991; Jha, 1980). India's GNP growth averaged only 3.7 percent in the 1970s, which was slow for a newly industrializing economy. The lack of dynamism could be attributed to pervasive government-mandated barriers to entry and expansion throughout the economy. Although growth accelerated to 5.2 percent in the early 1980s, many economists suggested that those results reflected high aggregate investment imposed by government planners rather than efficient investment and, possibly, also reflected an early entrepreneurial response to limited economic liberalization in the very late 1970s.[26] Central planning had enjoyed some successes; the share of GNP invested, even in this very poor country, rose steadily from 13 percent in 1970 to almost 21 percent in 1985. Further, public investment as a share of GDP climbed from 7.5 percent in the 1970s to 9.6 percent in the early 1980s. The need for access to modern technology was an important factor in favor of liberalization by sector, including opening up to multinationals, which had been unwelcome since the early 1970s.

Pragmatic economic incentives to privatize were low in 1984, at least by my comparative measures, although some Indian economists might have disagreed. The central government balance for 1984 was –6.5 percent of GNP. In any case, Indian leaders had an advantage over Latin American ones in financing deficits; the intrinsic inefficiency of India's state-owned financial sector had pragmatic advantages for the central government, which extracted substantial resources from banks through a form of indirect taxation. Indian central government debt securities paid below-market interest, but commercial banks, nationalized in 1969, were obliged to hold large quantities of debt securities. These coerced "prudential" investments plus cash reserve requirements had totaled 27 percent of commercial bank time and savings deposits in 1970 but were up to 46 percent by 1985 (Center for Monitoring the Indian Economy [CMIE], 1991: table 17.11, n.p.). The central government also financed itself by borrowing at low rates from the Reserve Bank of India (the central bank) and from banks themselves. In 1970, net bank credit to the state had been only 1 percent of GNP, but by 1980 it was 4 percent and remained near that level through the decade (CMIE, 1991). In fact, privatization of commercial banking increased the strain on public finances, at least through the medium term. Foreign debt as a share of GDP ratio was only 12 percent in 1980 but jumped to 19 percent in 1985. At –$6.6 billion in 1985, the trade balance was the main problem. Inflation, although worrisome to Indian leaders, was not near the hyperinflation level.

Gandhi's domestic political incentives to privatize were low. Chosen prime minister within hours of his mother's assassination in 1984, Rajiv Gandhi's normal political "honeymoon" period was extended by public sympathy for his loss. The new prime minister energetically deregulated during his first six months in office. An Oxbridge-trained engineer, Gandhi (like Mexico's Salinas) believed market-oriented reforms would improve efficiency. Gandhi effectively stopped pushing for his new economic policies within the first year, however, as political opposition coalesced. Business depended on protected domestic markets and often also on extensive "sweetheart" contracts with state enterprises as purchasers or suppliers. Over half of the middle class held government jobs, as did the unionized (and politicized) workers in state-owned manufacturing facilities. The economic basis of entire regions depended on the artificial exclusion of medium- and large-scale producers using contemporary technology from competition with traditional craft producers, especially in the textile sector. Since the nationalization of commercial banks in 1969 and their subsequent enforced move to the countryside, many of the comparatively prosperous farmers of the politically crucial north Indian Hindi heartland had come to rely on subsidized credit from wholly government-owned banks. Consequently, strong and easily mobilized opposition from entrenched interests existed to potential privatization. The Indian state, de facto, remained ideologically and practically committed to employing as many citizens as possible.[27]

International political pressures for privatization were also low. Since independence, India had delinked itself substantially from the international capitalist economy and was therefore less dependent on external goodwill than any of the Latin American countries. Even in 1988, despite a looming balance-of-payments crisis, Gandhi avoided approaching the IMF, fearing any hint of bending to foreign pressure would cause him to lose the election planned for early 1989.

Gandhi's Congress Party, which had formed all but two postindependence Indian governments, lost the 1989 election. The short-lived administrations of minority coalition leaders Prime Ministers V. P. Singh (1990) and Chandra Shekhar (1990–1991) were similar in their moderately left (in the Indian context) political complexions, and I treat them as a single case. In 1990, intrinsic economic incentives to privatize continued to be moderate. The reputations of state firms and protected private producers were no brighter than before, although historically high economic growth—averaging 6.2 percent from 1985 to 1989—continued into the late 1980s. Investment funds were not obviously lacking: public investment as a share of GDP averaged an impressive 10.4 percent. On the other hand, renewed economic growth made the strains on the infrastructure more apparent. The need for modern technology to modernize sectors from telecommunications to airlines to electricity generation was becoming acute.

Pragmatic economic incentives to privatize as Singh came to office remained low, although they had worsened incrementally since the previous administration. The central government's balance for 1990 was –7.0 percent. Banking policies continued to support government fiscal needs: by mid-1989 over 53 percent of deposits were reserved by the central government for its own needs, which was unfortunate for the efficiency of financial intermediation but useful for financing the state. The debt to GDP ratio was 23 percent, high by Indian standards but fairly moderate by world standards. The continuing trade imbalance (–$6.0 billion in 1990), however, made the debt potentially ominous.

Domestic political incentives to privatize were extremely low under Singh and Shekhar. Both men headed minority coalition governments. The political bases of each were among left intellectuals, disadvantaged castes and minorities, and, in rural areas, constituencies not normally favoring economic liberalization. Neither leader had anything to gain politically by endangering workers' jobs through privatization.

Events conspired, however, to push international political reasons to privatize to the moderate level. Iraq's invasion of Kuwait and the U.S.-led response propelled Shekhar reluctantly toward the United States, even granting U.S. war planes refueling rights. The Gulf War caused a double economic shock to India. First, large numbers of Indian guest workers in Kuwait and Saudi Arabia had become refugees, hastily fleeing with few possessions. Many lacked the wherewithal even to travel home; eventually, the Indian government diverted planes from its national carrier, the SOE Air India, to collect them from camps in Jordan and elsewhere—at considerable public expense. Moreover, throughout the 1980s India had received about $2 billion annually as worker remittances, overwhelmingly from the Gulf—an amount equal to almost a third of the trade deficit. The Gulf crisis plus the simultaneous collapse of substantial nonhard currency trade with the Soviet Union led to a debt crisis in 1991. Shekhar's leftist government reluctantly accepted a loan from the feared and often despised IMF, and traditionally fiscally prudent India's international credit rating was downgraded. Foreign governments quickly suggested regulatory changes that might be needed to attract new money.

Shekhar's government collapsed in early 1991. Separatists in the southern state of Tamil Nadu assassinated Rajiv Gandhi, who had been favored to win the next election. This event brought the Congress Party a sympathy victory, and Narasimha Rao (assumed office March 1991), a comparatively unknown party elder, assumed the office of prime minister. Rao encountered moderate intrinsic economic motives to privatize; little in the performance or operating conditions of public firms had altered in just over a year. Pragmatic economic incentives, however, had gone from low to moderate, principally because the foreign debt had crossed the symbolic 30 percent of GDP mark during the previous government and was now 36 percent. Other pragmatic economic conditions were unchanged.

Domestic political incentives confronted by Rao remained low, although less so than before. Rao also headed a minority government that depended on the support of either the economically conservative Hindu revivalist Bharatiya Janata Party (BJP) to the right or the Janata Dal/National Front group of Singh to the left. Although he adroitly distanced himself from the divisive religious politics of the BJP, the Congress Party's Rao relied on BJP support to push through fundamental changes in the Indian political economy. The de facto Congress-BJP economic legislative alliance supported domestic market-oriented changes benefiting business and the urban middle classes (such as delicensing production, liberalizing imports, and instituting phased liberalization of tight foreign exchange controls), but the BJP opposed measures of international liberalization. Typical of the intense political opposition privatization provoked was the fate of the November 1991 report issued by the government-appointed Narasimha Commission, which urged significant financial privatization by sector. The left parties immediately organized a one-day strike, closing banks nationwide. Financial reforms were further delayed by a huge stock market and banking scandal in which local affiliates of multinational banks were prominent players, to the delight of the antiprivatization forces. In 1992, at Rao's request, the Confederation of Indian Industry—a major national business association—drew up a novel plan to allow members of the elite civil service to be seconded to private-sector managerial positions, thus protecting their jobs in the event of public-sector downsizing. Senior bureaucrats opposed the plan, and nothing came of it.

Finally, international political incentives to privatize remained moderate. The collapse of the Soviet Union meant the disappearance of a major trading partner and strategic ally against both China and Pakistan. Although the United States tilted less toward Pakistan, President Bill Clinton insisted that India sign the Nuclear Non-Proliferation Treaty, which India considered discriminatory. Once the Rao government had made the politically costly decision to pursue domestic economic liberalization, including privatization by sector, greater international economic integration was a logical next step. Pragmatism suggested a softer line toward foreign investment.

Analysis

Small sample size and inevitable subjectivity of the indicators make my analysis provisional. Even so, several intriguing trends emerge. First, as Table 7.4 makes clear, later administrations privatized more than earlier ones, regardless of the country examined. This finding should probably be taken as evidence of the importance of the global context in which each country's policymakers operated. In three of the four countries, direct international pressures to privatize increased; even in the fourth, Brazil, Collor administration policymakers surely felt some status needs to conform to the latest practices in development circles, which obviously included privatization (see especially Biersteker, 1992).

Second, the intrinsic economic, or efficiency-related, incentives to privatize were not stronger in the later administrations but were roughly constant in all four countries throughout the decade. Furthermore, low, moderate, and high intrinsic reasons to reduce the state productive sector all occurred in conjunction with the moderate to vigorous privatization of the later administrations. Moreover, Table 7.5 reports a small negative correlation between intrinsic reasons to sell public-sector firms and actual privatization outcomes. If my coding is correct, strong intrinsic economic motives to privatize appear neither sufficient nor, surprisingly, even necessary for active movement by policymakers to reduce the state's economic role. That is, convincing politicians that their state enterprises are poor performers is by no means equivalent to convincing them that public-sector firms ought to be sold or previously state monopoly sectors opened to private competitors.

Third, the pragmatic economic, largely government budget–related, incentives to privatize increased for one country but stayed constant—and high—for the other three. If a larger sample confirmed that trend, it would support the following intuitively plausible statement: pragmatic economic motives to privatize are necessary—although insufficient—for moderate to vigorous privatization. If a national leader is to brave the inescapable criticism likely to fall on him or her for allowing foreign investors, for example, to make off with the "national heritage" (whether in oil or the rights to open fast-food restaurants), then the leader needs to expect some concrete benefits. The potential to solve—or, more likely, ameliorate—such pressing problems as huge budget deficits, large foreign or domestic public debts, or

Table 7.5   Correlations of Incentives with Privatization Outcomes

Incentives to Privatize	Correlation with Actual Privatization[a]
Intrinsic economic	−0.25
Pragmatic economic	0.47
Domestic political	0.73
International political	0.57
Combined economic	0.19
Combined political	0.80

Note: a. Correlations were calculated by coding incentives as either 1, 2, or 3, corresponding to low, moderate, and high. Privatization outcomes were coded as 1, 2, 3, or 4, corresponding to little, minor, moderate, or vigorous. Combined economic and combined political incentives were calculated as means of economic and political incentives, respectively.

near hyperinflation is a potentially powerful inducement to a senior politician and his or her economic team to bite the bullet. More cynically, a looming macroeconomic crisis goads politicians to want to be seen by the general public as doing something, relevant or not. The correlation between pragmatic economic incentives and privatization outcomes is positive but unimpressive.

Fourth, the domestic and international political incentives to privatize jumped in three of the four countries. Furthermore, each of the two (of nine) administrations that engaged in vigorous privatization had strong overall political incentives, coded "moderate" on one political dimension and "high" on the other, to do so. Thus, in Argentina, Menem privatized vigorously because he needed to court the business community quickly, and he also recognized that in the short to medium run the unions and the nonrevolutionary Left would have few viable options to achieve national influence if they abandoned him. In Mexico, Salinas sought to bolster his position, first, within the PRI by weakening the patronage resources available to the traditional machine politics, the party "dinosaurs," and, second, by demonstrating to the U.S. Congress that Mexico was willing to pursue free trade fairly vigorously, thus putting pressure on the United States to ratify the North American Free Trade Agreement. Both Menem and Salinas, thus, expected political benefits from selling state firms.

The data per se do not allow me to rank definitively the relative importance of domestic versus international political motives for emerging democracies to privatize, although Table 7.5 reports a stronger correlation of privatization with domestic political incentives (0.73) than with international ones (0.57). I speculate, however, that relatively large countries with fairly extensive domestic markets such as Argentina, Brazil, Mexico, and India enjoy at least some freedom of choice with respect to heeding or disregarding global influences and pressures, at least compared with smaller countries such as, for example, Ecuador, Bolivia, or even Sri Lanka. For Brazil and India in particular, dramatic moves toward privatization or any other radical economic policy changes are unlikely to occur unless the politician responsible believes he or she can reap some concrete domestic political benefits from the policy shift. (In fact, in the three-and-a-half-year period after this study ended, the Brazilian government under Itamar Franco and particularly under Fernando Henrique Cardoso appeared to be finding more domestic political reasons to press forward with privatization, which in the future seems likely to become vigorous.[28])

In sum, the empirical evidence clearly suggests that economic motives alone will probably be insufficient to inspire most democratic politicians to brave the political risks associated with privatization. Since the cases included no countries in which economic reasons to privatize were absent, however, we cannot conclude that political motives alone would be both necessary and sufficient to activate state shrinking. Nonetheless, these cases do allow me to argue that political incentives to privatize are at least necessary. In fact, combining the two political incentives yields the strongest relationship: a correlation of 0.80 with actual privatization (Table 7.5).

In this chapter I have provided empirical evidence in support of a central tenet of the "rational choice" school (Bates, 1988): politicians will respond to demands of their key political constituencies before those same politicians will implement "needed" economic reforms their core constituencies do not care deeply about. The rational choice model suggests that politicians worry more about their electoral popularity than about economic performance per se. Pragmatic and especially intrinsic economic incentives to privatize influence policymakers because economic outcomes eventually (and legitimately) affect citizens' evolutions of their elected leaders. What I have termed *intrinsic economic* incentives to privatize turn only upon the performance of the firm, sector, or organizational task to be spun off, whereas *pragmatic economic* incentives incorporate larger macroeconomic variables that might plausibly be positively influenced by privatization (government deficits and debt, foreign debt, and hyperinflation); it is reasonable to suppose that pragmatic economic incentives are stronger than intrinsic economic incentives largely because the pragmatic consequences of privatization (or the lack of privatization) are salient to a larger number of voters. For example, not everyone will be aware that a state-owned mining company is being run inefficiently, but serious problems with government finances that result in either a slide into hyperinflation or draconian spending cuts across the board will be widely perceived by voters. Understanding the attraction of continued electoral success for senior political leaders enables us to make theoretical sense of the findings of our empirical investigation that political incentives to privatize appear the most compelling and powerful, followed by pragmatic economic incentives, with intrinsic economic incentives coming in last.

I close the analysis with a few comments on an explanatory road not taken. My research design focused on the presence or absence of four types of incentives in the *environments* of the chief executives studied. Missing from the investigation were the *ideas and preferences of political leaders* and their senior economic policy advisers. Although this study has strongly confirmed the power of the rational choice analytical model, it should not be taken as evidence that ideas and cognitions are irrelevant or epiphenomenal. In fact, one aspect of the study suggests that policymakers' ideas were very important; there is every reason to believe that what Goldstein and Keohane (1993) term "causal" ideas also played a significant role in actual decisions to privatize. Throughout the 1980s, internationally visible leaders such as Margaret Thatcher, Ronald Reagan, and Lech Walesa used their bully pulpits to suggest expansion of the private sector as a solution for economic stagnation, corruption, and other ills. The later the date, the more likely it was that those ideas would seem not only familiar but even reasonable to decisionmakers in developing countries.

This study might have followed Hall (1989) and colleagues, who analyzed the unequal transmission of Keynesian ideas to the United States and Western Europe in the decades following World War II. I could have asked, Why did the *idea* of "privatization" as a solution to a variety of economic ills make greater headway in Mexico and Argentina through the early 1990s than it did in Brazil or India? One reason not to investigate ideas is that they are notoriously difficult to uncover reliably. The public statements of politicians are usually unhelpful in evaluating whether changing cognitions influenced policy choices. Menem loudly proclaimed himself a convert to the doctrine of a streamlined, minimalist state in the economic sphere, whereas Rao equally firmly reminded people that he was still a socialist— yet both men privatized to a substantial degree. Another, more profound reason not to include the role of ideas in the research design was that, in this case, they would not likely have changed the research findings. Diverse political incentives to chief executives would still explain the differences among the cases.

The potential usefulness of this chapter, thus, can be summarized as follows. I have examined privatization outcomes and the incentives to chief executives and their senior economic advisers to shrink the state's directly productive role in four large, newly industrializing, developing country democracies—three in Latin America and the fourth well outside the region but whose elected leaders confronted many similar problems. My findings confirm the perhaps obvious but frequently neglected wisdom that political considerations motivate public policy choices as much as, and often more than, purely economic considerations do, even apparently compelling considerations such as public-sector enterprises that objectively are performing at very low levels of efficiency. Reformers, both within developing countries and in the international community, who would promote market-oriented economic liberalization, therefore, would do well to take account of the political environment confronted by actual policymakers, who may be thinking of the next election or other popularity tests they must face. Real-world politicians, after all, do not live by technical feasibility studies alone.

A Note on Democracy and Privatization

In this chapter I have explored politicians' motives to privatize, concluding that political incentives, or the need to woo core domestic constituencies and sometimes foreign governments and international organizations, are usually more important than pragmatic economic incentives. Pragmatic economic incentives, in turn, are normally more compelling to policymakers than are intrinsic economic reasons to shrink the state's direct role in production.

During the period covered by the study, only India was an established democracy. Argentina and Brazil had recently democratized, whereas Mexico remained a soft, semiauthoritarian regime undergoing incremental political liberalization. Does this mean the presence or absence of democracy is irrelevant in politicians' decisions to privatize? Surely not. Political regime type, like privatization, is best understood as a continuum rather than a dichotomous variable with only two values of "democracy" and "authoritarian regime." At any point along the continuum (or continua), national political leaders make policy choices in accordance with their beliefs about the preferences of their core constituencies. The difference between an elected leader and one who has come to power through a coup or other nondemocratic means is *not* that one must consider the desires of his or her supporters and the other need not. Rather, differences lie in the *membership* of the crucial regime support coalition. In the extreme case, a military dictator must retain only the loyalty of the senior officer corps and his or her palace guard, which constitute the relevant constituency. Each of the four countries considered in this chapter was either democratic or democratizing; leaders in each country had a multitude of social groups—including owners of capital and possessors of votes—whose loyalty they had to retain.

The process of democratization, that is, does not alter the structure of incentives political leaders confront in making economic policy decisions. It does, however, dramatically shift the identities of the crucial political actors whose support national politicians need. During the period from the mid-1980s through 1992, none of these four countries experienced a dramatic political regime shift—although Argentina did in 1983 and Brazil did in 1985. A discussion of incentives to privatize in, say, Poland, however, would have highlighted the difference in the relevant domestic constituencies before and after the end of Communist rule. The particular problems new or fragile democracies have with liberalizing economic reforms have to do with the broader constituencies they must please, compared with many authoritarian regimes, and the propensity of newly politically incorporated groups to expect some material benefits as a consequence of their newfound political weight (Armijo, Biersteker, and Lowenthal, 1994). My finding that politicians assess not only the economic but also the political rationality of alternative public policy choices should thus apply to democrats and authoritarians alike. When making economic decisions, rulers must consider the logic not only of the market but also of the polity.

Notes

1. My thanks to those who made useful comments on various versions of this chapter, including, in alphabetical order, Barry Ames, Gregor Binkert, Alberto Bisso, Charles Blakely, Christopher Bosso, Luiz Carlos Bresser Pereira, Ardeshir Contractor, Eileen Crumm, Kenneth P. Jameson, Luigi Manzetti, Robert McCombs, Eileen McDonagh, Kaizad Mistry, Philip Oxhorn, David Pion-Berlin, Ravi Ramamurti, Carlos Ribeiro, José Serra, and Pamela Starr. Remaining mistakes are mine.

2. Except as noted, economic statistics throughout are from statistical publications of the World Bank, including *World Development Report* (various years); *World Tables* (various years); and *Trends in Developing Economies 1993 Extracts,* Vol. 2 (1993). Figures on state enterprise deficits are from Pinheiro and Schneider (1993: 13), those on public investment as a share of GNP are from Pfeffermann and Madarassay (1992: 4–18), and those on the productivity of investment are from Frieden (1991: 80).

3. Figures on the public share of gross fixed capital formation for Argentina, Mexico, and India are from Short (1984). Short's percentage for Brazil is 22.8 percent from the country's national accounts, which perversely include state-owned enterprise (SOE) investment with private-sector investment. The estimate for Brazil cited here, therefore, comes from Trebat (1983: 122) and includes investment by federal government direct administration plus large SOEs owned by the central government.

4. A logically possible variant of this reasoning is that privatization enhances efficiency through less politics. The argument asserts that privatization will improve economic efficiency by reducing the politically determined pressures and temptations faced by state enterprise management. Politicians who oversee state production may otherwise be tempted to pressure public-sector managers to misappropriate public-sector resources—including government jobs, contracts, and goods and services—to reward the politicians' friends and punish their enemies. At the same time, public-sector managers try to extract rents, or bribes, from those in the general public who wish to do business with state firms. These pressures and temptations

are assumed to be diminished or absent in privately owned businesses. Incumbent policymakers, however, should be relatively unlikely to seek efficiency by intentionally reducing their own opportunities to use the state for patronage. This reason should be relatively unimportant, therefore, in policymakers' motives to privatize and thus is not a part of the research design.

5. Selling off state assets is not a long-run solution to the structural problems of public finances, but it can provide a crucial short-term infusion of funds. For a skeptical view of the efficacy of privatization as a solution to the public sector's resource problems, even in the short to medium run, see Pinheiro and Schneider (1993).

6. A budget balance of even –5.0 percent of GNP is worrisome. For comparison, the U.S. balance was –2.4 percent in 1980 and –4.8 percent in 1991. The need to discriminate among these cases, most of which had fiscal worries, suggested a higher cutoff level.

7. The World Bank considers a debt to GDP ratio of 30 percent or more to represent "moderate" indebtedness, whereas 50 percent or greater is "severe" indebtedness.

8. The coding of quantitative indicators is inevitably somewhat arbitrary. Cutoff levels were chosen with two aims: to accord with my qualitative sense of the relative severity of macroeconomic problems in the different administrations and to discriminate among the cases.

9. On aid conditionality, see Stallings (1992); Kahler (1992).

10. It is hard to imagine a scenario in which an international actor would pressure a developing country government to *avoid* privatization because of an interesting anomaly in the incentive structure surrounding advanced country attitudes toward privatization abroad. Potential benefits (profits to investors, savings to the government budget, and better service for customers) are shared by both developing country citizens and foreigners, but potential costs (lost jobs for SOE employees, loss of economic policy autonomy for the central government, and disrupted and sometimes reduced service to customers) fall almost exclusively on nationals of the privatizing country.

11. See also Biersteker (1992); Ghosh (1991); and Schneider (1990) for useful attempts at cross-nationally comparative definitions.

12. The Argentina cases here and throughout the chapter draw on Armijo (1994); Erro (1993); Huser (1994); Lewis (1990); Manzetti (1993); Norden (1990); Petrecolla, Proto, and Gerchunoff (1993); Pion-Berlin (1992); *Latin American Weekly Report (LAWR)*; *Latin American Regional Reports: Southern Cone*; and the *Financial Times*.

13. The Argentine government privatized the YPF itself in mid-1993 for $3 billion, thus carrying its privatization further in sectoral terms than Mexico's.

14. The Mexican cases here and throughout draw on Bazdresch and Elizondo (1993); Frieden (1991); Langston (1990); Schneider (1990); *LAWR*; and *LARR: Mexico and Central America*.

15. On Brazilian SOEs and privatization, see Abreu and Werneck (1993); Baer and Villela (1992); Pinheiro and Oliveira Filho (1991); Ramamurti (1992); Ribeiro (1992); Schneider (1990); Trebat (1983); *LAWR*; and the *Financial Times*.

16. On Indian SOEs and privatization, see Chitale (1992); Echeverri-Gent (1990); Encarnation (1989); Kohli (1990); the *Financial Times*; *India Today*; and *Economic and Political Weekly*.

17. Another important restriction in Indian law was the lack of free "exit" from most types of production. To protect employment, plants and businesses, once

operating, could not be closed, downsized, or even relocated without explicit government permission, which was difficult to obtain.

18. Because both Singh and Shekhar had short tenures and represented largely the same interests to the left of the Congress Party, I treat their administrations as a single period.

19. A related liberalizing move in early 1992 ended the "freight equalization scheme" by which government-owned railways charged firms identical rates to move specified raw materials (such as iron ore) and intermediate industrial inputs (such as steel) over both long and short distances for the purpose of spreading industrialization more widely around the country. This change instantly rendered several public-sector steel mills, located far from suppliers and markets, nonviable.

20. Menem also found a good mixture of carrots and sticks to use with the military. On the one hand, he pardoned the top brass that had been imprisoned under Alfonsín for their roles in the Malvinas-Falklands fiasco in the early 1980s (and, implicitly, for ordering the "dirty war" in which at least 10,000 suspected leftist sympathizers "disappeared" between 1976 and 1982). On the other, he reacted strongly against a military rebellion in December 1990 rather than attempting to negotiate as Alfonsín had done in similar situations. Further, persistent rumors suggest that officers in charge of the major SOEs managed by the military may have accepted large payoffs from the government to accept privatization of those firms. See Manzetti and Blake, 1996.

21. Although the Peronist Party has long had "right-wing" elements, this designation refers primarily to social conservatives (including even some neofascists) rather than to devotees of free trade and small government.

22. Trebat (1983: 115–152) concluded that state firms made investment decisions mainly on market (rather than purely political) considerations, that the productivity of SOE investment in terms of value-added was high, and that SOE production was complementary to, rather than in competition with, private investment.

23. Lamounier and Bacha (1993: table 12). The public was also becoming frustrated with deteriorating levels of service caused by lack of investment. See Pinheiro and Schneider (1993: 22).

24. Reasonable observers can differ. Pinheiro and Schneider (1993: 21) wrote: "Privatization was a major issue in the 1989 election, and President Collor made it one of his top priorities." This strikes me as an exaggeration.

25. By the end of the third year of the Collor presidency, the opposite was true: the cumulative effect of seven failed shock-style economic reforms in as many years had left the population cynical and uncooperative.

26. See Ahluwalia (1991). For an opposing view, see Adams (1990). Because of the rather poor record for the 1970s and despite the early 1980s upturn, I evaluate the overall macroeconomic scenario Gandhi inherited as one that provided an incentive to privatize.

27. India's distributionist economic policies, although arguably macroeconomically suboptimal, may have been essential to maintaining democracy, an extraordinary achievement in such a poor country. See Armijo (1997).

28. In May 1996, the Cardoso administration pushed forward with its largest ever privatization, that of the Rio de Janeiro–based electricity generation and distribution firm, the Light, which was sold for $2.1 billion to a consortium whose controlling interest was held by a French public-sector utility company. See Armijo and Jha (1997).

8

Capital Flows, Fixed Exchange Rates, and Political Survival: Mexico and Argentina, 1994–1995

Pamela K. Starr

In late December 1994, with its foreign reserves rapidly running out, the Mexican government abandoned the fixed-rule exchange rate regime that had formed the cornerstone of what had been a strikingly successful battle against inflation (annual price increases fell from 159 percent in 1987 to only 7 percent in 1994). The need to abandon this exchange rate policy was driven by the Mexican government's failure to adjust its domestic monetary policy to changing conditions in international financial markets. But how could an economic team whose management skills had been repeatedly praised by both investors and financial analysts suddenly make such a grave mistake?

The Mexican Central Bank has argued that the country could do little to protect itself from such a sudden, negative shift in international financial markets. Rising world interest rates and a sudden collapse of international confidence in the peso generated by political instability in Mexico combined to produce a speculative run on the currency in late 1994 (Gil-Diaz and Carstens, 1996; Banco de México, 1995). This explanation is less than satisfactory. If international conditions were the key explanatory factor, then other countries with similar exchange rate regimes should have been equally unable to adjust to shifts in international markets. In Argentina, however, that did not occur. Faced with rising international interest rates and a drop in confidence in the peso created by a political stalemate that threatened to produce a fiscal crisis, the Argentine government, after an initial delay, moved quickly and decisively to readjust its domestic economic policies to protect the peso's fixed rate of exchange. What explains these different reactions? How could Argentina's democratic government, with presidential elections only months away, pay the political costs produced by the sharp tightening of monetary policy needed to protect a fixed exchange rate from sudden capital outflows when a more authoritarian regime in Mexico was unable to weather the political costs of recession on the eve of presidential elections?

In this chapter I argue that the explanation for these distinct policy responses is found in the structure of the electoral coalitions backing each government and the relative stability of the electoral environment in each country. In Argentina, the government of Carlos Menem relied on the support of an electoral coalition whose essential core was composed of voters with a shared fear of inflation and that operated in a relatively certain electoral environment. This combination of factors substantially reduced the political costs of adjustment on the eve of presidential elections. The Mexican government, by contrast, depended on the support of an electoral coalition whose economic concerns extended beyond fighting inflation. Although those voters strongly favored efforts to sustain economic stability, they were equally, if not more immediately, concerned about economic growth. This combination of preferences produced a coalition whose cohesion was vulnerable in hard times. The Mexican election also took place in an atmosphere of uncertainty. Sharp divisions within the ruling party, recent electoral reforms, and a weak candidate reduced the government's confidence in its capacity to emerge victorious and thus its willingness to take chances as the polling date approached. The political costs of adjustment in the midst of a presidential election campaign were higher, and hence established more significant obstacles to adjustment, in Mexico than in Argentina.

To illuminate this argument, I first identify the nature of the international financial system in which Argentina and Mexico operated during the early 1990s and the exchange rate strategies the two countries employed to maximize their economic opportunities in this global setting. I then look at how each country implemented its exchange rate strategy—a fixed exchange rate in Argentina and a fixed-rule exchange rate regime in Mexico. I next consider the role of economic forces in the events under analysis, demonstrating that economic forces were undoubtedly partially responsible for the deviant policy actions taken by the two countries in response to external pressures on their exchange rates. Mexico clearly faced a greater economic imbalance and thus a more costly adjustment than did Argentina. A purely economic approach to the policy puzzle at hand, however, fails to explain fully the depth of Mexican reticence or the suddenness of the Argentine decision to adjust. I then shift attention to the political forces responsible for these essential details of the adjustment story, identifying differences in the structure and functioning of the electoral coalitions of Menem in Argentina and of the Institutional Revolutionary Party (PRI) in Mexico and distinctions in the political environment surrounding elections in each country, and illuminating how those differences shaped economic policy decisions. In the final section I consider the lessons of the Mexican and Argentine cases regarding the capacity of countries with democratic regimes and liberalizing political systems to maintain a fixed or a fixed-rule exchange rate regime in a world economy increasingly dominated by a high degree of mobility in capital flows.

Exchange Rate Policy and the International Financial System

Changes in the structure of international finance since the mid-1980s have altered the ability of Latin American countries to access capital on international markets. During that period, capital flows have become more mobile, and competition for international funds has increased. As a consequence, Latin American countries that hoped to tap global capital markets to help finance development have had to adopt policies capable of augmenting the profitability of investments within their borders.

During the first two decades following World War II, international capital flows were tightly controlled to mitigate against the sort of financial instability that contributed to financial collapse during the early 1930s. Beginning in the 1970s and gaining speed during the 1980s, however, a process of financial deregulation swept through the international market. As governments gave up their powers to restrict capital flows, the character and operation of international financial markets changed dramatically. Deregulation produced a more liberal, market-dominated environment in which capital flows increasingly followed the dictates of the market rather than the preferences of politicians. In a deregulated environment, the composition of capital flowing across borders also changed; direct and portfolio investments quickly overtook commercial bank lending and loans from international financial institutions as the dominant source of capital on international markets. Capital movements thus ceased to be dominated by the perceptions of a very few lenders and instead responded increasingly to the profitability concerns of a multitude of individual investors (from multinational firms to the managers of large investment funds to small investors). These changes in the behavior of international financial markets established a new set of constraints on Latin America's capacity to access international capital. As the suppliers of capital multiplied and the tools at governments' disposal to manage capital flows declined, access to global capital came increasingly to rely on market perceptions of the security and profitability of investments in a region that had given birth to the debt crisis of the 1980s.

The 1980s also witnessed an increase in global demand for international capital.[1] Although most Latin American countries were absent from international capital markets in the wake of the debt crisis, expanding budget deficits in industrial countries created a new demand for such capital. When Latin America initiated its return to international capital markets in the late 1980s, therefore, it faced much greater competition for available funds than it had in the past (Griffith-Jones and Stallings, 1995). With this expanded competition for capital and the growing influence of market forces over the international distribution of capital, Latin American countries faced a new challenge as they reentered international capital markets in the late 1980s and early 1990s. More than ever, they were forced to find a mechanism that would make them stand out as a viable investment opportunity in a highly competitive market.

Faced with this policy challenge, Mexico and Argentina implemented similar economic strategies. As part of a broad market-based reform, each country began to liberalize its financial markets and determined to fix its exchange rate; in December 1987, Mexico initiated a policy reform that culminated in the adoption of a fixed-rule exchange rate regime, and in April 1991 Argentina adopted a fully fixed exchange rate. The objective of these policy shifts, in conjunction with trade liberalization and privatization, was to persuade international investors of the sincerity of each country's commitment to a stable macroeconomic environment (something that had been lacking in the recent past). With a fixed or a fixed-rule exchange rate, an expansionary monetary policy could produce a drain on a country's international reserves. To avoid insolvency under such an exchange rate regime, a country must thus pursue a stable monetary policy; it must contain inflationary pressures and the associated threat of broader economic instability. A commitment to a fixed or a fixed-rule exchange rate, if successfully implemented, would thereby imbue reform with a measure of credibility that would reduce the anticipated risk of investing in the Mexican and Argentine markets and thereby help those countries attract international capital in the highly competitive environment of the 1990s.

This strategy for providing a credible commitment to macroeconomic stability, however, does not come free of costs. First, a fixed exchange rate adopted to produce credibility in international markets, not surprisingly, tends to become the linchpin of investor confidence. It thus becomes extremely difficult for the government to modify the exchange rate without undermining its credibility. Rather than mitigating market pressures on a country's international reserves, a devaluation in these circumstances is just as likely to stimulate further outflows of capital. For Mexico and Argentina, therefore, devaluation was not considered an adjustment option.

Second, a fixed exchange rate regime sharply limits a government's ability to attenuate the domestic consequences of international economic disequilibria. If international interest rates were to rise, for example, domestic rates would also need to rise to protect the foreign exchange reserves essential to preserving the country's capacity to protect the value of its currency. The ability of the government to use fiscal policy to mitigate the recessionary consequences of rising interest rates is also tightly constrained. As recession kicks in, tax revenues will fall. To keep the broad fiscal deficit (the financial deficit) at a level that can be financed without an increase in the money supply, the government must often reduce its spending. In other words, both monetary policy and fiscal policy under a fixed or a fixed-rule exchange rate system tend to be procyclical rather than countercyclical; they tend to reinforce rather than mitigate the recessionary pressures imported from abroad.

An exchange rate policy that undermines government capacity to prevent living standards from declining in an election season, however, entails serious political risks. The fact that the government of Carlos Menem in Argentina seemed better able than the Mexican government during 1994 and early 1995 to withstand the political costs associated with declining living standards thus provides an opportunity to investigate the political conditions under which this exchange rate strategy can be sustained.

Benefits and Costs of Fixed Exchange Rates in the Presence of Highly Mobile Capital: The Experiences of Mexico and Argentina

During the late 1980s and early 1990s, economic reform built on fixed or fixed-rule exchange rate systems produced visible benefits for both Mexico and Argentina. The emergence of macroeconomic stability protected by a commitment to the monetary and fiscal policies required to protect a fixed exchange rate reduced the risk of investing in the two economies just as interest rates in industrial country markets began an extended decline in early 1991. As international investors searched for higher rates of return on their investments, economic reform transformed Mexico and Argentina into promising investment targets. This sequence of events produced a massive flow of capital into both the Mexican and Argentine markets. Between 1991 and 1993, nearly $25 billion entered the Argentine market, and over $82 billion surged into Mexico.

Each country used a portion of this foreign capital to help modernize economies that had enjoyed little investment for more than a decade. Imports of both capital goods and intermediate goods (production inputs) boomed. Argentina and Mexico also used a portion of their foreign capital windfall to finance imports of consumer goods. Each hoped the expanded availability of imported consumer products would help to control price inflation by increasing competition in the domestic economy and thereby encouraging domestic producers to become more efficient. In economies that had just emerged from a prolonged economic crisis, however, pent-up demand for imported goods combined with easy access to international capital to drive the current account deep into deficit. Argentina's current account registered a surplus of $4.6 billion in 1990 but deficits of $5.4 billion in 1992 and $7.1 billion in 1993—over 3 percent of gross domestic product (GDP). In Mexico, the current account deficit totaled $14.9 billion in 1991 and $23.4 billion by 1993—6.4 percent of Mexico's total national production (IMF, 1996).

Growth and investment in the Mexican and Argentine economies thus became heavily dependent on inflows of international capital. If those inflows were to subside because of changes in international economic conditions or, worse, if they were to cease suddenly because of an abrupt reversal in market perceptions of the profitability of investments in the Mexican or Argentine economy, the consequent adjustment—particularly in light of the policy constraints imposed by the fixed or fixed-rule exchange rate regime used in each country—would be economically painful and politically costly. Beginning in 1994, such unfavorable changes in the structure and perceptions of international financial markets began to emerge. Starting with an initial uptick in February 1994, U.S. interest rates began an upward trend that persisted into early 1995. The rising profitability of investments in the United States created an incentive for investors to move away from higher-risk markets in developing countries. The sudden success of Brazil's Real Plan beginning in July 1994 also threatened to divert investment funds away from Mexico and Argentina. The reemergence of price stability in the Brazilian economy followed by the election of the plan's author, Fernando Henrique Cardoso, to the presidency renewed investor enthusiasm for Brazil.

For Mexico and Argentina, two economies heavily dependent on large capital inflows, these developments signaled the need to adopt a set of painful policy adjustments to ensure a continued inflow of capital in this new international context. To preserve its competitive position as a desirable site for portfolio investment and thereby to protect its foreign reserves and fixed exchange rate, each country would have to raise domestic interest rates. The resulting drop in economic activity in advance of presidential elections, however, carried potentially significant political costs in both countries.

In Mexico, rising international interest rates corresponded with internal developments that rattled market perceptions of the country's political and economic stability. In late March 1994, Luis Donaldo Colosio, the presidential candidate of Mexico's ruling party, was assassinated. The first assassination of a prominent politician in over fifty years, coming only three months after a guerrilla uprising in the southern state of Chiapas, deeply shook investor confidence. Over $11 billion flowed out of Mexico in the weeks following the assassination. This massive outflow of capital ceased in early May but only after the Mexican government agreed to absorb much of the perceived risk associated with investing in a potentially unstable political environment by converting peso-denominated government bonds (CETES) into dollar-denominated securities (*tesobonos*). In other words, although the government allowed the peso to depreciate 11 percent (the maximum allowed under Mexico's fixed-rule regime) and permitted interest rates on Mexican government securities to rise nearly 7 percent, it was insufficient to entice investors back into the market in the aftermath of the Colosio assassination. Rather than allow interest rates to rise further to attract capital back into Mexico, the government moved to protect the domestic economy from the deep recession such a strategy would produce: it decided instead to attract investors by absorbing much of the exchange rate risk produced by the assassination and thereby contain interest rate increases.

This strategy to stabilize an economy buffeted by an unexpected political shock could have been effective if investor confidence had revived rapidly (as occurred in late 1993 following the U.S. Senate's approval of the treaty establishing the North American Free Trade Agreement). The growing attractiveness of investment opportunities outside of Mexico and the threat of continued instability within Mexico—evidenced by a wave of high-profile kidnappings, visible discord within the ruling party, and the unresolved uprising in Chiapas—however, ensured that the bullishness on Mexico evidenced by investors during 1993 would not soon return. Rather than abandon a short-term strategy designed to deal with a temporary crisis of confidence, however, the Mexican government continued to exchange peso-denominated CETES for the dollar-denominated *tesobonos* (as a percentage of total outstanding government securities, *tesobonos* increased from 13 percent in March to 63 percent in July 1994 [Hale, 1995: 48]). With presidential elections scheduled for late August, the Mexican government consciously avoided any further adjustments to changing international market conditions to avoid the recession adjustment would inevitably entail.

As election day approached, the Mexican government reinforced its efforts to avoid a recession by increasing the supply of credit in the economy and thereby bringing interest rates down. Although the government sustained a fairly restrictive fiscal policy throughout 1994, monetary policy was another matter. The Bank of Mexico oversaw a marked expansion in domestic credit during the six months preceding the late August elections (IMF, 1995; Sachs, Tornell, and Velasco, 1995; Heath, 1995). That expansion is visible in the growth of Central Bank credit provided to both the government and the private sector and in the resulting increase in the monetary base (an average increase of 22 percent for the March–August 1994 period; Banco de México [1995 and 1996]). Expansion also came despite the sharp drop in foreign reserves Mexico suffered during the spring. The Bank of Mexico thus followed an explicit policy of sterilizing capital out-flows—increasing domestic credit to compensate for outflows of international capital—to sustain domestic economic activity.

This policy of emitting *tesobonos* and increasing domestic credit despite declining foreign reserves was the opposite of what would have been required to protect Mexico's fixed-rule exchange rate regime. Rather than tightening monetary policy to protect the foreign reserves needed to back the peso, Mexico risked a further loss of reserves by expanding domestic credit and increasing its short-term international liabilities. These actions were not merely the policy mistakes of bad economists—the managers of Mexican monetary policy knew exactly what they were doing. Their previous writings clearly identify a restrictive monetary policy as the appropriate response to declining foreign exchange reserves under a fixed or a fixed-rule exchange rate regime (Gil-Diaz and Carstens, 1996; Banco de México, 1994). Further, Mexican monetary policy from late 1992 until late 1993 had followed those prescriptions to protect the peso from a rapid-ly rising current account deficit. The policy decisions taken in 1994 thus very consciously put at risk an essential component of Mexico's successful economic reform effort—its fixed-rule exchange rate regime.

At first blush, the reason for this course of events seems disarmingly simple: the Mexican government was unwilling to risk the potential political consequences of a recession in the weeks preceding a presidential election. The government thus relaxed monetary policy to ensure an electoral victory with the intention of carrying out the needed economic adjustment after the election. This explanation based on electoral cycles has at least two shortcomings. First, if the election had been the only reason for the loosening of monetary policy, there should have been a policy correction soon after the election; such a postelection tightening never came, however. A second shortcoming of the electoral cycle explanation is found in a paral-lel set of developments in Argentina. Facing a very similar set of con-straints—reduced access to the international capital needed to finance a bulging current account deficit in months preceding presidential elec-tions—Argentina adopted a different policy response. After the sort of delay one would expect during an election cycle, Argentina suddenly and sharply tightened both its monetary and fiscal policy to protect the value of the peso despite the consequences for economic growth.

Like their Mexican counterparts, Argentine officials initially attempted to mitigate the domestic economic consequences of rising world interest rates throughout most of 1994. Although world rates pushed up Argentine domestic interest rates notably during 1994,[2] the economic authorities clearly attempted to mitigate the domestic economic consequences of the changes in international capital markets. The Argentine government did not place bonds on world markets throughout the March–June period to avoid the repercussions of the rising rates of interest required to complete those sales. The government also abandoned its initial auction of 90-day treasury bills in August, after only a small proportion of the planned issue had been sold, rather than accept the higher than anticipated interest rate demanded by the market.[3] As a consequence, capital inflows declined by 36 percent during 1994, despite the need to finance a current account deficit that was growing at a torrid pace (during the first half of 1994 the deficit increased 127 percent over the first semester of 1993).

The Argentine government also did little to reverse the rapid slide of its budget balance from surplus to deficit during 1994. Within days of issuing a series of statements in mid-April insisting on the need for austerity given the unfavorable international climate, the expanding current account deficit, and an anticipated drop in government revenues (emanating from a recent tax reform), the government reversed its position. Rather than cut spending, the government allowed a primary budget surplus of $1.7 billion registered during the second quarter of 1994 to virtually evaporate by the end of the third quarter and to fall into deficit during the last three months of the year. This deficit, at a time when the status of international capital markets made financing difficult, translated into higher interest rates on Argentine government bonds in late 1994 and the unavoidable necessity of entering the market to place those bonds. In response to these developments, the Argentine government again announced a series of austerity measures in early September and again backed away from their implementation. Economy Minister Domingo Cavallo instead announced that Argentina would forgo the final two tranches of its loan from the International Monetary Fund (IMF) to achieve "greater freedom in economic decisions" (*Latin American Weekly Report,* October 20, 1994: 4–5). In short, the government aimed to free itself from the fiscal constraints contained in its agreement with the IMF at a time when it preferred to avoid spending cuts.

On November 17, however, the Argentine government suddenly and dramatically changed its policy course. Following a larger than anticipated jump in U.S. interest rates, the government acted decisively to close a $1.3 billion budget gap—it issued a decree that terminated all discretionary spending in the federal government and parastate industries for the last six weeks of 1994 (Economic Report, 1996; *El Cronista Comercial* [Mexico City], 1994). The resulting shortage of pesos in the economy produced a rapid rise in domestic interest rates. Although the Central Bank mitigated the increase by injecting pesos into the economy, interest rates rose 2.75 percent within two weeks—nearly as much as the total increase during the preceding nine months.[4]

A month later, the Argentine economy was pummeled by the "tequila effect"—the shock wave that rattled international financial markets in the aftermath of the late December devaluation of the Mexican peso. Fearing other debtors would be unable to meet their obligations, investors lost confidence in emerging markets, especially those in Latin America. Argentina's current account deficit and budgetary difficulties on the eve of the May 1995 presidential elections further unsettled investors. This dramatic drop in investor confidence in the safety of the Argentine market translated into an outflow of $4 billion in just the first three months of 1995—which represented four times the outflow for the first eleven months of 1994 and 25 percent of Argentina's foreign reserve holdings.

The response of the Menem government to these events dramatically deepened the austerity program begun so dramatically in late 1994. Interest rates shot up further (between mid-December 1994 and February 1995, call money rates nearly doubled to 19 percent), and government spending was slashed another $1 billion, which included large wage cuts for federal workers. These steps had dramatic consequences for the Argentine economy. Economic growth plummeted from +6.2 percent in the last quarter of 1994 to –4.6 percent and –3.7 percent in the second and third quarters of 1995, respectively. Unemployment rose from 10.8 percent in May 1994 to nearly 19 percent one year later, and the banking system teetered on the verge of collapse (Economic Report, 1996: 19). At the same time, however, these drastic measures helped to slash Argentina's current account deficit (the trade account moved from a $4.8 billion deficit in 1994 to a $1 billion surplus in 1995) and prevented a resurgence of inflation in the economy. In short, beginning in late November 1994, the Menem government did what was necessary to protect the value of the peso despite the sharply negative consequences for the living standards of Argentine voters.

Alternate Explanations
of Monetary Policy Decisions

Why would Menem's democratic government be willing to risk a deep recession on the eve of presidential elections to protect the fixed exchange rate of the Argentine peso, whereas a more authoritarian regime in Mexico perceived this course of events as too costly politically? These events appear to run counter to the conventional wisdom about the relative capacity of governments to implement stabilization and adjustment programs. Although dissenting voices are increasingly evident in the literature

(Remmer, 1991; Nelson, 1994b, 1994c), analysts have long argued that the insulation from popular pressures authoritarian political structures provide better enables those regimes to implement economically painful and politically unpopular policy measures. In the cases of Argentina and Mexico, however, it was the Mexican government that operated in the more authoritarian political setting. The government enjoyed the support of a political party with a machinelike capacity to deliver votes in good times and bad (from its founding in 1929 through 1982, the party never delivered less that 70 percent of the national vote to its candidate for the presidency[5]). Although the power of that machine was clearly in decline by 1994, its capacities still far exceeded those of its Argentine counterpart. Why was the government with the seemingly greater institutional capacity to withstand voter discontent the one that was incapable of implementing needed adjustment measures?

One possible explanation for this analytic puzzle is the Mexican crisis itself. Many in the popular press have argued that Mexico could have adjusted its economy as effectively as Argentina did if it had faced a crisis of similar magnitude to the tequila effect. From this perspective, the crisis convinced the Argentine people that the only option was a radical economic adjustment. The massive outflow of capital in the first weeks of 1995 renewed fears of hyperinflation and thus erased the popular opposition to the recession produced by the government's adjustment program. It follows that without the crisis President Menem would have been unable to oversee the needed adjustment in the economy and win reelection. Although there is undoubtedly some measure of truth to this argument—the crisis clearly reduced dramatically the political costs of recession in Argentina—it cannot explain why the Argentine government initiated its adjustment strategy a month *before* the Mexican devaluation. The Mexican crisis cannot be the source of events that preceded it.

A second, more satisfying explanation argues simply that the imbalance in the Mexican economy was much greater, and thus would have been more costly both economically and politically to correct, than its Argentine equivalent. Abundant evidence supports the role this factor played in these two cases. On the eve of the marked changes in the international financial system that occurred in 1994, the Mexican economy was burdened by stagnant growth, a current account deficit totaling 6.4 percent of GDP, and a banking system weighed down by a portfolio of nonperforming loans that reached 9 percent of total lending. The Argentine economy at the end of 1993, by contrast, enjoyed dynamic growth, a current account deficit of only 3.3 percent of total economic activity, and a healthier financial sector. Adjusting monetary policy to shifts in the international financial system would thus have been much more costly in terms of economic growth for Mexico than for Argentina. The depth of Mexico's economic difficulties prompted both analysts and Mexican policymakers to argue that circumstances suggested a gradualist approach to economic adjustment in Mexico as opposed to the shock adjustment implemented by Argentina beginning in late 1994 (Hale, 1995; Banco de México, 1995).

This explanation raises the question, however, of why no policy response of any sort ever materialized in Mexico. Although the Mexican government did adopt short-term measures in April 1994 to mitigate the outflow of capital following the Colosio assassination, it took no further steps during the next six months to adjust the domestic economy to an increasingly difficult international context (after increasing a quarter of a percentage point in February and March, the U.S. federal funds rate shot up half a percentage point in both May and August and another three-quarters of a point in November). To the contrary, the government consciously sterilized capital outflows, continued to emit *tesobonos,* refused to cut government spending despite evidence that the budget would end the year in deficit, and oversaw a large decline in domestic interest rates from August through October. In short, the Mexican government made no move to implement adjustment policies gradually during the May–October period; instead, it avoided all adjustment throughout the period despite deteriorating conditions in international financial markets and thereby placed the stability of the peso at risk.

Electoral Coalitions and the Fear of the Unknown

The factors responsible for the different approaches to exchange rate management taken by Mexico and Argentina during 1994 and 1995 must be able to explain why the Menem government in Argentina decided that the political consequences of recession were manageable and the Mexican government reached the opposite conclusion. The explanation of the distinct political calculus of these two governments lies in the structure of the electoral coalitions backing each government and the amount of electoral uncertainty each government encountered.

Superficially, the political coalitions backing the two governments seem fairly similar. Each relied on electoral support provided by a political party with machinelike qualities that operated particularly well in rural areas. Each was also constructed from the vestiges of populist coalitions concentrated in urban areas whose characteristics mutated during the neoliberal reform process.[6] This situation enabled each government to take advantage of its historically close relationship with organized labor to minimize opposition to economic reform despite its costs in terms of worker wages and benefits. Each government was then able to exploit its implementation of market-oriented economic reforms with labor quiescence to win the support of a key segment of the private sector. This revamped core of the populist component of the political coalitions backing the Menem government in Argentina and the PRI government in Mexico was essential to the success of each government's effort to stabilize the domestic economy. The core could not, however, ensure government survival in truly contested presidential elections. Neither postpopulist coalition, even in conjunction with the vote-getting power of the party machinery in rural areas, accounted for enough votes to ensure nationwide electoral victories.[7] Each government thus had to construct a broader, less stable electoral coalition in the runup to elections to guarantee its political survival. The character of the two electoral coalitions was significantly different, and it is here where the explanation for the distinct approaches to exchange rate management is found.

Mexico

The structure of the PRI's electoral coalition during 1994 reflected the dual concerns of most Mexican voters. Not unlike voters elsewhere, Mexicans tended to support the candidates who seemed most able to oversee an improvement in living conditions. High inflation throughout the late 1980s had taught Mexican voters the importance of price stability, but the slow growth that accompanied declining price levels during the early 1990s also reminded citizens of the importance of higher incomes to their standard of living. Mexican voters, therefore, were not fixated on inflation as the main threat to their living standards, as was the case in Argentina. Although the Mexican economy had experienced a bout of hyperinflation in the late 1980s, inflation peaked in 1987. The weight of inflation was never sufficiently great to threaten the Mexican economy with collapse, and inflation fell quickly after the initiation of a highly successful stabilization program in December 1987. During the two years preceding the 1994 elections, prices rose an average of only 10 percent a year. The Mexican experience with inflation, therefore, was less traumatic than that in several other Latin American countries, including Argentina, and it was safely in the past. By late 1993, Mexican voters did not see inflation as the single overriding threat to economic welfare. Although price stability continued to be a concern, it also seemed relatively assured. The more immediate threat to Mexican living standards seemed to be the unemployment and low wages produced by slow growth.

Although economic growth had been relatively healthy in the early stages of Mexico's stabilization efforts, it was only 2.8 percent in 1992 and had fallen to below 1 percent in 1993—well below the approximate 3 percent rate needed to provide jobs for new entrants into the labor market. In late 1992, the Mexican government implemented a restrictive monetary policy to help reduce the country's ballooning current account deficit. As domestic interest rates rose, economic activity dropped. This planned recession, however, was deeper than intended by Mexican economists because of a brewing crisis in the banking sector that produced a much larger drop in lending than anticipated. The economy barely registered growth in the second quarter and contracted in the third quarter.[8]

Anemic economic growth helped to alter the policy preferences of Mexican voters. They had been promised an economic miracle at the end of their years of sacrifice in the interest of price stability. With the arrival of a recession instead, many Mexicans felt deceived and cheated as they struggled to make payments on the mountain of debt incurred during the previous two years. Businesspeople in particular were highly critical of a policy that pursued price stability at the cost of economic growth. As the number of bankruptcies rose, so did resentment among those in the private sector over what they perceived as the government's overzealous pursuit of low inflation.[9]

This shift in Mexican preferences away from the battle against inflation and toward a renewed emphasis on economic growth was also strikingly evident in government-sponsored opinion surveys taken in advance of the 1994 presidential election. The surveys showed that the vast majority of voters were worried much more about unemployment and low wages than about renewed inflation.[10] Anemic growth in a society with a rapidly expanding workforce, high indebtedness, and expectations of good times rather than bad and without a healthy fear of renewed inflation led to growing dissatisfaction with economic policies designed to protect the value of the Mexican peso by pursuing low inflation and a reduced current account deficit. The anti-inflationary foundation of the PRI's electoral coalition during 1994, therefore, was relatively weak, much weaker than that in Argentina (as the next section will demonstrate).

The electoral consequences of low rates of growth were particularly problematic for the PRI in urban areas. The foundation of the party's political machine had always been its ability to mobilize support from unionized workers and peasants. The urban poor and Mexico's middle class, however, were always beyond the reach of the machine, which thus operated less effectively in urban areas. Traditionally, the PRI had minimized the threat of electoral opposition from those sectors of Mexican society by providing them with economic opportunities through an expanding economy and by controlling the supply of viable opposition candidates through payoffs and intimidation. Under these circumstances, urban actors tended to acquiesce to the PRI system either by not voting or by voting for candidates known to have no real chance of victory. The 1988 presidential election, however, demonstrated the vulnerability of this strategy of coalition maintenance in economic hard times.

In 1988, six years of crisis in the Mexican economy, compounded by a painful stabilization program initiated just seven months in advance of the presidential elections and the first viable opposition candidate since 1954, produced an electoral disaster for the PRI. It is generally accepted that the ruling party candidate either won the election by a very slim margin or did not, in fact, win it. Not only did the PRI lose solidly among the middle classes (professionals and small business owners) and the urban poor, but the labor sector of the party also failed to deliver votes as effectively as in the past. Only electoral alchemy assured a solid victory.

This experience taught the new administration of Carlos Salinas a powerful lesson—the PRI political machine could no longer guarantee election victories in economic hard times. The administration thus focused its coalition-building efforts on constituencies in which the party machine had failed to mobilize support and specifically targeted voters who had previously abstained from the election process. President Salinas's central tool in this effort was the creation of economic opportunities, especially in urban areas, through an economic program that delivered stability, growth, and expectations of a better future.[11] The administration's striking success on the economic front during its first three years in office enabled it to reconstruct a potent electoral coalition. The effectiveness of that strategy was clearly evident in the 1991 midterm elections. Relying on the power of the party machine in rural areas and a campaign strategy that tirelessly reminded urban voters of how much better off they were than they had been just three years earlier, the PRI realized an impressive electoral recovery.[12]

As the 1994 elections approached, however, the viability of the strategy was threatened by an economic slowdown and reduced voter fears of inflation. Public dissatisfaction with the government and its policies grew as the consequences of the 1993 recession began to touch the lives of Mexican citizens, and the loudest voices raised in protest came from those urban actors the Salinas administration had worked so hard to bring into the PRI coalition—small and medium-sized business owners and the broader urban middle class. Anemic growth was clearly threatening the cohesion of the Salinas coalition, and in combination with the continuing political presence of Cuauhtemoc Cárdenas—the nearly victorious opposition candidate in the 1988 presidential election—it raised the specter of a repetition of 1988's near disaster in 1994.

Beyond the tenuous cohesion of its electoral coalition, the PRI also confronted an uncertain electoral environment in the months preceding the 1994 elections. The profound economic crisis in the 1980s had not only undermined the institutional cohesion of the PRI's electoral coalition but had also weakened the legitimating power of elections long perceived as of dubious fairness. The same sense of economic desperation that drove urban voters to break with the past and vote against the PRI in large numbers in

1988 also undermined their tolerance for rigged elections. As long as the PRI system seemed to be working in the interest of most urban actors, they had no incentive to demand change. As crisis modified those perceptions during the 1980s, however, urban voters began to demand a real voice in determining who would govern them. The intensity of this call for reform increased dramatically in the aftermath of the bitterly contested and highly suspect official outcome of the 1988 elections. In these circumstances, the PRI's traditional practice of manipulating the vote to ensure its victories would have to be revised if the legitimating power of the electoral process were to survive.

The Salinas administration thus agreed to a series of electoral reforms that dramatically reduced the ability of the PRI to manipulate the vote count.[13] The PRI still retained many advantages during the campaign (favored access to the media, large supplies of human and financial resources, and the power of incumbency), but it also faced the uncertainties associated with a new electoral strategy needed to mobilize support from sectors of society beyond the reach of the party machinery. Would the party's advantages in campaigning be sufficient to ensure the cohesion of its restructured coalition on election day? Electoral reform meant the PRI would have to face these uncertainties without its traditional ace in the hole—the tool that had saved the day in 1988. With its power to manipulate events on election day sharply circumscribed, the PRI thus faced an entirely new reality—the possibility that it could lose.

The uncertainty produced by electoral reform and an electoral coalition whose cohesion relied heavily on the government's ability to provide the jobs, good wages, and consumer demand generated by a growing economy sharply circumscribed the government's policy options as elections approached. Any effort to protect the value of the peso by relying on a tight monetary policy and thus persistent recession in the Mexican economy was likely to have serious electoral consequences. It was therefore not surprising that in September 1993 the Salinas government decided to relax its year-old effort to reduce Mexico's large current account deficit. In its annual renewal of the Pacto—the accord among the government, business, and labor that established the means by which economic stability would be maintained—the government promised to increase spending, reduce taxes, and loosen the restraints on wage increases. The strategy contained in the 1993 Pacto implied a modest boost to the economy that the government hoped would be transformed into a large boost following the approval of the North American Free Trade Agreement by the U.S. Congress.[14] The approval of this treaty created an inflow of capital and a drop in domestic interest rates that spurred an economic expansion. President Salinas emphasized the growth objectives of the new Pacto in his speech announcing it to the nation. It was time, he argued, to reap the harvest of the national effort to defeat inflation by reactivating the economy.

The happy electoral outcome this strategy was designed to produce, however, was seriously threatened in the first months of 1994 by political instability, divisions within the ruling party, and weak PRI candidates for the presidency. As political uncertainty increased, investors hesitated to spend money in Mexico, thereby producing higher interest rates, renewed stagnation in the economy, and the risk that the urban component of the PRI coalition would defect before election day.

On January 1, 1994, a rebel uprising in the southern state of Chiapas set in motion a sequence of events that overshadowed the campaign of the ruling party's candidate for the presidency and raised the specter of a split within the ruling party only seven months prior to the August elections. Unable to defeat the rebels quickly by military means, the Salinas administration turned to negotiations. The president chose Manual Camacho to lead the government's negotiations with the rebels. The former mayor of Mexico City and a finalist in the selection of the PRI presidential candidate for 1994, Camacho quickly arranged a cease-fire and an amnesty for the rebels. Those actions calmed investor fears of political instability, preserved an incipient recovery in the Mexican economy, and made Camacho the man of the hour. As he continued his efforts to establish a permanent peace in Chiapas, Camacho used his newfound political prominence to renew his campaign for the presidency. Although he never explicitly expressed a desire to replace the party's presidential candidate, Camacho was perpetually evasive when asked about his intentions despite an apparent request from the president in late January to declare publicly his disinterest in the position (*Acción,* no. 286, January 31, 1994: 12). It was not until March 22 that Camacho finally declared he would not seek the presidency in 1994.

Camacho's machinations overshadowed and undermined the campaign of the party's official candidate, Luis Donaldo Colosio. Beset by internal weaknesses, the Colosio campaign seemed unable to emerge from Camacho's shadow. Colosio experienced a sharp drop in public support and serious doubts about his ability to defeat the leading opposition candidate, Cuauhtemoc Cárdenas, in the August election.[15] The consequence of this political uncertainty for the Mexican economy was stagnation. After expanding at a healthy pace during the first two months of 1994, rising interest rates quickly cut off the economy's budding recovery by March. In this uncertain and tense political environment, magnified further by the government's inability to win a peace treaty in Chiapas, Colosio was assassinated on March 23.

As mentioned previously, in the wake of Chiapas and the power play by Camacho, the first assassination of a high-level politician in Mexico since 1928 sent shivers down the spine of the investment community. In the month following the assassination, $11 billion flowed out of the Bank of Mexico, and interest rates on peso-denominated government bonds rose more than 6 percent. In an economy already teetering on the edge of renewed recession, if the government did nothing to mitigate the consequences of those developments, a deep recession just five months prior to the elections was a near certainty.

The assassination also laid bare a sharp division within the ruling party. Many of the reforms carried out during the Salinas administration had been strongly opposed by a large segment of the PRI. Those politicians, often identified as the old guard or the "dinosaurs," believed the Salinas reforms—the economic and especially the political reforms—threatened the very survival of the political system on which national stability, as well as their personal power and prosperity, depended. Although those party members had bowed to the tradition of party unity and tolerated Salinas's reform effort during his presidency, they were not equally willing to accept the perpetuation of the policies for another six years. Much of the old guard was thus incensed by Salinas's November 28, 1993, decision to appoint Colosio as the PRI's presidential candidate. Rather than appoint a compromise candidate—an individual acceptable to both Salinas and the old guard—Salinas chose a protégé, an individual who owed his entire political career to Salinas's patronage. The old guard interpreted the action as an attempt by Salinas to perpetuate his policies and political influence beyond his term in office. The new presidential candidate's acceptance speech seemed to verify their suspicions. Colosio parroted the policy aims enunciated by Salinas in his final state of the union address less than two months earlier—policy statements that explicitly excluded the preferences of the old guard.[16]

This discord within the party exploded into the public eye in the wake of the Colosio assassination. Elements within the old guard tried to take advantage of the political chaos produced by the killing to force Salinas to choose a candidate more to their liking. The day after the assassination, about twenty party veterans (mostly ex-governors and ex-legislators) sent a letter to Salinas insisting that they had the right to participate in the selection of Colosio's successor; the letter was followed by pronouncements of support for a rival of Salinas's preferred candidate. After nearly a week of uncertainty in which Salinas weighed his options and measured his power within the party, he successfully imposed his preferred candidate, Ernesto Zedillo. This success came at a price, however. To preserve party unity and thereby protect the party's aura of invincibility and ensure the effective functioning of its political machine during the campaign, Salinas apparently agreed to give the old guard substantial influence over the coming campaign. Salinas agree to send one of his most trusted and powerful advisers, Chief of Staff José Cordoba, out of the country for the remainder of the year to reduce his influence over the campaign, and representatives of the old guard quickly occupied key campaign posts.[17] Given the old guard's preference for political survival above all else, as well as its sharp criticism of the economic costs associated with many of the Salinas reforms (particularly low real wages and the problems faced by small and medium-sized businesses), its central role in the campaign presented another obstacle to any government attempt to protect the peso through recessionary policies.

The political capacity of the Mexican government to raise interest rates sufficiently to protect its foreign reserves during spring and summer 1994 was further constrained by the weakness of the PRI's presidential candidate. Zedillo was a noncharismatic technocrat and a poor public speaker who was ill at ease on the campaign trail. Those characteristics produced a dramatic drop in the polls for the PRI candidate during the first weeks of the campaign and a strikingly poor performance in a national debate with his two closest challengers in mid-May.[18] By late spring, only three months before election day, his capacity to garner even a plurality of votes was unclear at best. Although Zedillo's polling numbers improved substantially in June and July, his ability to win by a large enough margin to ensure the legitimacy of the elections by overpowering public suspicions of the government's promise of a free and fair election remained uncertain. The government feared that even if Zedillo won the election, a small margin of victory would not prevent the opposition from convincingly claiming fraud and calling for social unrest to demand new elections, which could lead to ungovernability and force the Salinas administration to accept the formation of an interim or a coalition government.

Under these circumstances, the Salinas administration's economic policy options were sharply constrained by political necessities. The survival of a PRI government relied on the cohesion of an electoral coalition composed of voters controlled by the party machine and an all-important segment of urban swing voters. The electoral loyalty of the first group depended on party unity to ensure the effective operation of the machine. The votes of Mexico's urban actors depended directly on their belief that PRI governance would expand their economic opportunities, which by 1994 translated into the government's capacity to deliver economic growth. The uncertainty of the electoral environment as a result of electoral reforms, rebellion in the south, a weak presidential candidate, and a skeptical electorate meant the PRI government needed to hold its coalition together in its entirety to assure victory in the August elections. Disputes and divisions within the party and a political assassination, meanwhile, raised fears that the efficiency of the PRI machine would lag as it had done in 1988.

Given these electoral constraints, it is not surprising that the Mexican government chose to mitigate the recessionary consequences of rising international interest rates and declining investor confidence throughout spring and summer 1994. Following the postassassination jump in interest rates, the government was able to force interest rates down two full percentage points by election day by sterilizing capital outflows to prevent a large contraction in the money supply (largely through a huge increase in development bank lending) and replacing peso-denominated government bonds with dollar-denominated securities.[19] The payoff was an economy that expanded 4.8 percent in the second quarter of 1994 and 4.5 percent in the third quarter and, on August 21, an absolute majority of the vote for Zedillo—nearly double the total of his nearest rival.

In the aftermath of the election, interest rates continued to fall, and the economy continued to expand at a rapid pace. If the election had been the only obstacle to economic adjustment, one would have expected a very different set of economic developments. Clearly, the constraints on economic policy options extended into the postelection period. In part, the policy limitations were both economic and political. On the economic side, further devaluation of the peso, whether a one-off devaluation or an increase of the slide within the fixed-rule system, seemed unwise. During the election campaign, the government had transferred nearly two-thirds of its internal debt into dollar-denominated securities; an immediate postelection devaluation would thus significantly increase the government's liabilities in pesos and threaten to create a large fiscal deficit. It also seemed unwise to devalue the Mexican currency unless that move was coupled with a stabilization program that included significant increases in domestic interest rates; such increases, however, were considered too dangerous.

By late 1994, the Mexican banking system was in a very delicate situation. Nearly 9 percent of outstanding loans in the system were past due, over three times the international standard for an unhealthy banking institution and measured according to Mexico's more generous accounting methods. The Mexican government had also been forced to bail out two banks. A rapid rise in interest rates leading to a downturn in the Mexican economy thus threatened to spark a full-blown crisis in the financial system.

Beyond these economic constraints to adjustment in the weeks following the election, the Salinas government was also limited by political considerations. In an effort to solidify the support of key urban voters prior to election day, Zedillo had repeatedly promised Mexicans a return to economic growth under his administration and had warned of an economic catastrophe if his opponents were to win the election. Although it was successful on election day, the Zedillo team recognized that the strategy did little to produce loyal support among swing voters in the postelection period. Urban voters had given the PRI the opportunity to make good on its promises of stability and growth, but they remained skeptical and were ready to defect if they were let down or spurned. The Zedillo team seemed to fear that any sudden implementation of an adjustment program could convince these voters that the PRI had intentionally deceived them during the campaign, which could produce fodder for the public protests of electoral fraud called—thus far with only minor success—by Cárdenas, one of the losing presidential candidates. Ungovernability could ensue. The Zedillo team thus argued successfully for a delay of any adjustment measures in the transition period.[20] The new Pacto, announced on September 24, set in stone a compromise position—there would be no change in the fixed-rule exchange rate regime, and inflation would fall farther, but there would also be no tightening of monetary policy, and growth would continue at the 4 percent rate. The Mexican government thus opted to roll the dice one more time—to sustain a risky economic strategy a bit longer to ensure the perpetuation of PRI governance.

Argentina

The electoral coalition backing Carlos Menem and his Peronist Party during 1994 and 1995 differed significantly from its Mexican counterpart despite substantial similarities in their membership structures. Although both coalitions were composed of voters concerned with improving their living standards through stable prices and rising incomes, the relative weight placed on those two objectives was significantly different in each coalition. The initial formation of Menem's neoliberal electoral coalition was not unlike that of the Salinas coalition—individuals joined the coalition gradually as a direct consequence of Menem's ability to bring down inflation (from over 3,000 percent in 1989 to only 4.3 percent in 1994) and to restore hope for a better future. The coalition also incorporated individuals with a multitude of competing second-order policy interests and the tendency toward coalition instability that entailed in light of the budgetary constraints imposed by a fixed exchange rate monetary system.

The stability of Menem's electoral coalition, however, enjoyed two essential advantages over the Salinas coalition. First, even though the stability of the Menem coalition suffered as voters' fears of inflation began to fade during 1993 and 1994, the scar in Argentine society left by hyperinflation was still prominent. It had only been five years since price increases of 3,600 percent in a single year (the year prior to Menem's inauguration) had effectively brought the Argentine economy to its knees, and it had only been three years since hyperinflation had disappeared. That experience had radically reshaped the preferences of Argentines. Even as their identities as workers, professionals, low-level managers, and businesspeople gradually resurfaced, Argentine voters retained a preference for a government that would preserve price stability. This continuing concern with inflation was evidenced in an October 1994 poll. When asked to identify the top problems facing the next president of Argentina, five of ten Argentines still mentioned the need to maintain fiscal and monetary stability.[21] As changing international economic conditions and risk assessments began to generate pressure for economic adjustment during 1994, voter memories of the recent and extremely costly consequences of hyperinflation reduced the political risk associated with implementing austerity prior to a presidential election. By playing on voters' latent fear of inflation, the Menem government was able to restabilize the anti-inflationary foundation of its electoral coalition—an option unavailable in Mexico.

The stability of the Menem coalition also benefited from a relatively secure electoral environment. Whereas during 1994 Mexico was in the process of gradually opening up an authoritarian system to more democratic practices, the Argentine political system had been democratic for more than a decade; the uncertainties associated with the outcome of free and fair elections were thus more familiar there. The politicians who populated the Menem government had a better sense of how to operate effectively in a democratic environment than their Mexican counterparts and also had more confidence that they could do so successfully. Uncertainty was an accepted part of the Argentine political system rather than something new and potentially threatening.

The relative certainty of the electoral environment in Argentina combined with the latent yet powerful fear of renewed inflation among Argentine voters significantly reduced the political risk associated with instituting economic austerity only months before a presidential election. To say the political risk associated with economic austerity was lower in Argentina than in Mexico, however, does not mean it was absent; the inevitable uncertainties associated with elections persisted. More important, throughout 1994 it was not obvious that price stability continued to dominate the policy preferences of Argentine voters; to the contrary, the government faced growing popular demands for renewed policy attention to income levels. Policies designed only to preserve price stability were thus not perceived by Argentine policymakers to be an assured path to coalition cohesion. Not surprisingly and not unlike the Salinas administration, the Menem government attempted to evade the recessionary consequences of adjusting to shifts in the international economy throughout 1994. In November 1994, just six months prior to the elections, however, the Menem government rapidly and dramatically reversed course—a decision the Mexican government refused to take under similar circumstances.

As international interest rates began their gradual upward march in early 1994, the Argentine trade deficit began to reflect the costs of an overvalued currency. Trade figures for 1993 (released in early March 1994) showed a deficit 40 percent above government expectations (*Latin*

American Monitor [*LAM*], April 1994: 3). The Menem government's ability to respond to this emerging economic instability, however, was constrained by political realities. The drop in the annual rate of inflation from triple digits in 1991 to single digits by the end of 1993 had begun to reorient the policy preferences of Argentine voters. Unions began to agitate against the costs of economic reform, businesses called for increased government assistance, and the middle class demanded an end to rising government corruption. More tangibly, the imposition of fiscal austerity measures produced violent protests in several northwestern provinces in late 1993 and the fear that such protests would spread. Plans to dismiss thousands of provincial employees and a lack of money to pay those who remained (even as provincial officials gave themselves a pay increase) incited riots in one province and violent protests in two others. The central role of provincial voters in the Menem coalition and the disturbing realization that votes once perceived as assured might now be in jeopardy forced the government to respond strongly. The Menem government dismissed one provincial governor and—more important for exchange rate stability—sent an emergency aid package, with a promise of more to come, to the affected provinces and to others that seemed headed in the same direction.

In early 1994, the need to solidify the provincial vote as quickly as possible and to garner support elsewhere in society was caused by the approach of nationwide elections for a Constituent Assembly. In late 1993, Menem reached an agreement with the leading opposition party, the Radicals, to undertake a reform of the Argentine constitution that would include a provision to permit presidential reelection, thereby enabling Menem to run for a second term. Given that only one-third of the Argentine electorate supported Menem's reelection gambit, winning a majority of seats in the assembly was far from assured for Menem and his Radical Party allies. The implementation of austerity measures prior to the April 10 election thus entailed a large political risk but did not involve a great economic risk since the imbalance in the Argentine economy during the austral autumn was emergent rather than catastrophic. The Menem government thus opted to postpone adjustment.

Immediately after the election, in which the government secured a comfortable majority, it seemed economic adjustment would move to the center of the policy stage. Concerned about the rapidly growing trade deficit and rising U.S. interest rates that threatened to slow capital inflows, Economy Minister Domingo Cavallo warned his fellow cabinet members that the "bonanza is over." Recognizing that declining capital inflows would impede growth and thereby reduce government revenues (in combination with tax cuts implemented in late 1993), on April 12 the government issued a decree capping most government spending. At the same time, Cavallo implied that the government would do nothing to mitigate this economic slowdown, suggesting that the country should expect the economy to expand by only 3.5 percent in 1994 (down from 6 percent in 1993) (*LAM,* May 1994: 3-4; *Latin American Weekly Report* [*LAWR*], May 19, 1994). Within days, however, this promise of adjustment was abandoned.

A mid-April reassessment of the government's political needs produced a dramatic policy reversal. Although it had won the April elections, a closer analysis of the results revealed serious problems for the Menem administration. The Peronist Party suffered marked setbacks throughout the northwest, losing in three northwestern provinces and experiencing major setbacks in two others (including Menem's home province). In addition, continuing unrest in the region promised future losses if nothing was done to attenuate the costs of adjustment (*LAWR,* April 29, 1994; (Economist Intelligence Unit [EIU], second quarter, 1994: 11). Voters had also castigated the administration for seemingly rampant government corruption. Only weeks before the election, a scandal had broken involving bribes and extortion in the medical care system for pensioners. A new opposition coalition, the Frente Grande, used the scandal as ammunition in a campaign dominated by criticism of corruption and the unfairness it produced in the distribution of the costs associated with economic reform. This anticorruption campaign produced dramatic results: the Frente increased its share of the vote from just 2.5 percent in the October 1993 legislative elections to 13.5 percent (and a startling 37 percent in Buenos Aires) just six months later. Even though voters probably felt more free to express their discontent during the April elections when little of great importance seemed to be at stake than they would during a presidential election, the message and danger for the Menem government were unmistakable: concerns about corruption were clearly undercutting the stability of Menem's electoral coalition.

Menem's coalition also faced a brewing threat from within the ranks of the Peronist Party. A prominent member of the party with a reputation for honesty and integrity, as well as effective economic management, launched a campaign to challenge Menem for the party's presidential nomination. José Octavio Bordón's call for an open party primary forced Menem to divert resources to shore up his support within the party. This internal party challenge also served as a timely reminder that the Peronist Party was not composed of automatons who blindly followed the president; many in the party were increasingly concerned about the political costs of economic reform in their traditional constituencies. Within the executive mansion, this situation raised concerns that the Constituent Assembly might introduce changes to the reforms Menem and the leadership of the Radical Party had agreed to in late 1993 (Menem was particularly concerned that provincial representatives might introduce a plan to increase the percentage of federal tax revenues sent to the provinces and thereby undermine efforts to keep the federal budget in balance; see *LAM,* July 1994: 3). Menem's capacity to maintain control of his troops during the assembly's deliberations would inevitably be further undermined if a recession were to magnify the costs of economic reform in Argentine society. A postponement of economic adjustment efforts thus seemed prudent.

Beginning April 22, the statements and actions of Menem and Economy Minister Cavallo clearly demonstrated the government's decision to reverse its economic policy course. On that date, Cavallo announced that the economy was likely to grow 6 to 7 percent annually for several more years (gone was the estimate of 3.5 percent announced only days earlier). He also dismissed any threat to the economy from reduced capital inflows as a result of higher U.S. interest rates and began to argue that the trade deficit was a sign of strength rather than weakness in the economy (*LAWR,* May 5 and 19, 1994). The president followed those statements with a proposal (in a May 1 speech before the Congress) for a three-year investment of $7 billion to fight poverty. In the words of the governor of the Province of Buenos Aires, the party had determined that it "must take action to increase work opportunities, raise production, and boost growth," especially in the provinces.[22] To achieve these objectives, the Menem government proposed not to increase government spending dramatically but instead to shift funds from other purposes. A reduction in spending, however, was out of the question. In the words of Cavallo, "Public spending cannot be brought down any further" (*LARR,* June 2, 1994: 3).

This decision to abandon economic adjustment efforts was reinforced by events throughout the winter. A poll taken in June 1994 showed a collapse in both Menem's personal popularity and public optimism about the economy. Menem's numbers fell from 61 percent in December to only 37 percent in June, and public expectations of an improving economic situation fell from 43 percent to 28 percent in the same period (*LAM,* August 1994). In a further reflection of the government's declining popularity, 60,000 Argentines turned out on July 6 to protest high unemployment and fiscal austerity. Further fueling the fire of discontent was the late July release of the May unemployment figures. For the first time ever, Argentine unemployment registered in the double digits (10.8 percent). In response, labor unions called a general strike for August 2. Although the strike was only partially effective in Buenos Aires, adherence was high in Argentina's more industrialized provinces (Cordoba and Rosario). On the heels of this semisuccessful one-day urban strike came a very successful ten-day strike by farmers demanding government assistance in rescheduling their debts, access to affordable credit, and action to block unfair foreign competition. In early September, Argentine industrialists joined the expanding chorus of critical voices. Although broadly supportive of its economic policies, the first Argentine Industrial Conference went on record criticizing the government's trade policy and the cost of credit (*LARR,* September 15, 1994).

As persistent political pressures continued to delay adjustment, instability in the Argentine economy deepened. Economic figures released in
July pointed out not only the double-digit unemployment rate but also the
highest inflation rate of the year, a trade deficit expanding at a torrid pace,
and a decline in industrial output.[23] At the same time, rising world interest
rates and the consequent drop in capital inflows to Argentina tightened the
domestic money supply and thereby raised domestic interest rates (this
dilemma deepened in August when the sudden success of stabilization
efforts in Brazil increased the attractiveness of stabilization to investors).
Most serious, however, was a sharp decline in government revenues coupled with spending increases. Tax reductions announced in late 1993
designed to increase the productivity of Argentine firms had cut into government revenues significantly by mid-1994. Revenues also suffered from
an unanticipated fall in sales taxes at midyear. At the same time, the government felt compelled to transfer more funds to the provinces (an 8 percent increase through the first nine months of 1994) and was forced by a
court ruling to increase substantially its payments to retirees. The consequence was a budget careening toward deficit. A comfortable surplus during the first half of the year fell sharply in the third quarter and was no
longer sufficient to cover the government's debt obligations.

Bad news on the budget front was particularly problematic for economic stability. A balanced budget was essential to investor confidence in
the Argentine government's commitment to the fixed value of the peso. As
the budget figures weakened, capital inflows were thus likely to decline
further, producing a slowdown in economic activity. The government also
encountered difficulties financing its emerging fiscal deficit. The recent
rise in world interest rates would translate into higher financing costs for
the Argentine government and upward pressure on domestic interest rates if
Argentina floated bond issues internationally. To avoid these growth-
inhibiting consequences of international borrowing, the Argentine government delayed entering the market to the greatest extent possible (the government stayed out of the market completely during the second quarter and
entered only tepidly during the third quarter).[24] Another option would have
been to issue bonds in the domestic market, but here, too, the government
encountered limited demand.[25] Again, the government chose to restrict supply to keep prices up and interest rates low rather than to finance its deficit
fully. The Menem government thus postponed any effective response—
through either adjustment or financing—to its burgeoning fiscal deficit
throughout the winter for fear that any response would undermine economic growth and thereby weaken government control of the Constituent
Assembly by feeding the emergent instability within the Menem coalition.

With the August 24 promulgation of a new constitution that permitted
presidential reelection, it appeared that the political constraints to stabiliza-

tion had been loosened sufficiently for the government to act. In early September, the government announced a plan to eliminate the budget deficit by the end of the year through spending cuts and revenue increases. The plan required that all government ministries cut spending by 10 percent and freeze hiring for the remainder of the fiscal year and compelled the provinces to implement austerity measures. On the revenue side, the plan called for a continuation of a recently initiated crackdown on tax evaders. As in April, however, this effort to respond to growing economic instability proved very difficult to implement. The campaign against tax evasion met with strong opposition in the provinces, as it forced hundreds of businesses to close. Provincial governments and their employees also chafed under the coercive tactics employed by the federal government to encourage the privatization of money-losing firms owned by the provincial governments. As protests spread, the government retreated—it suspended the antievasion program and reduced its pressure for economic reform in the provinces. It seems that with presidential elections only eight months away and the president's popularity sagging (in early September, only 36 percent of the electorate said they would vote to reelect Menem), the government determined it could not risk alienating the provincial party machines and the votes they could deliver in the May polls.

The decision to delay once again needed adjustments in economic policy, however, was insufficient to rebuild Menem's electoral strength. Although the strategy might have protected provincial loyalty, it did little to address the source of the weakening support in the president's broader electoral coalition. To the contrary, the cohesion of the coalition depended not only on a fear that inflation might return but also on the conviction that Menem was the individual most capable of protecting the population from that eventuality. If it appeared that the Menem government's economic management could threaten the economic stability so cherished by most Argentine voters, Argentines would begin to question their support of Menem. The appearance of economic mismanagement could thus torpedo the foundation of Menem's electoral support. Delayed adjustment was a very risky electoral strategy.

To mitigate that risk, the government attempted to shape the public perception of its management of the economy. Beyond the now commonplace insistence that the trade deficit was a positive development for the economy, Economy Minister Cavallo began to argue that a short-term budget deficit was not a threat to economic stability. What mattered were the budget figures for the entire year, which he insisted would be balanced. In late September 1994, the government also announced its decision to forgo the last two installments of a loan from the IMF, arguing that since it could now obtain credit in private markets it no longer needed to accept loans from the IMF. The dubious nature of that justification was made abundantly clear by the difficulties the government had encountered over the preceding six months in its attempt to obtain the amount of credit it needed at a price it was willing to pay. The decision to suspend its agreement with the IMF was motivated instead by a desire to avoid the embarrassment and associated political costs of having to acknowledge publicly its inability to meet the fiscal targets contained in the loan agreement.

This strategy—to avoid adjustment through a series of ad hoc economic policy maneuvers designed to preserve provincial support and to rely on a public relations campaign to ease popular fears about the wisdom of that approach—could not be sustained forever. Ultimately, the absence of adjustment would deepen economic instability sufficiently to raise doubts within the members of Menem's electoral coalition about his ability to preserve economic stability. This eventuality occurred sooner rather than later. In early October, a leaked IMF report drew public attention to those facts the government had hoped to hide. Occupying the headlines of all of the Buenos Aires newspapers, the report indicated that the government had missed several spending targets established in its agreement with the IMF, and it criticized the fiscal policy management that had produced this outcome. The government's statistical agency added fuel to the fire when it announced late in the month that the fiscal surplus had evaporated during the third quarter of the year. These two revelations burst the government's public relations balloon, producing great concern among both investors and Argentine voters about the survival of the fixed exchange rate and, thus, of broader economic stability in Argentina.

This marked change in the economic policy environment significantly increased the political-economic risk of not dealing with the budget deficit and thus somewhat modified the government's strategy. On November 1, the Menem administration sent a bill to Congress to revise the budgets for 1994 and 1995. The bill contained three provisions that together defined the new approach of the Menem-Cavallo team. First, the government openly acknowledged that the 1994 budget would end the year with a deficit and that financing that deficit could no longer be postponed; it thus requested congressional approval of a $1.3 billion increase in the government's borrowing limit for the year. The acceptance of a short-term fiscal imbalance and the increase in domestic interest rates its financing would produce was coupled with two other provisions designed to prevent the persistence of that imbalance in 1995. The first called for strict limits on the amount of money the government would be required to pay out to retirees, and the second gave the executive superpowers to reorganize government agencies and to privatize without congressional approval for four years.[26]

Led by members of the president's party, Congress balked. It stripped the superpowers provision from the bill, voiced its displeasure with the spending cap on social security payments, and rearranged other spending priorities in the budget package. In the face of this congressional challenge, the executive threatened to move forward with or without congressional cooperation and resurrected the "phantom" of inflation. The economy minister announced that he would be forced to impose a "savage adjustment" on the economy by decree if the Congress did not pass the bill in its original form, and the president noted that his government would be forced "to veto everything which signifies an excessive increase in public spending." Cavallo also insisted repeatedly that if Congress refused to pass the bill, "inflation will return."[27] Recognizing the threat inaction posed to the cohesion of its electoral coalition, the government turned up the heat on a reticent Congress. By raising the specter of inflation and blaming the Congress for this renewed threat, Menem and Cavallo could revive the government's electoral coalition in two ways: the coalition would reignite the fear of inflation among Argentines while painting the Menem-Cavallo team as the white knights protecting Argentine economic stability from the irresponsible behavior of Congress. At the same time, however, the government hoped to limit the negative impact this revised strategy would have on the support it would ultimately need from party politicians. As late as November 15, government officials thus continued to insist that they were willing to wait for the Congress to act (rather than bypassing the Congress by legislating through decree), even though the time and compromise doing so required would delay the effective resolution of the building budget crisis.

Another sudden change in the policy environment, however, once again modified the government's policy calculus. On November 16, the U.S. Federal Reserve announced a higher than anticipated increase in U.S. interest rates (a rise of three-quarters of a percentage point). Fearing the impact this increase would have on capital inflows, interest rates, growth, and, ultimately, investor confidence in Argentina's fixed exchange rate, the government moved decisively. The following day, President Menem issued a decree launching the austerity program he had been avoiding since March. The decree froze all discretionary government spending for the remainder of the year with the objective of eliminating the entire $1.3 billion deficit in forty-five days. Cavallo also made clear the government's intention to persist with austerity into 1995: "From here until the elections and throughout 1995 [government agencies] are not going to obtain extra funds."[28] The Menem government seemed to have calculated that the political risk of continued delay outweighed the risk of implementing an austerity program in the runup to presidential elections.

That calculation makes sense only in light of the anti-inflationary core of the government's electoral coalition. The Argentine government had instituted the sort of austerity program the Mexican government had refused to implement throughout 1994 despite the fact that the measures of instability were somewhat higher in the Mexican economy than in Argentina.[29] The government's willingness to take this political risk when faced with a significantly smaller threat to the peso's parity reflected the anti-inflationary composition of Menem's electoral coalition and the peculiar mixture of political costs and benefits that produced. Not only were the costs of inaction perceived to be high (inaction would undermine Menem's reputation for responsible economic policy management), but the costs of action seemed manageable. Just as the April 1991 initiation of Argentina's successful stabilization program had crafted a winning electoral coalition in just five months (Menem's job approval ratings had measured only 20 percent in March 1991), the government hoped the preservation of embattled price stability could reconstruct its electoral support in time for the May elections.

The political risk embodied in this strategy was also lessened by the electoral environment in which it was implemented. The recent revisions to the Argentine constitution had established the direct election of the president (done previously through an electoral college system) and created a second round in the presidential election if no candidate obtained either 45 percent of the vote or 40 percent with a 10 percent lead over the next candidate. The totality of the reform, however, left the basic rules of democratic politics in Argentina unchanged. Also, despite the continuing disputes between Menem and provincial party leaders over adjustment and funding priorities in the provinces, there was no question about the relative capacity of the Peronist Party machine to deliver votes once the two sides reached an agreement.

Finally, the opposition was in disarray. The Radical Party was highly discredited by its collaboration with the government in the reform of the constitution (its vote count fell from 30 percent in October 1993 to 20 percent in April 1994). This electoral disaster produced turmoil within the party and led one faction to consider forming an electoral alliance with the government. The party managed to unify sufficiently to choose a single presidential candidate, but that candidate's viability was severely undermined in late February 1994 by the collapse of the provincial economy when he was governor. The second opposition force, Frepaso, was an alliance of former Peronists and a series of small parties on the left. Although it ultimately chose a strong candidate, it did not do so until late February 1994. During the last months of 1994, however, Frepaso was torn by internal disputes over who its candidate should be. Although both the Radicals and Frepaso complained about the rising costs of sustaining an economic strategy built on a fixed exchange rate, ultimately neither offered a credible alternative.

The electoral environment surrounding the Menem government's decision to take the political risk associated with adjustment on the eve of elections actually mitigated that risk. Relative stability in both the basic rules of politics and the operational capacity of the ruling party, as well as a fairly weak opposition, combined to produce greater electoral certainty in Argentina than in Mexico.

After the Menem government had decided to opt for adjustment, the political risk associated with that strategy was further reduced by the Mexican peso crisis and the huge outflow of capital from the Argentine economy the crisis produced. Given their long experience with devaluations preceded by large capital outflows, Argentines correctly perceived this development as a serious threat to economic stability. Menem actively played on those potent memories in his presidential campaign and thereby reconstituted his electoral coalition with phenomenal success. The president constantly reminded voters of the horrors of the hyperinflationary past and that he was the one who had brought economic stability to Argentina. He asked voters if they were willing to change horses in the middle of the treacherous stream they were now fording. They were not. Menem won a decisive victory in May despite a rapidly contracting economy and an explosion of unemployment.

Conclusion

The experiences of Mexico and Argentina offer some preliminary lessons about the benefits and costs associated with fixed exchange rates in middle-income developing countries and about the compatibility of this common component of economic liberalization with democratic politics. In the short term, fixed exchange rates can dramatically increase the credibility of anti-inflationary efforts in countries with a reputation for lax monetary management. This credibility can produce a dramatic increase in capital inflows, especially in periods of an abundant supply of international capital, which can help to finance economic expansion.

The medium-term costs of fixed exchange rates in an international financial environment dominated by a high degree of capital mobility, however, can be great. If the fixed exchange rate is used as an anchor to pull down domestic price increases, as in both the Mexican and Argentine cases, its real value will become overvalued, thereby undermining the competitiveness of exports, generating a current account deficit, and creating a great dependence on capital inflows to finance the imbalance. More important for the central theme of this book, unregulated flows of short-term investment capital impose tight policy constraints on governments that have adopted a fixed exchange rate. Any action the market sees as threatening macroeconomic stability will quickly translate into a rapid outflow of capital that, if sufficiently large, will threaten the fixed value of a country's currency. To sustain a fixed exchange rate in the current international financial environment, therefore, governments must enjoy sufficient political flexibility to be able to withstand the recessionary consequences of macroeconomic inflexibility in the face of rising international interest rates, a sudden collapse of investor confidence, or any other international financial development that reduces the inflow or produces an outflow of capital.

This raises the question of the conditions under which governments are likely to possess the political flexibility necessary to sustain a fixed exchange rate and survive in office. The Mexican and Argentina cases suggest that this condition will be much easier to attain in the short-term wake of a hyperinflationary crisis than in the medium or long term. The generalized nature of the pain caused by hyperinflation, as well as the benefits derived from its elimination, made it relatively easy for the successful slayer of the inflationary dragon to quickly construct a broad base of political support.[30] The two cases considered in this chapter also indicate, however, that it is difficult to preserve the cohesion of an anti-inflationary coalition over time in a democratic setting. Success in the battle against inflation will undermine the policy consensus that brought together an otherwise disparate cross section of society into a single electoral coalition. As coalition members begin to focus once again on incomes rather than prices in the struggle to improve their living standards, their willingness to tolerate the slow growth associated with an overvalued exchange rate and the periodic recessions produced by shifts in world capital markets will wane. This seemingly inevitable breakdown of the anti-inflationary policy consensus will tend to destabilize the foundation of societal support backing the government and thereby undermine the political flexibility essential for the successful maintenance of a fixed exchange rate.[31]

Despite this dynamic, the comparison of monetary management in Argentina and Mexico during 1994 indicates that under certain conditions it is possible to produce the political flexibility needed to sustain a fixed exchange rate in the face of capital outflows. In late 1994, the Menem government was able to recraft a policy consensus within its electoral coalition to protect the fixed rate of the peso. This success came as a consequence of the residual fear of inflation in the Argentine electorate because of its relatively recent and highly traumatic experience with hyperinflation. In fact, the Menem government found that the anti-inflationary core of its electoral coalition effectively forced it to take actions designed to protect the value of the peso. This foundation of political flexibility was augmented by the relative certainty of the electoral environment surrounding the May presidential elections. Although the constitutional reform had mandated the direct election of the president, it had made few other changes in the rules governing elections in Argentina. The mechanisms by which parties and candidates would garner votes remained unchanged, and the opposition was in disarray.

The situation was very different in Mexico. Greater popular confidence in the government's final victory against inflation prevented the Salinas administration from replicating the Menemist strategy for rebuilding policy consensus within its electoral coalition. Political flexibility was also hindered by the uncertainty surrounding the August 1994 presidential poll. The electoral clout of the traditional bases of the ruling party had weakened dramatically in recent years, forcing the PRI to employ a new strategy designed to win support from segments of society that had previously abstained from politics. A series of three electoral reforms during 1993 and 1994 had also placed limits on many of the PRI's traditional mechanisms for winning votes. Uncertain about the capacity of its new strategy to win votes under new electoral rules, the Salinas administration determined to do too much rather than not enough to win votes. As political flexibility fell, so did its capacity to protect an effectively fixed exchange rate as capital flowed out during 1994.

This explanation of Argentina's success and Mexico's failure to preserve a fixed exchange rate in the face of capital outflows on the eve of presidential elections does not correlate neatly with the argument that democracy tends to undermine the policy flexibility needed to implement efficient economic policies. Authoritarian Mexico failed, whereas democratic Argentina succeeded. This outcome suggests that political regime types are too nebulous a concept to predict effectively the manner in which the political setting constrains economic policy choices. Having said this, the cases do support the broader contention that democratic practices tend to undermine policy flexibility whereas authoritarian practices increase it. The relatively high degree of uncertainty characteristic of the Mexican electoral environment during 1994 was the consequence of a painfully slow but very real process of political liberalization. Mexico remained a soft authoritarian regime during 1994, but it was also experiencing an expansion of democratic practices. In Argentina, successful implementation of the measures needed to preserve macroeconomic instability in late 1994 was a result of authoritarian practices rather than democratic procedures. The Menem administration decided that the time needed to construct a policy compromise within the Argentine legislature and the likely nature of that compromise would be too costly for economic stability in Argentina and thus legislated the needed fiscal adjustment by executive decree.

The experiences of Mexico and Argentina thus suggest that the maintenance of a fixed exchange rate in the presence of mobile capital tends to be incompatible with democratic practices. This conclusion, however, should not be construed to mean financial liberalization is inherently incompatible with political liberalization; instead, it suggests that financial liberalization based on a fixed exchange rate appears incompatible with democratic practices. To avoid the tradeoff between macroeconomic stability and political survival within a democratic context evident in both the Mexican and Argentine cases, countries would be well advised to avoid fixed exchange rates. They should opt instead for a regime that incorporates enough flexibility to compensate for the inevitable economic inefficiencies produced by the compromise and delays inherent in a democratic decisionmaking process.

Notes

1. On the globalization of finance, see Helleiner (1994). Its impact on developing countries is illuminated in Griffith-Jones and Stallings (1995).
2. Interbank rates increased from an annual average of 5.7 percent during the second quarter of 1993 to an average of 8.1 percent for the second quarter of 1994 and to over 10 percent during July and August (EIU, third quarter, 1994: 20).
3. The government sold only slightly more than half of the units placed up for auction rather than discount the price (raise the interest rate) sufficiently to sell the entire lot. The government offered 6.4 percent on its peso-denominated bonds, whereas the market demanded 7.9 percent (EIU, third quarter, 1994: 27).
4. Call money rates rose from 7.5 percent during November to 10.25 percent during the first half of December (Economic Report, 1994: 173; and *El Cronista Comercial* [Mexico City], Internet edition, December 2, 6, 8, and 19, 1994).
5. Presidential election results found in Handelman (1997).
6. On the distinction between the rural and urban characteristics of the coalitions constructed by the Peronist Party in Argentina and the PRI in Mexico, see Gibson (1997).
7. Although estimates of the base of assured votes the Peronist Party and the PRI could anticipate vary, most fall in the 25 percent to 35 percent range. See McGuire (1995).
8. As the tight monetary policy of the Banco de México undercut economic growth, it also inhibited the capacity of debtors (firms and individuals) to make loan payments. For a banking system that had overlent in 1992 and had incurred significant losses speculating in Mexican bonds, the losses added up quickly. Between August 1992 and August 1993, the past-due accounts of the Mexican banking system grew 150 percent (*Accion,* no. 767, September 6, 1993: 2).
9. Even in early 1994, after the Mexican government had shifted its economic policy toward an increased emphasis on growth in advance of the August presidential elections, a private-sector publication reported that the "immense majority" of Mexican firms remained "resentful of the government's fiscal harassment and the difficult situation their firms are going through" (*Accion,* no. 784, January 17, 1994: 1).
10. When asked "what issues should become a top priority for the next Mexican president," respondents to nationwide opinion surveys conducted for the PRI campaign mentioned "create new jobs" far more often than anything else (52 percent); the second-most-common answer was "improve wages" (23 percent).

Concerns about economic stability (12 percent) and reducing inflation (6 percent) trailed badly. Cited in Oppenheimer (1996: 153).

11. For the urban poor, the Salinas administration added an antipoverty program known as the National Solidarity Program, or Pronasol, designed specifically to help those populations that had voted for the opposition in 1988. On Pronasol, see Cornelius, Craig, and Fox (1994); and Dresser (1991).

12. In the 1988 elections, the PRI majority in the Chamber of Deputies had fallen from 68 percent of the seats to just over 50 percent. Following the 1991 elections, the PRI gained sixty seats, and its majority rebounded to a comfortable 61 percent.

13. The content and political implications of these reforms are discussed in Alcocer V. (1995).

14. Although some government officials favored a larger fiscal expansion to pump up the economy ahead of the elections, Finance Minister Pedro Aspe and Bank of Mexico director Miguel Mancera strongly opposed that approach. The economic cabinet thus agreed on a modest expansion that would use up the budget surplus without creating a deficit. Although some private economists argued that the new Pacto would produce a small budget deficit, they agreed that it would be easily financed and thus would not have inflationary consequences (Ramirez de la O, 1993).

15. According to a MORI/Este Pais poll, Colosio's support fell from around 40 percent in mid-February to 32 percent by the beginning of March. Cited in *Latin American Regional Report* (*LARR*), March 31, 1994: 3. Doubts about Colosio's ability to win the election were common fare in the print media and were expressed by Colosio's campaign manager, Ernesto Zedillo, in a letter written March 19, 1995, and published in the newspaper *Reforma* (Mexico City) on October 3, 1995.

16. Evidence of Salinas's effort to perpetuate his influence beyond the end of his term in office was also provided by José Angel Gurria, a member of the Salinas technocratic team. In a private meeting with Japanese businesspeople, Gurria is reported to have assured them that there would be no break with Salinas's economic policies in a Colosio administration. Instead, Colosio would guarantee twenty-four years of policy continuity because his successor would also emerge from the Salinas cabinet (*Proceso* [Mexico City], no. 892, December 6, 1993: 11, 13).

17. In the days following the unveiling of the new official party candidate, Salinas loyalists were replaced in several key party and campaign posts by loyalists of Carlos Hank Gonzalez, a prominent representative of the old guard. Ignacio Pichardo Pagaza occupied the post of party secretary-general and later took over as Zedillo's campaign manager. Hank loyalists also occupied the party's secretariat for electoral action and retained the secretariat of finance.

18. Polls published in *Este Pais* and *Reforma* show that Zedillo's popularity dropped approximately 10 percent from early April to late May. See *Este País* (Mexico City), August 1994: 2; *Reforma,* April 15 and May 29, 1994.

19. Figures on development bank lending and money supply from Bancode México, *Indicadores Economicos* (December 1995: 1–9); interest rate and growth figures are from Banco de México (1995: 17, 75); figures on government securities are in Hale (1995: appendix 14).

20. The Zedillo team's preoccupation with avoiding a recession in the transition period can be seen in its persistent public promises of growth, rumors of sharp disagreements between Zedillo's supporters and Pedro Aspe and Miguel Mancera (finance minister and Central Bank president, respectively, and proponents of a tight monetary policy to protect the fixed-rule exchange rate regime) over economic

strategy in the weeks following the election, and the comments of one member of the Zedillo economic team, Guillermo Ortiz, who implied that a bit more flexibility in exchange rate policy might even be acceptable to promote growth.

21. Poll taken by Centro de Estudios de Opinion Publica in Argentina's main urban areas. Cited in *LAM* (November 1994).

22. Governor Eduardo Duhalde, quoted in *LARR* (June 2, 1994: 3).

23. Prices rose nearly 1 percent in July, the trade deficit for the first four months of 1994 was up 400 percent from the same period in 1993, and industrial output fell 1.4 percent in June. See *LAM* (July 1994).

24. Republica Argentina (1995: 113).

25. The government's difficulties placing bonds in the domestic market in the quantity and at the price it preferred are detailed in a series of articles in the newspaper *La Nación* (Buenos Aires) from late August to late October 1994 (see in particular August 23 and September 22, 1994).

26. The contents of the budget reform bill are found in *La Nación* (October 30, 1994).

27. Both officials were quoted in *El Cronista Comercial*, Cavallo in the November 15 and 16, 1994, issues and Menem in the November 17, 1994, issue on the Internet at www.cronista.com.

28. Cited in Univ. of Buenos Aires, *Microseminarios* 176 (Nov. 14–20, 1994). Posted on the Internet at http:\\www-informatik.uni-muenchen.de/rec/argentina.

29. In both countries, the budget deficit (financial deficit) as a percentage of GDP was well under 1 percent throughout 1994. They also experienced a two-thirds dropoff in capital inflows in the third quarter of 1994 relative to the same period a year earlier (68 percent for Argentina and 66 percent for Mexico). But the Mexican current account deficit totaled 7.5 percent of GDP at the end of the third quarter, whereas the Argentine deficit was only 3.6 percent. This meant that although both countries suffered a significant drop in capital inflows, macroeconomic stability was significantly more dependent on those inflows in Mexico than in Argentina. Data derived from IMF (1996).

30. This empirical evidence reinforces Rodrik's (1994) argument that trade liberalization is more common in high inflationary settings. According to Rodrik, the political costs associated with the redistribution of resources inherent in a commercial opening can be minimized when consumers perceive the costs of inflation to be greater than the redistributive costs and liberalization is sold as an essential inflation-fighting tool.

31. The Argentine and Mexican experiences with monetary liberalization thus reinforce Nelson's (1994) conclusion that the policy consensus behind economic reform is increasingly difficult to sustain as reform moves from implementation to consolidation because of the shrinking circle of individuals who perceive of themselves as the beneficiaries of reform.

Part 4

Conclusion

9

The Logics of Liberalization

Philip Oxhorn & Pamela K. Starr

Latin America continues to face myriad economic, political, and social problems. The recent tangible successes achieved by countries in the region in reactivating their economies, consolidating democratic institutions, and (at least in some cases) paying back the social debt accumulated during most of the 1980s have created the appearance that national and international forces are irresistibly propelling the region toward growing market-based economies and stable democracies. Such a conclusion, however, would be misleading. Political and economic liberalizations have not always coincided neatly in Latin America. Liberal economic policies during the late nineteenth and early twentieth centuries were most often associated with authoritarian regimes or highly restricted democracies. During the 1940s and 1950s, the relationship between liberalization processes was reversed—political liberalization was associated with growing state influence in Latin American economies. Over the years, the region has also been subjected to much more instability in the realm of politics than in its broad pattern of economic development.[1] In short, Latin American history offers no evidence of an inevitable association between market economics and democratic practices.

The studies presented in this volume imply further that the current dual transition in Latin America may be no more than a happy conjunctural coincidence. The studies suggest that no clear, much less obvious, relationship exists between political and economic liberalizations. The specific experiences of the four countries that were the focus of the various chapters (Argentina, Brazil, Chile, and Mexico) belie the inevitability of a future based on robust democracies and vibrant markets. Chile is the closest to realizing the new "liberal utopia." Yet, it began its transformation under one of the most repressive military regimes in the history of Latin America and relies on more regulatory barriers to free markets than its eastern neighbor, Argentina. Chilean democracy also reflects the country's particular path to liberalization. Despite the fact that Chile's democratic tradition is unrivaled in much of the world and includes the strongest institutionalized party system in the region (Mainwaring and Scully, 1995), it remains saddled with the legacies of an authoritarian past—a restricted form of democracy and historically high levels of social inequality and exclusion.

At the opposite extreme, Argentina's military failed so miserably in its efforts to liberalize the economy that a weak democratic regime that did little to reform the state-led model of development became the only viable option for governing the country. Yet, despite growing economic problems and Argentina's historically weak political parties and democratic tradition, the democratic regime was not only able to survive but was ultimately able to implement far-reaching economic liberalization.

The ambiguity only grows when we consider the Brazilian case. The so-called Brazilian economic miracle of the 1970s was ushered in by a military regime on the basis of decidedly illiberal economic policies. Following the 1985 transition, democracy has survived despite notoriously weak political parties, high levels of corruption, and the inability, if not unwillingness, to implement significant economic liberalization.

Finally, the Mexican experience demonstrates that an authoritarian regime can retain power even as it pursues, first, state-led development and, when that exhausts itself, far-reaching economic liberalization. Moreover, growing popular frustrations with the costs of economic liberalization have produced increasing pressures for expanded political liberalization since the mid-1980s, suggesting that increased political liberalization might become an obstacle to continued economic liberalization.

Economic and political liberalizations are thus neither necessarily mutually reinforcing nor inevitably incompatible. The relationship between the two is instead rather ambiguous, but that should not imply that the interaction between political and economic liberalization is random. It is not. Rather, it is a reflection of the autonomous character of the logics that underlie these two distinct, albeit related, processes. Clearly, liberalization implies the expansion of choice, but the logic of increasing individual choice in a political setting differs from that in an economic environment. As Waisman demonstrates in this volume, economic liberalization is governed by a logic of *differentiation,* whereas a logic of *mobilization* is at the core of political liberalization. Ideally (and perhaps historically in Western Europe), the two logics should complement one another, with economic differentiation providing a structural foundation for the subsequent political mobilization of a multiplicity of autonomous actors associated with strong, vibrant civil societies. Currently in Latin America, however, tension exists between the two, particularly in those countries that developed large, state-led industrial structures as a result of the import-substituting model of industrial development (which includes the four countries of focus in this volume). In those countries, the economic differentiation associated with the shift to a market-based development strategy contributes to an excessive fragmentation of civil society (Oxhorn and Ducatenzeiler, Waisman, Garretón, and Barrera in this volume) that can undermine the consolidation of democracy. At the same time, political mobilization empowers those sectors with the most to lose from economic liberalization with the capacity to block needed reforms (Waisman, Faucher, and Kingstone in this volume).

In highlighting the tension between the political and economic components of dual transitions in Latin America, the chapters in this volume also clearly demonstrate that such tension does not inevitably generate conflict between them. Instead, the studies presented here help us to better understand the way the logics of liberalization interact by suggesting a series of mediating factors that together determine how that tension plays out. The first principal conclusion to draw from this book is that because political and economic liberalizations are governed by distinct underlying logics, any factor that influences the liberalization process may have a different impact in the economic realm than in the political realm. Characteristics of both the national and international environments at the time of liberalization will shape the relationship between political and economic liberalizations. The studies in this volume point to five relevant factors: two structural characteristics of the policy environment—extreme socioeconomic inequality and a changing sociopolitical matrix—and three more conjunctural factors—the degree of economic crisis, the character of ruling coalitions, and the nature of political institutions.

In Latin America, liberalization has taken place within the context of the region's extreme socioeconomic inequality. Economic liberalization in such an environment tends to favor those with wealth and influence and thus tends to concentrate rather than differentiate assets (Chapter 1). An increasingly unequal distribution of wealth, however, also weakens the mobilizing logic of political liberalization if those with grievances find they are unable to protect their interests by influencing government policy (Chapter 4). If the political order fails to respond to popular grievances, confidence in the utility of democracy will suffer, thereby undermining the process of democratic consolidation (Acuña and Smith, 1994). In particular, such a situation is ripe for the emergence of the kinds of nondemocratic tendencies that have plagued the region historically. We can already see this in the popularity of Alberto Fujimori's 1992 autogolpe in Peru, as well as in the high levels of popular support for the attempted military coup in Venezuela the same year. Less obvious (and therefore perhaps more ominous) are the high levels of popular support for expanding the military's role in securing domestic law and order in countries as diverse as Brazil and El Salvador.

A second factor shaping the relationship between political and economic liberalizations is the nature of the sociopolitical matrix within which liberalization occurs. The current period of liberalization, according to Garréton in this volume, is characterized by a sociopolitical matrix that is in flux.[2] The previous pattern governing relations among the state, the system of representation, and social actors has been disrupted, and new patterns are beginning to emerge. A new matrix, however, has not yet been consolidated. Essentially, this means the very nature of political representation and power is still being contested (Chapter 4). Thus, there is no guarantee that today's democratic regimes will eventually be consolidated. Nevertheless, economic liberalization has continued more or less unabated, further highlighting the autonomy of the two logics involved. The fact that the two processes have recently tended to coincide more than ever before is an encouraging development that has opened new opportunities for a positive, mutually reinforcing relationship between economic and political liberalizations that did not exist in earlier historical periods. Yet, we reiterate that it is not inevitable that Latin American countries will be able to take advantage of these opportunities.[3]

Within the environment created by socioeconomic inequality and a sociopolitical matrix that is in flux, the interaction between political and economic liberalizations is also shaped by more conjunctural characteristics of the political-economic setting. One such factor is economic crisis. Conventional wisdom teaches that an economic crisis tends to undermine a government's legitimacy and thereby to impair its capacity to overcome the obstacles to economic reform and renewed growth erected by entrenched interests. In a democratic setting, governments should find this challenge even more formidable, and their inability to resolve an economic crisis should be expected to hinder the consolidation of democracy. Severe economic crises, however, appear to enable rather than obstruct liberalizing reforms (Chapters 5 and 8; Stokes, 1996; Rodrik, 1994). A deep crisis can overcome or weaken public opposition to the potential costs associated with needed economic reforms. As the damage caused by the illness increases, the pain associated with the cure ultimately appears minor by comparison. Although any such public reaction to a severe economic crisis will inevitably have a limited life span, its short-term impact can be profound. Thus freed of significant opposition, the government can effectively implement policies to liberalize the economy. If the reforms help to renew economic growth, their success will augment the popularity and perceived legitimacy of the government, thereby helping to consolidate public support for democratic governance.

A second conjunctural factor evident in the studies contained in this volume is the nature of the ruling coalition. Not unlike the impact of socio-economic inequality, the composition of the coalition of actors backing a government will greatly influence the precise content of an economic reform program (Chapters 5, 7, and 8). Since governments will find it difficult to implement policies that damage the interests of key supporters, they will attempt to design a reform program that avoids this eventuality. The exact character of a government's liberalizing efforts will thus reflect the requirements of political survival as much as those of economic growth. The growth-enhancing potential of economic liberalization thus relies on the political needs of the ruling coalition. Only if those demands are complementary will economic liberalization tend to reinforce democratic consolidation.

The structure of a country's political institutions is the final force identified in this book as shaping the outcome of dual transitions. Institutions such as party systems and electoral laws establish the rules that govern the interaction among the multiplicity of actors in a polity. Their character, as clearly demonstrated by Kingstone in this volume, can either hinder or promote the formation of the stable governing coalitions that are indispensable to effective governance in a democratic setting. In the absence of such coalitions, governments will find it difficult to withstand the political costs associated with implementing essential yet unpopular reforms (most visibly in the Brazilian case, balancing the federal budget). The nature of political institutions thereby indirectly affects the capacity of governments to implement effective economic reform, even when such reform is necessary for the consolidation of democracy. More generally, as argued in several chapters, political institutions must also play a vital role in effectively incorporating the various segments of civil society into policymaking processes. Otherwise, the potential contradictory logics of economic and political liberalizations will result in the undermining of still fragile democratic regimes and perhaps even of the success of the economic reforms themselves.[4]

This paradox points to a second conclusion that follows from the studies presented here: at least in the current period, the success of economic liberalization appears to depend on limiting either the ability or the willingness of those affected most negatively by economic reform to influence policy. This conclusion is supported more or less clearly in every chapter, and it implies at least some limits to political liberalization during a dual transition. Moreover, the "winners" and "losers" often cut across all social sectors (Chapter 3), suggesting potentially severe restrictions on the political voice of large segments of the population (Ducatenzeiler and Oxhorn, 1994).

This conclusion implies that political barriers to economic reform are likely to be particularly significant during the middle phase of the liberalization process (Nelson, 1994a). In the near term, successful reform will stabilize the economy. As declining inflation reduces the losses suffered by the vast majority of society, economic reform develops its own natural constituency. In the medium term, however, the warm feeling resulting from price stability begins to fade (Rodrik, 1994; Acuña and Smith, 1994; and Chapter 8), and structural adjustment policies begin to threaten directly the livelihoods of well-organized sectors of society (employees of soon to be privatized state-owned industries, producers dependent on a domestic market soon to be opened to international competition, and the like). Further, during this transitional period the ultimate beneficiaries of structural reform are often unaware that they will someday benefit.

This medium-term conflict between the logics of political and economic liberalizations has been attenuated in much of Latin America as a consequence of hyperinflation and capital flows. Societies that suffered severe economic losses because of hyperinflation were traumatized by the experience. Fear of renewed inflation makes a population hesitant to use its electoral clout to penalize a government whose policies damage citizens' immediate economic interests if such action is seen to threaten price stability (Chapter 8). Although temporary, this constraint on popular pressures can significantly reduce the political costs associated with implementing structural reforms in a democratic context. Equally, the sudden availability of international capital beginning in the early 1990s reduced the tension between political and economic reforms. Capital inflows helped to produce growth during the early, historically recessionary phases of economic reform. As growth mitigated the costs of stabilization and reform, it also increased the popularity of those economic policies. The risk associated with such reliance on international capital, as demonstrated vividly in Mexico in 1995, however, is that the flows can reverse themselves (often for reasons independent of the national context) and thereby sharpen, rather than attenuate, the political obstacles to economic reform.

The obstacles to economic reform have also been overcome in the Latin American setting through authoritarian means (Ducatenzeiler and Oxhorn, 1994), especially in Mexico and Chile. In other cases, channels for political participation were restricted with the aid of a hyperinflationary crisis in a democratic framework that undermined the collective strength of key actors within civil society, particularly organized labor. In either case, economic liberalization (and the crisis that generally preceded it) often weakened the political representation of those groups most likely to challenge economic reform policies.[5]

Ultimately, it may not be a question of an inevitable tradeoff between the market and democracy but instead a question of the *types* of democracy and market that are compatible.[6] More specifically, to the extent that markets are unregulated, thereby allowing the logic of profit maximization and economic power to reign increasingly unopposed, will democratic regimes have to limit the political influence of the large numbers of citizens who lack the economic resources to participate effectively in such markets? Important questions for the future of the region (to which we will return) are thus whether the limits placed on political representation—and on political liberalization more generally—during a dual transition are inevitable or avoidable, whether they are permanent or reversible, and if they are avoidable and reversible, how that might be achieved.

This brings us to a third general conclusion that follows from the previous two: any apparent affinity between economic and political liberalizations in Latin America in recent years may be more the result of coincidence than of any inevitability. The studies presented here clearly indicate that economic liberalization does not necessarily increase democracy. Equally, the autonomous logics governing political and economic liberalization suggest that democracy may not be a necessary precondition for economic liberalization. Instead, the severity of economic crisis and its associated threat to regime stability were most often sufficient incentives to initiate economic liberalization throughout Latin America, regardless of the type of political regime in power. The price stability and improved economic performance that emerged from successful reform efforts helped authoritarian regimes in Chile and Mexico to weather the worst period of political crisis, just as similar economic successes in Brazil and Argentina (as Chapters 5 and 8 suggest) helped to eliminate a threat to political stability in a democratic setting.

The specific policy choices made by governments in their effort to build a stable, market-based economy also seem largely independent of regime type. Chapters 7 and 8 clearly demonstrate that authoritarian Mexico faced many of the same pressures in shaping government policy decisions as did more democratic countries. Chapter 8 notes further that Mexico's authoritarian regime (during the 1993–1994 period) was actually more susceptible to the sort of popular pressures that undermine the optimality of economic policy decisions—pressures most often associated with democratic governments—than was a democratic regime in Argentina. Moreover, Chapter 6 shows that some democratic regimes can be an obstacle to needed economic change, even when such change appears to be in the interest of the majority of the population. The cases analyzed in this volume thus suggest that patterns of "contestation" and "participation"[7] may either favor special interests that are able to block needed economic change at the expense of the rest of society (Brazil) or allow for the adoption of those policies at particular points in time (Argentina, Chile, and Mexico). In either case, they appear to vary, at best, only superficially with actual regime type. A political environment conducive to effective economic liberalization thus seems unrelated to the relative degree of democracy.

This third conclusion suggests that Latin American governments, whether they realize it or not, have been literally "muddling through" the myriad problems associated with the aftermath of the debt crisis, the exhaustion of the import-substituting model of development, and unconsolidated democratic institutions. The sometimes contradictory policy paths followed by countries that purport to pursue a similar objective—the simultaneous transition to political democracy and a market-based economy—suggest that policymakers are unaware of the potentially contradictory relationship between political and economic liberalizations (and often mistakenly assume that the two are largely complementary). It is our hope that the insights in this book about the interplay between political and economic liberalizations will call policymakers' attention to the tendency of these two reform efforts to conflict, especially in the medium term, but with the recognition that their precise interaction varies with the nature of the policy setting in which they are implemented. The studies in this volume illuminate five key factors that shape the reform environment and that governments can attempt to take into account to design policies well suited to their particular national contexts—policies that will encourage, rather than inadvertently undermine, a synergy between the two reform processes.

Our third conclusion is also consistent with the argument that political democracy in Latin America has been the contingent outcome of a variety of factors (Karl, 1990). There can be no doubt that diverse forces have converged to increase the likelihood that both economic and political liberalizations will be pursued in Latin America during the 1990s. Those forces include the discrediting of military governments and other nondemocratic political alternatives in the hemisphere, the end of the Cold War and greater international pressure for democratization, and a new and growing consensus on the economic policies best suited to underwrite Latin American development as the next millennium dawns (Chapter 3; Williamson, 1990c).[8] In the current period, democratic regimes have also had the advantage of being new, which has allowed for the emergence of new elites with only a minimal stake in the previous development model or economic strategy and the consequent capacity to implement alternative (sometimes radical) policies to deal with pressing economic problems (Geddes, 1995).[9] At the same time, although we disagree with the view that political instability merely reflects cycles of economic policy failure (Malloy, 1987), one cannot dismiss the possibility that the advantage might shift to "new" authoritarian regimes if the region passes through another severe economic crisis. Although we hope the "myth of authoritarian advantage" can be put to rest (Maravall, 1994), all of the studies in the current volume confirm that we cannot take political democracy for granted.

Even in an environment as conducive to a successful dual transition as the 1990s have been, however, of the four cases analyzed in this volume only Chile and Argentina can be said to have conformed to this new "ideal"—and they did so from radically different starting points and at very distinct paces. Further, even though two key sources of pressure encouraging political and economic liberalization in the Latin American context are international in character (the end of the Cold War and the rise of a neoliberal consensus), they have not led to similar attempts to undertake dual transitions elsewhere in the developing world, with the important exception of Eastern Europe.[10] The evidence once again leads us back to the conclusion that more is going on than most current studies of political and economic liberalization recognize. By examining some core assumptions of the conventional wisdom about the relationship between market economies and political democracy, this volume has begun to illuminate the underlying mechanism driving the current process of dual transitions toward both free markets and free polities.

In emphasizing the contingent nature of any relationship between economic and political liberalizations, we have deliberately emphasized that the two processes are as likely to diverge as to reinforce one another. In closing, we wish to highlight some of the insights offered in this book on ways the current coincidence between the two processes can be transformed into a truly virtuous circle of economic development and political democracy. At the most abstract and general level, such a transformation requires taking steps to ensure the health of democratic actors. As all of the chapters suggest, particularly those by Oxhorn and Ducatenzeiler, Waisman, Garretón, and Barrera, the majority of Latin Americans must be incorporated into the policymaking process through democratic institutions at the level of the state and civil society. Too often, the literature on economic development and democratization assumes that democratic institutions are somehow the inevitable result of economic development, especially if that development is based on free markets. As the present book makes very clear, this is not true, and in the worst cases the relationship may even be the reverse as economic liberalization leads to a weakening of democratic institutions. Whereas such incorporation will inevitably lead to changes in economic policies (indeed, this is one measure of the effectiveness of such incorporation), one should not assume that such changes will be detrimental to economic development. That was not the case historically in Western Europe, where economic prosperity may even have been the *outcome* of such incorporation (Schmitter and Karl, 1991); the limited evidence from Chile suggests the same may be true in Latin America as well (Weyland, 1997).

Such a positive outcome, in Chile as well as Western Europe, was the result of strong systems of representation. In particular, political party systems that covered the entire spectrum of societal interests were institutionalized, and other actors in civil society (business associations as well as labor organizations, social movements, special interest groups, and so on) were able to influence policy decisions. This outcome, in turn, will require that Latin American countries overcome current problems of representation, as well as more historical ones that go back decades.

Although it is beyond the scope of this concluding chapter to sketch solutions to the challenge of strengthening (and in some cases creating) party systems and civil societies, it is important to emphasize that the policymaking process itself will be one factor favoring (or blocking) such developments. In this sense, the clearest economic policy recommendation emanating from the case studies in this volume reflects our second and third conjunctural factors shaping the relationship between political and economic liberalization—the nature of the ruling coalition and the structure of political institutions. Chapters 6, 7, and 8 demonstrate that economic liberalization can be implemented effectively in a democratic setting as long as the reform is designed to work within the constraints imposed by political reality. Those constraints vary from country to country because the nature of political coalitions and institutions, as well as the broader policy environment, vary. The precise manner in which market-based reforms are structured and implemented in each case will also have to vary if reforms are to be consistent with the consolidation of democratic practices.

In other words, Latin American democracies should be hesitant to implement a cookie-cutter approach to neoliberal reform. As Chapter 5 demonstrates, neoliberal reform has gone forward in Brazil (beyond the deep economic crisis) in part because of the incremental pace at which it has been carried out. The Cardoso government realized, in Faucher's words, that "the democratic road to economic [reform] lies with a leader's ability to design a reform program that fits the nature and quantity of political support available." Only a gradualist approach could be successful in Brazil's particular democratic context. Equally, Chapter 7 illuminates multiple paths to effective privatization in four countries. No one approach was necessarily better than the other except with regard to how effectively it meshed with the political needs of the government undertaking reform and thus with the capacity of the government to both sustain reform and survive politically.

Beyond the need to strengthen party systems and civil society, Chapter 2 also points to the need to strengthen the regulatory power of the state. Capitalist markets in Latin America have proven to be more efficient mechanisms for generating wealth than has the state, yet their operation is not without flaws. Latin America's developing markets tend to produce perverse incentives that can undermine efficiency, generate vulnerabilities, hinder the development of human capital, and distort the distribution of wealth. The Latin American state thus must develop the capacity to regulate markets in a limited yet essential way to minimize the human and economic costs of market failures and thereby promote complementarity rather than conflict between markets and democracy.

Chapter 8 counsels a deeper sort of caution: it is possible that specific reforms within the neoliberal policy package will intensify the tendency for conflict between political and economic reform and thereby prove incompatible with democratic practices, even if economic liberalization in general is not. Starr demonstrates that this is the case with fixed exchange rates in a context of great capital mobility. Whether coupled with a currency board as in Argentina since 1991, based on a fixed set of rules as in Mexico until the end of 1994, or even constructed through a narrow target zone as in Brazil under the Real Plan, fixed exchange rates will be difficult, if not impossible, to sustain in a democratic setting with the high degree of capital mobility characteristic of the 1990s. Under these circumstances, financial liberalization should be accompanied by a more flexible exchange rate regime.

Latin America can thus aspire to both democracy and market economies, but this end point in the reform process is far from assured. If Latin American policymakers continue to muddle blindly through the reform process, they are as likely to oversee political and economic reforms that undermine one another as they are to see a happy complementarity between the two. The distinct autonomous logics that govern political and economic liberalization require that policymakers and analysts of reform must more carefully consider the impact of the constellation of forces shaping the reform process in the political as well as economic realms. Only then will it be possible to design economic reforms that are consistent with democratic practices and to deepen democracy without threatening economic liberalization.

Notes

1. It is possible to discern three fundamental shifts in Latin America's approach to development since the mid-nineteenth century. Economic liberalization and relatively free markets dominated from then until the Depression. Beginning in the 1930s, that pattern was gradually displaced by the growth of the developmentalist state with a concomitant increase in the state's penetration of society through the 1960s. Since the mid-1970s, there has been a secular trend back toward economic liberalization and free markets, with a significantly reduced role of the state in both the economy and society. In contrast, the ten countries in South America plus Mexico experienced an average of almost six changes of political regime from 1900 through 1990. If authoritarian (and stable) Mexico and Paraguay are excluded, the average is almost seven—and this figure does not include political instability that did not result in a regime change. Calculated from Rueschemeyer, Stephens, and Stephens (1992: table 5.1, 160–161).

2. In this sense, the current situation may be similar to that of the 1930s,

when economic and political instability resulted from the collapse of the world economy in 1929 (Chapter 2).

3. We will return to the future possible relationship between economic and political liberalizations at the end of this chapter.

4. We will return to this point later.

5. On this point, see Oxhorn and Ducatenzeiler (1998); as well as Chapters 2 and 4 in this volume. Brazil appears to be the major exception, with the result that economic liberalization has been fairly limited. See Chapters 5 and 6.

6. This question is addressed at length in Oxhorn and Ducatenzeiler (1998).

7. Cf. Remmer (1996), as discussed in Chapter 1.

8. A markedly distinct national and international context during the 1960s and early 1970s contributed to the emergence of military regimes throughout Latin America—the discrediting of democratic governments and the existence of a variety of "credible" authoritarian alternatives, the heating up of the Cold War and growing levels of international support (especially from the United States) for authoritarian governments, and a relatively high level of consensus among economic policymakers surrounding the necessity of a developmental state (O'Donnell, 1973; Hirschman, 1979).

9. This is perhaps another reason Brazil has been so slow to adopt neoliberal reforms: the nature of the transition and the weakness of the political system allowed for an unusually high level of continuity in the political elite with the return to democracy. See Hagopian (1996).

10. Many developing countries entered the 1980s with either a market-based economy or a political democracy, thus eliminating the need for a dual transition. Many others, especially in Africa and the Middle East, however, were characterized by closed, state-dominated economics and authoritarian political regimes, yet they failed to attempt simultaneous liberalization.

Bibliography

Abreu, Marcelo de P., and Rogério L. F. Werneck, 1993. "Privatization and Regulation in Brazil: The 1990–92 Policies and the Challenges Ahead," in Werner Baer and Michael E. Conroy, eds., "Latin America: Privatization, Property Rights, and Deregulation—I," special issue of *Quarterly Review of Economics and Finance* 33.

Accolla, Peter, 1989. "Privatization in Latin America, 1988–1989." U.S. Department of Labor, Bureau of International Labor Affairs, Washington, D.C., Foreign Labor Trends 89–20.

Acuña, Carlos H., and William C. Smith, 1994. "The Political Economy of Structural Adjustment: The Logic of Support and Opposition to Neoliberal Reform," in William C. Smith, Carlos H. Acuña, and Eduardo A. Gamarra, eds., *Latin American Political Economy in the Age of Neoliberal Reform.* New Brunswick: Transaction Books and the North-South Center, pp. 17–66.

Adams, John, 1990. "Breaking Away: India's Economy Vaults into the 1990s," in Marshall Bouton and Philip Oldenburg, eds., *India Report 1990.* Boulder: Westview, pp. 77–100.

Afonso, Jose Roberto R., and Sulamis Dain, 1987. "O Setor Publico e as Financas Publicas na America Latina: O Caso do Brasil," paper presented at Coloquio Franco-Latinoamericano sobre Finanzas Publicas y Desarrollo, IIAP-IEI/UFRJ-CEPAL, Rio de Janeiro, November.

Ahluwalia, Isher Judge, 1991. *Productivity and Growth in Indian Manufacturing.* New Delhi: Oxford University Press.

———, 1985. *Industrial Growth in India: Stagnation Since the Mid-Sixties.* New Delhi: Oxford University Press.

Alcocer V., Jorge, 1995. "Recent Electoral Reforms in Mexico: Prospects for a Real Multiparty Democracy," in Riorden Roett, ed., *The Challenge of Institutional Reform in Mexico.* Boulder: Lynne Rienner, pp. 57–75.

Allison, Graham T., 1971. *Essence of Decision: Explaining the Cuban Missile Crisis.* Boston: Little, Brown.

Almond, Gabriel, and Sidney Verba, 1963. *The Civic Culture: Political Attitudes and Democracy in Five Nations.* Princeton: Princeton University Press.

253

Altimir, Oscar, 1995. "Inequality, Employment and Poverty in Latin America: An Overview," paper presented at the conference "Poverty in Latin America: Issues and New Responses," Kellogg Institute for International Studies, University of Notre Dame, South Bend, Indiana, September 30–October 1.

———, 1993. "Income Distribution and Poverty Through Crisis and Adjustment." *CEPAL*, United Nations Working Paper, Santiago, Chile, September.

———, 1990. "Development, Crisis and Equity," *CEPAL Review* 40, April, pp. 7–28.

———, 1981. "La pobreza en América latina," *Revista de la CEPAL* 13, April, pp. 65–91.

Aragão, Murillo de, 1995. "Ação dos Grupos de Pressão nos Processos Constitucionais Recentes no Brasil," paper presented at the Latin American Studies Association, September 28–30, 1995.

———, 1992. "Ação dos Grupos de Pressão nos Processos Constitucionais Recentes no Brasil," paper presented at the seventeenth International Congress of the Latin American Studies Association, Los Angeles, California, September.

Armijo, Leslie Elliott, 1997. "India: Democratic Integrity and Financial Molasses," in Richard Bingham and Edward W. Hill, eds., *Government and Business Finance: Global Perspectives on Economic Development*. Newark: CUPR Press of Rutgers University.

———, 1996. "Inflation and Insouciance: The Peculiar Brazilian Game," *Latin American Research Review* 31, no. 3, pp. 7–46.

———, 1994. "Menem's Mania? The Timing of Privatization in Argentina," *Southwestern Journal of Law and Trade in the Americas* 1, no. 1, pp. 1–28.

Armijo, Leslie Elliott, and Prem Shankar Jha, 1997. "Center-State Relations in India and Brazil: Privatization of Electricity and Banking," *Revista de Economia Política* 17, no. 3, pp. 120–142.

Armijo, Leslie Elliott, Thomas J. Biersteker, and Abraham F. Lowenthal, 1994. "The Problems of Simultaneous Transitions," *Journal of Democracy* 5, no. 4, October, pp. 161–175.

Baer, Werner, 1995. *The Brazilian Economy: Growth and Development*. New York: Praeger.

Baer, Werner, and Annibal V. Villela, 1992. "Privatization and the Changing Role of the State in Brazil," paper presented at the seventeenth International Congress of the Latin American Studies Association, Los Angeles, California, September.

Banco de México, 1995 and 1996. *Indicadores Economicos*. Banco de México, México, DF., April, December, and February.

———, 1995. *Informe Anual, 1994*. Banco de México, México, D.F.

———, 1994. *Informe Anual, 1993*. Banco de México, México, D.F.

Baño, Rodrigo, 1985. *Lo Social y lo Politico, un Dilema Clave del Movimiento Popular*. Santiago: Facultad Latinoamericana de Ciencias Sociales (FLASCO).

Bardhan, Pranab, 1984. *The Political Economy of Development in India*. Oxford: Blackwell.

Barrera, Manuel, 1998. "Macroeconomic Adjustment in Chile and the Politics of the Popular Sectors," in P. Oxhorn and G. Ducatenzeiler, eds., *What Kind of Market? What Kind of Democracy? Latin America in the Age of Neoliberalism*. University Park: The Pennsylvania State University Press, pp. 21–41.

———, 1994. "Política de ajuste y proceso de democratización en Chile: Sus efectos sobre los trabajadores," *Mexicana de Sociología*, Universidad Nacional Autónoma de México, 56 (January–March), pp. 105–129.

Bates, Robert H., ed., 1988. *Toward a Political Economy of Development: A Rational Choice Perspective.* Berkeley: University of California Press.

Bates, Robert H., and Anne O. Krueger, eds., 1993. *Political and Economic Interactions in Economic Policy Reform: Evidence from Eight Countries.* Oxford: Blackwell.

Bazdresch, Carlos P., and Carlos Elizondo, 1993. "Privatization: The Mexican Case," in Werner Baer and Michael E. Conroy, eds., "Latin America: Privatization, Property Rights, and Deregulation—1," special issue of *Quarterly Review of Economics and Finance* 33, pp. 45–66.

Beccaria, Luís, 1993. "Estancamiento y distribución del ingreso," in Alberto Minujin, ed., *Desigualdad y exclusión, desafíos para la política social en la Argentina de fin de siglo.* Buenos Aires: UNICEF/Locasa.

Bekerman, Marta, 1986. "Financial Sector and Industrialization in Argentina: A Conflictive Relationship," paper presented at the thirteenth International Congress of the Latin American Studies Association, Boston, Massachusetts, September.

Belassa, Bela, 1986. *Toward Renewed Economic Growth in Latin America.* Washington, D.C.: Institute for International Economics.

Biersteker, Thomas J., 1992. "The Logic and Unfulfilled Promise of Privatization in Developing Countries," mimeo, Watson Institute, Brown University, Providence, R.I.

Block, Fred, 1987. *Revising State Theory.* Philadelphia: Temple University Press.

Bresser Pereira, Luiz Carlos, 1996. "Managerial Public Administration: Strategy and Structure for a New State," communication presented at the fiftieth Resumed Session of the United Nations General Assembly, "Public Administration and Development," New York, April 16.

———, 1993. "The Failure to Stabilize," paper presented at the conference "Brazil: Economic, Political and Social Reform," Institute of Latin American Studies, University of London, London.

———, ed., 1991. *Populismo Econômico. Ortodoxia, Desenvolvimentismo e Populismo na América Latina.* São Paulo: Nobel.

Bresser Pereira, Luiz Carlos, José María Maravall, and Adam Przeworski, 1993. *Economic Reforms in New Democracies: A Social-Democratic Approach.* New York: Cambridge University Press.

Bresser Pereira, Luiz Carlos, and Yoshiaki Nakano, 1994. "The Political Origin of Economic Problems," paper presented at the conference "Latin America: What Kind of Market? What Kind of Democracy?" McGill University, Montreal, April 6–8.

———, 1984. *Inflação e Recessão.* São Paulo: Brasiliense.

Camou, Antonio, 1995. *Gobernabilidad y Democracia.* Mexico City, D.F.: Instituto Federal Electoral.

Canclini, N. García, 1989. *Culturas hibridas. Estrategias para entrar y salir de la modernidad.* Mexico: Grijalbo.

Cardoso, Fernando, and Enzo Faletto, 1979. *Dependency and Development in Latin America.* Berkeley: University of California Press.

Center for Monitoring the Indian Economy (CMIE), 1991. *Basic Statistics Relating to the Indian Economy,* Vol. I: *All India.* New Delhi: Center for Monitoring the Indian Economy, August.

CEPAL (Comisión Económica para América Latina y el Caribe), 1994. *Panorama social de América Latina.* United Nations, Santiago, Chile, November.

———, 1992. *Equidad y Transformación productiva. Un enfoque integrado.* United Nations, Santiago, Chile.

———, 1990. *Magnitud de la Pobreza en América Latina en los Años Ochenta.* Santiago: CEPAL and Programa de las Naciones Unidas Para el Desarrollo.

———, 1989. *Transformación Ocupacional y Crisis Social en América Latina.* Santiago: United Nations.

———, 1988. "Equidad, Transformación Social y Democracia en América Latina," CEPAL mimeo. Santiago: United Nations.

Chitale, Varsha Bharoo, 1992. "Privatization in India," mimeo, Bangalore, Vyasa Bank.

Collier, David, ed., 1979. *The New Authoritarianism in Latin America.* Princeton: Princeton University Press.

Collier, Ruth Berins, and David Collier, 1991. *Shaping the Political Arena.* Princeton: Princeton University Press.

Comisión Nacional Bancaria y de Valores, 1995. *Boletín estadistica de banca multiple.* Mexico City, D.F.: Comisión Nacional Bancaria y Valores, December.

Cook, Maria Lorena, Kevin J. Middlebrook, and Juan Molinar Horcasitas, 1994. "The Politics of Economic Restructuring in Mexico: Actors, Sequencing, and Coalition Change," in Maria Lorena Cook, Kevin J. Middlebrook, and Juan Molinar Horcasitas, eds., *The Politics of Economic Restructuring: State-Society Relations and Regime Change in Mexico.* San Diego: Center for U.S.-Mexican Studies, University of California, San Diego, pp. 3–52.

Coppedge, Michael, 1993. "Institutions and Democratic Governance in Latin America," paper presented at the conference "Rethinking Development Theories in Latin America," University of North Carolina at Chapel Hill.

Cornelius, Wayne A., Ann L. Craig, and Jonathon Fox, eds., 1994. *Transforming State-Society Relations in Mexico: The National Solidarity Strategy.* San Diego: Center for U.S.-Mexican Studies, University of California, San Diego.

Crozier, Michel, Samuel Huntington, and Joji Watanuki, 1975. *The Crisis of Democracy: Report on the Governability of Democracies to the Trilateral Commission.* New York: New York University Press.

Dabéne, Olivier, 1994. *L'Amerique latine au Xxe siecle.* Paris: Armand Colin.

Dahl, Robert A., 1971. *Polyarchy: Participation and Opposition.* New Haven: Yale University Press.

———, 1961. *Who Governs: Democracy and Power in an American City.* New Haven: Yale University Press.

Dahrendorf, Ralf, 1988. *The Modern Social Conflict.* Berkeley: University of California Press.

Diamond, Larry, 1994. "Rethinking Civil Society: Toward Democratic Consolidation," *Journal of Democracy* 5, no. 3, April, pp. 4–17.

———, 1993. "Three Paradoxes of Democracy," in Larry Diamond and Marc F. Plattner, eds., *The Global Resurgence of Democracy.* Baltimore: Johns Hopkins University Press, pp. 95–107.

———, 1992. "Economic Development and Democracy Reconsidered," in Gary Marks and Larry Diamond, eds., *Re-examining Democracy: Essays in Honor of Seymour Martin Lipset.* Newbury Park: Sage, pp. 93–139.

Diamond, Larry, and Juan J. Linz, 1989. "Introduction: Politics, Society, and Democracy in Latin America," in Larry Diamond, Juan Linz, and Seymour Martin Lipset, eds., Vol. 4, *Democracy in Developing Countries: Latin America.* Boulder: Lynne Rienner, pp. 1–58.

Dias Carneiro, Dionísio, 1987. "Passivo do Governo e Déficit Público no Período 1970/1985," in E. Lozardo, ed., *Déficit Público Brasileiro: Política Econômica e Ajuste Estrutural.* Rio de Janeiro: Paz e Terra.

Díaz, Alvaro, 1994a. "Tendencias de la reestructuración económica y social en Latinoamérica," *Revista Mexicana de Sociología*, no. 4, October–December.

——, 1994b. "Las Transformaciones de la Estructura Social en Chile," Sur Profesionales mimeo, Santiago.

Díaz Alejandro, Carlos, 1983. "Open Economy, Closed Polity?" in Diana Tussie, ed., *Latin America in the World Economy*. Hampshire, England: Gower, pp. 21–53.

Diniz, Eli, 1995a. *Governabilidade, Democracia e Reforma do Estado: Os Desafios da Construçao de uma Nova Ordem no Brazil dos Anos 90*. Rio de Janeiro: IUPERJ.

——, 1995b. "Relaçoes Executivo-Legislativo," *Cadernos de Conjunture* (Rio de Janeiro), no. 51, May.

Dornbusch, Rudiger, 1995. "Progress Report on Argentina," in Rudiger Dornbusch and Sebastian Edwards, eds., *Reform, Recovery, and Growth: Latin America and the Middle East*. Chicago: University of Chicago Press, pp. 223–237.

——, 1991. "Lessons That Mexico Can Learn from Brazil," *Financial Times*, October 16.

Dornbusch, Rudiger, and Sebastian Edwards, eds., 1991. *The Macroeconomics of Populism in Latin America*. Chicago: University of Chicago Press.

Dornbusch, Rudiger, Ilan Goldfajn, and Rodrigo Valdes, 1995. "Currency Crises and Collapses," *Brookings Papers on Economic Activity*, no. 2.

Dornbusch, Rudiger, and Alejandro Werner, 1994. "Mexico: Stabilization, Reform, and No Growth," *Brookings Papers on Economic Activity*, no. 1.

dos Santos, M., 1994. *Estrategias de gobernabilidad en la crisis*. Comparative report on the RLA 90/011 Project, PNUD-UNESCO-CLACSO, June.

dos Santos, Wanderley Guilherme, 1996. "Exercício Findo—1995: Avaliação do primeiro Ano do Governo Fernando Henrique Cardoso," in *O Primeiro Ano do Governo de Fernando Henrique Cardoso*. Rio de Janeiro: Instituto Universitário de Pesquisas do Rio de Janeiro, no. 53, January, UFRJ.

Dresser, Denise. 1991. *Neopopulist Solutions to Neoliberal Problems: Mexico's National Solidarity Program*. Current Issues Brief Series, no. 3. La Jolla, Calif.: Center for U.S.-Mexican Studies, University of California.

Ducatenzeiler, Graciela, and Philip Oxhorn, 1994. "Democracia, autoritarismo y el problema de la gobernabilidad en América Latina," *Desarrollo Económico* 34, April–June, pp. 31–52.

Echeverri-Gent, John, 1990. "Economic Reform in India: A Long and Winding Road," in Richard E. Feinberg, John Echeverri-Gent, and Friedemann Müller, eds., *Economic Reform in Three Giants: U.S. Foreign Policy and the USSR, China, and India*. New Brunswick: Transaction, pp. 103–134.

Eckstein, Susan, 1988. *The Poverty of Revolution: The State and the Urban Poor in Mexico*, 2d ed. Princeton: Princeton University Press.

——, 1982. "The Impact of Revolution on Social Welfare in Latin America," *Theory and Society* 11, pp. 43–94.

Economic Report, 1996. *Preview Economic Report for 1995*. Buenos Aires: Republica Argentina, Ministerio de Economic y Obras Servicios Publicos, Secretaria de Programación Economica.

Economist Intelligence Unit (EIU), 1993–1995. *Country Report: Argentina*. London: EIU, various issues.

——, 1993. *Country Report: Brazil*. London: EIU.

——, 1992–1995. *Country Report: Mexico*. London: EIU, various issues.

Encarnation, Denis J., 1989. *Dislodging Multinationals: India's Strategy in Comparative Perspective*. Ithaca: Cornell University Press.

Erro, David G., 1993. *Resolving the Argentine Paradox: Politics and Development, 1966–1992*. Boulder: Lynne Rienner.

Escobar, Arturo, and Sonia Alvarez, eds., 1992. *The Making of Social Movements in Latin America*. Boulder: Westview.

Espinoza, Vicente, 1993. "Pobladores, Paricipación Social y Ciudanía: Entre los Pasajes y las Anchas Alamedas," *Proposiciones* (Santiago) 22.

Evans, Peter B., 1995. *Embedded Autonomy: States and Industrial Transformation*. Princeton: Princeton University Press.

———, 1979. *Dependent Development: The Alliance of Multinational, State, and Local Capital in Brazil*. Princeton: Princeton University Press.

Evans, Peter B., Dietrich Rueschemeyer, and Theda Skocpol, eds., 1985. *Bringing the State Back In*. Cambridge: Cambridge University Press.

Fajnzylber, Fernando, 1990. *Unavoidable Industrial Restructuring in Latin America*. Durham: Duke University Press.

Faucher, Philippe, 1993. "Políticas de Ajuste ou Erosão do Estado no Brasil?" *Dados* 36, no. 3, pp. 393–418.

Faucher, Philippe, and Blanca Heredia, 1995. "Unequal Exposure: Market Power and Trade Policy in Brazil and Mexico," paper presented at the twentieth International Congress of the Latin American Studies Association, Washington, D.C., September.

Feinberg, Richard E., 1988. "The Changing Relationship Between the World Bank and the International Monetary Fund," *International Organization* 42, no. 3, Summer, pp. 546–560.

Ffrench-Davis, Ricardo, and Stephany Griffith-Jones, eds., 1995. *Coping with Capital Surges: The Return of Finance to Latin America*. Boulder: Lynne Rienner.

Figueiredo, José, and Gerry Rogers, 1994. "Patrones de Precariedad laboral y Deprivación," *Economía y Trabajo en Chile, 1992–94*. Santiago, Programa de Economía del Trabajo.

Flynn, Peter, 1993. "Collor, Corruption and Crisis: Time for Reflection," *Journal of Latin American Studies* 25, pp. 351–371.

Frieden, Jeffry A., 1991. *Debt, Development, and Democracy: Modern Political Economy and Latin America, 1965–1985*. Princeton: Princeton University Press.

Frischtak, Leila L., 1994. *Governance, Capacity and Economic Reform in Developing Countries*. World Bank Technical Paper no. 254. Washington, D.C.: World Bank.

Garcia, N., and V. Tockman, 1985. *Acumulación, Empleo y Crisis*. Santiago: PRE-ALC.

Garretón, Manuel Antonio, 1996. "Social Movements and the Process of Democratization: A General Framework," *International Review of Sociology* 6, no. 1, pp. 39–49.

———, 1995a. "Democratización, desarrollo, modernidad. ¿Nuevas dimensiones del análisis social?" in M. A. Garretón and O. Mella, eds., *Dimensiones actuales de la Sociología*. Santiago: Bravo y Allende.

———, 1995b. "Transformacion del Estado en America Latina," *Espacios, Revista Centroamericana de Cultura Politica*, no. 6, October–December.

———, 1994a. *La faz sumergida del iceberg. Estudios sobre transformación cultural*. Santiago: CESOC.

———, 1994b. "Redefinición de gobernabilidad y cambio político," *Síntesis, Revista de Ciencias Sociales Iberoamericanas*, no. 22, July–December.

————, 1989. *The Chilean Political Process*. Boston: Allen and Unwin.

Geddes, Barbara, 1996. "Initiation of New Democratic Institutions in Eastern Europe and Latin America," in Arend Lijphart and Carlos H. Waisman, eds., *Institutional Design in New Democracies*. Boulder: Westview, pp. 15–41.

————, 1995. "The Politics of Economic Liberalization," *Latin American Research Review* 30, no. 2, pp. 195–214.

Ghosh, D. N., 1991. "Incoherent Privatization, Indian Style," *Economic and Political Weekly,* May 25, pp. 1313–1316.

Gibson, Edward, 1997. "The Populist Road to Market Reform: Policy and Electoral Coalitions in Mexico and Argentina," *World Politics* 49, no. 3, pp. 339–370.

Gil-Diaz, Francisco, and Agustin Carstens, 1996. "Some Hypotheses Related to the Mexican 1994–95 Crisis," Banco de México Research Paper no. 9601, México, D.F.

Goldstein, Judith, and Robert O. Keohane, 1993. "Ideas and Foreign Policy: An Analytical Framework," in Judith Goldstein and Robert O. Keohane, eds., *Ideas and Foreign Policy: Beliefs, Institutions, and Political Change*. Ithaca: Cornell University Press, pp. 3–30.

Graham, Carol, 1994. *Safety Nets, Politics, and the Poor: Transitions to Market Economies*. Washington, D.C.: Brookings Institution.

Griffith-Jones, Stephany, and Barbara Stallings, 1995. "New Global Financial Trends: Implications for Development," in Barbara Stallings, ed., *Global Change, Regional Response: The New International Context of Development*. Cambridge: Cambridge University Press, pp. 143–173.

Haggard, Stephan, and Robert Kaufman, 1995. *The Political Economy of Democratic Transitions*. Princeton: Princeton University Press.

————, 1994. "Democratic Institutions, Economic Policy and Performance in Latin America," in Colin Bradford, ed., *Redefining the State in Latin America*. Paris: Organization for Economic Cooperation and Development (OECD).

————, eds., 1992. *The Politics of Economic Adjustment*. Princeton: Princeton University Press.

Hagopian, Frances, 1996. *Traditional Politics and Regime Change in Brazil*. Cambridge and New York: Cambridge University Press.

————, 1992. "The Compromised Consolidation: The Political Class in the Brazilian Transition," in Scott Mainwaring, Guillermo O'Donnell, and Samuel Valenzuela, eds., *Issues in Democratic Consolidation: The South American Democracies in Comparative Perspective*. Notre Dame: Notre Dame University Press, pp. 243–293.

Hale, David, 1995. "Lessons from the Mexican Peso Crisis of 1995 for the Post Cold War International Order," World Bank Report on Mexico, February.

Hall, John A., 1995. "In Search of Civil Society," in John A. Hall, ed., *Civil Society: Theory, History, and Comparison*. Cambridge: Polity, pp. 1–31.

Hall, Peter A., 1989. "Introduction," in Peter A. Hall, ed., *The Political Power of Economic Ideas: Keynesianism Across Nations*. Princeton: Princeton University Press.

Halperín Donghi, Tulio, 1987. *El espejo de la historia: Problemas argentinos y perspectivas hispanoamericanas*. Buenos Aires: Editorial Sudamericana.

Hamilton, Nora, 1982. *The Limits of State Autonomy: Post Revolutionary Mexico*. Princeton: Princeton University Press.

Handelman, Howard, 1997. *Mexican Politics: The Dynamics of Change*. New York, St. Martin's.

Hartlyn, Jonathan, and Samuel Morley, eds., 1986. *Latin American Political Economy: Financial Crisis and Political Change.* Boulder: Westview.

Heath, Jonathan, 1995. "The Devaluation of the Mexican Peso: Economic Policy and Institutions." Washington, D.C.: Center for Strategic and International Affairs, June.

Helleiner, Eric, 1994. *States and the Reemergence of Global Finance: From Bretton Woods to the 1990s.* Ithaca: Cornell University Press.

Helwege, Ann, 1995. "Poverty in Latin America: Back to the Abyss?" *Journal of Interamerican Studies and World Affairs* 37, pp. 99–123.

Heredia, Blanca, 1994. "Making Economic Reform Politically Viable: The Mexican Experience," in William C. Smith, Carlos H. Acuña, and Eduardo A. Gamarra, eds., *Democracy, Markets, and Structural Reform in Latin America.* New Brunswick: Transaction Publishers and the North-South Center, pp. 265–295.

Hirschman, Albert, 1979. "The Turn to Authoritarianism in Latin America and the Search for Its Economic Determinants," in David Collier, ed., *The New Authoritarianism in Latin America.* Princeton: Princeton University Press, pp. 61–98.

Huntington, Samuel, 1984. "Will More Countries Become Democratic?" *Political Science Quarterly* 99, Summer, pp. 193–218.

———, 1968. *Political Order in Changing Societies.* New Haven: Yale University Press.

Huser, Herbert C., 1994. "Reforma military revisión del pasado: The Civil-Military Relationship in Democratic Argentina," paper presented at the eighteenth International Congress of the Latin American Studies Association, Atlanta, Georgia, March.

Instituto dos Estudos para o Desenvolvimento Industrial, 1991. "Carga Fiscal, Competitividade Industrial e Potencial de Crescimento Econômico," *Mudar para Competir,* August.

International Advisory Services Group, 1991. "The Tax Burden and Effective Rates of Protection for Various International Producers." Washington, D.C.: International Advisory Services Group, May.

IMF (International Monetary Fund), 1995. *World Economic Outlook.* Washington, D.C.: IMF, March.

———, 1993–1996. *International Financial Statistics.* Washington, D.C: IMF.

Jalan, Bimal, 1991. *India's Economic Crisis: The Way Ahead.* New Delhi: Oxford University Press.

Jha, Prem Shankar, 1980. *India: A Political Economy of Stagnation.* New Delhi: Oxford University Press.

Kahler, Miles, 1992. "External Influence, Conditionality, and the Politics of Adjustment," in Stephan Haggard and Robert R. Kaufman, eds., *The Politics of Economic Adjustment.* Princeton: Princeton University Press, pp. 89–136.

Kanitz, Stephen Charles, 1991. "O Peso da Carga Tributária nas Empresas," study conducted for the periodical *Exame,* São Paulo, Brazil.

Karl, Terry, 1990. "Dilemmas of Democratization in Latin America," *Comparative Politics* 23, no. 1, October, pp. 1–21.

Kingstone, Peter, 1994. "Shaping Business Interests: The Politics of Neoliberalism in Brazil, 1985–1992," Ph.D. dissertation, University of California, Berkeley.

Kohli, Atul, 1993. "Democracy Amid Economic Orthodoxy: Trends in Developing Countries," *Third World Quarterly* 14, November, pp. 671–689.

———, 1990. "The Politics of Economic Liberalization in India," in Ezra N. Suleiman and John Waterbury, eds., *The Political Economy of Public Sector Reform and Privatization.* Boulder: Westview, pp. 364–388.

Kuznets, S., 1955. "Economic Growth and Income Inequality," *American Economic Review* 45, March, pp. 1–28.

Lamounier, Bolivar, and Edmar Lisboa Bacha, 1993. "Redemocratization and the Impasse of Economic Reform in Brazil," paper presented at Overseas Development Council Conference on Interactions Between Redemocratization and Market-Oriented Reforms in Latin America and Eastern Europe, Washington, D.C., April.

Lamounier, Bolivar, and Amaury de Souza, 1995. *O Congresso Nacional e as Reformas.* São Paulo: Relatório de Pesquisa, IDESP.

Langston, Joy, 1990. "Privatization in Mexico: An Early Appraisal," paper presented at the nineteenth International Congress of the Latin American Studies Association, Washington, D.C., September.

Leftwich, Adrian, 1994. "Governance, the State and the Politics of Development," *Development and Change* 25, pp. 363–386.

———, 1993. "Governance, Democracy and Development in the Third World," *Third World Quarterly* 14, no. 3, pp. 605–624.

Lewis, Paul H., 1990. *The Crisis of Argentine Capitalism.* Chapel Hill: University of North Carolina Press.

Lijphart, Arend, and Carlos H. Waisman, eds., 1996. *Institutional Design in New Democracies: Eastern Europe and Latin America.* Boulder: Westview.

Linz, Juan, 1975. "Totalitarian and Authoritarian Regimes," in F. Greenstein and N. Polsby, eds., *Handbook of Political Science,* Vol. 3. Reading, Mass.: Addison-Wesley, pp. 175–411.

Linz, Juan, and Arturo Valenzuela, eds., 1994. *The Failure of Presidential Democracy: Latin America.* Baltimore: Johns Hopkins University Press.

Lipset, Seymour Martin, 1994. "The Social Requisites of Democracy Revisited," *American Sociological Review* 59, February, pp. 1–22.

———, 1959. "Some Social Requisites of Democracy: Economic Development and Political Legitimacy," *American Political Science Review* 53, March, pp. 69–105.

Loaeza, Solidad, 1992. "The Role of the Right in Political Change in Mexico," in Douglas Chalmers, Maria Carmo Campello de Souza, and Atilio Boron, eds., *The Right and Democracy in Latin America.* New York: Praeger, pp. 128–141.

Lustig, Nora, 1994. "Solidarity and the Strategy of Poverty Alleviation," in Wayne Cornelius, Ann Craig, and Jonathan Fox, eds., *Transforming State-Society Relations in Mexico: The National Solidarity Strategy.* San Diego: Center for U.S.-Mexican Studies, University of California, San Diego, pp. 79–96.

———, 1992. *Mexico: The Remaking of an Economy.* Washington, D.C.: Brookings Institution.

Lynch, Juan, 1992. *Caudillos in Spanish America, 1800–1850.* Oxford: Clarendon Press.

Maciel, Claudio Schuller, 1990. "Padrão de Investimento Indústrial nos Anos 90 e Suas Implicações para a Política Tecnológica," in Luciano Coutinho and Wilson Suzigan, eds., *Desenvolvimento Tecnológico da Indústria e a Constituição de um Sistema Nacional de Inovação no Brasil.* Campinas: IPT/FECAMP contract-Instituto de Economia/UNICAMP, 1991.

Macpherson, Crawford B., 1977. *The Life and Times of Liberal Democracy.* Oxford: Oxford University Press.

Mainwaring, Scott, 1995. "Brazil: Weak Parties, Feckless Democracy," in Scott Mainwaring and Timothy R. Scully, eds., *Building Democratic Institutions: Party Systems in Latin America.* Stanford: Stanford University Press, pp. 354–398.

———, 1992. "Dilemmas of Multiparty Presidential Democracy: The Case of Brazil," paper presented at the Helen Kellogg Institute for International Studies, South Bend, Indiana, March.

———, 1991. "Politicians, Parties, and Electoral Systems: Brazil in Comparative Perspective," *Comparative Politics* 24, October, pp. 21–44.

Mainwaring, Scott, and Timothy R. Scully, 1995. "Introduction: Party Systems in Latin America," in Scott Mainwaring and Timonthy R. Scully, eds., *Building Democratic Institutions: Party Systems in Latin America.* Stanford: Stanford University Press, pp. 1–34.

Malloy, James, 1991. "Democracy, Economic Crisis and the Problem of Governance: The Case of Bolivia," *Studies in Comparative International Development* 26, no. 2, pp. 37–57.

———, 1987. "The Politics of Transition in Latin America," in James Malloy and Mitchell Seligson, eds., *Authoritarians and Democrats: Regime Transition in Latin America.* Pittsburgh: University of Pittsburgh Press, pp. 235–258.

Manzetti, Luigi, 1995. "Argentina: Market Reforms and Old-Style Politics," *North-South Focus* 4, no. 3, pp. 2–4.

———, 1993. *Institutions, Parties, and Coalitions in Argentine Politics.* Pittsburgh: University of Pittsburgh Press.

———, 1992. "The Political Economy of Privatization Through Divestiture in Lesser Developed Economies: The Case of Argentina," paper presented at the seventeenth International Congress of the Latin American Studies Association, Los Angeles, California, September.

Manzetti, Luigi, and Charles Blake, 1996. "Corruption and Market Reforms: New Means for Old Ways," *Review of International Political Economy* 3, December, pp. 662–697.

Maravall, José María, 1994. "The Myth of Authoritarian Advantage," *Journal of Democracy* 5, October, pp. 17–31.

Marshall, Thomas H., 1950. *Citizenship and Social Class and Other Essays.* Cambridge: Cambridge University Press.

Martins, Luciano, 1993. "Reform of Public Administration and Political Culture in Brazil: An Overview." Washington, D.C.: Inter-American Development Bank, Department of Operations.

McGuire, James W., 1995. "Political Parties and Democracy in Argentina," in Scott Mainwaring and Timothy R. Scully, eds., *Building Democratic Institutions: Party Systems in Latin America.* Stanford: Stanford University Press, pp. 200–246.

Mesa-Lago, Carmelo, 1989. *Ascent to Bankruptcy: Financing Social Security in Latin America.* Pittsburgh: University of Pittsburgh Press.

———, 1978. *Social Security in Latin America: Pressure Groups, Stratification and Inequality.* Pittsburgh: University of Pittsburgh Press.

MIDEPLAN, 1995. "Resulatados de Encuestas de Caracterización Socioeconómica Nacional, CASEN 1994, Segundo Informe," MIDEPLAN mimeo, Santiago, September.

Minujin, Alberto, and Gabriel Kessler, 1995. *La Nueva Pobreza en la Argentina.* Buenos Aires: Planeta.

Montclair, Stéphane, 1994. "Le quasi-impeachment du Président Collor," *Revue française de science politique* 44, no. 1, February, pp. 23–48.

Morandé, Pedro, 1984. *Cultura y Modernización en América Latina.* Santiago: Cuadernos del Instituto de Sociología, Universidad Católica de Chile.

Muller, Edward N., 1988. "Democracy, Economic Development, and Income Inequality," *American Sociological Review* 53, February, pp. 50–68.

Muñoz, Oscar, and Carmen Celedón, 1993. "Chile en transición: estrategia económica y política," in Juan Morales and Gary McMahon, eds., *La política económica en la transición a la democracia. Lecciones de Argentina, Bolivia, Chile, Uruguay.* Santiago: CIEPLAN.

Murillo, M. V., 1997. "Union Politics, Market-Oriented Reforms, and the Reshaping of Argentine Corporatism," in D. Chalmers, C. Vilas, K. Hite, S. Martin, K. Piester, and M. Segarra, eds., *The New Politics of Inequality in Latin America: Rethinking Participation and Representation.* Oxford: Oxford University Press, pp. 72–94.

Nelson, Joan, 1994a. "How Market Reforms and Democratic Consolidation Affect Each Other," in Joan Nelson, ed., *Intricate Links: Democratization and Market Reforms in Latin America and Eastern Europe.* Washington, D.C.: Overseas Development Council, pp. 1–36.

———, 1994b. "Linkages Between Politics and Economics," *Journal of Democracy* 5, no. 4, October, pp. 49–62.

———, ed., 1990. *Economic Crisis and Policy Choice: The Politics of Adjustment in the Third World.* Princeton: Princeton University Press.

———, ed., 1994c. *Intricate Links: Democratization and Market Reforms in Latin America and Eastern Europe.* Washington, D.C.: Overseas Development Council.

Norden, Deborah L., 1990. "Democratic Consolidation and Military Professionalism: Argentina in the 1980s," *Journal of Interamerican Studies and World Affairs* 32, no. 3, Fall, pp. 151–176.

Nylen. William R., 1992. "'Neoliberalismo para Todo Menos Eu': Brazil and the Neoliberal Solution," in Douglas A. Chalmers, Maria Carmo Campello de Souza, and Atilio Boron, eds., *The Right and Democracy in Latin America.* New York: Praeger.

OECD (Organization for Economic Cooperation and Development), 1995. *La gestion publique en mutation: Les réformes dans les pays de l'OCDE.* Paris: OECD.

O'Donnell, Guillermo, 1996. "Illusions About Consolidation," *Journal of Democracy* 7, April, pp. 34–51.

———, 1994. "Delegative Democracy," *Journal of Democracy* 5, no. 1, January, pp. 56–69.

———, 1993. "On the State, Democratization and Some Conceptual Problems: A Latin American View with Glances at Some Postcommunist Countries," *World Development* 21, no. 8, August, pp. 1355–1369.

———, 1992. "Transitions, Continuities and Paradoxes," in Scott Mainwaring, Guillermo O'Donnell, and Samuel Valenzuela, eds., *Issues in Democratic Consolidation: The South American Democracies in Comparative Perspective.* Notre Dame: Notre Dame University Press, pp. 17–56.

———, 1988. "State and Alliances in Argentina, 1956–1976," in Robert Bates, ed., *Toward a Political Economy of Development.* Berkeley: University of California Press, pp. 176–205.

———, 1973. *Modernization and Bureaucratic Authoritarianism: Studies in South American Politics.* Berkeley: Institute of International Studies, University of California, Berkeley.

O'Donnell, Guillermo, and Philippe Schmitter, 1986. *Transitions from Authoritarian Rule: Tentative Conclusions About Uncertain Democracies.* Baltimore: Johns Hopkins University Press.

Oliveira, Gesner, 1991. "Condicionantes e Diretrizes de Política para a Abertura Comercial Brasileira." São Paulo: IPEA Research Project, CEBRAP, February.

Oliveira, Gesner, and Celso Toledo, 1995. "The Brazilian Economy Under the Real: Prospects for Stabilization and Growth," paper presented at the nineteenth International Congress of the Latin American Studies Association, Washington, D.C., September.

Oppenheimer, Andres, 1996. *Bordering on Chaos.* New York: Little, Brown.

Oszlak, Oscar, 1981. "The Historical Formation of the State in Latin America: Some Theoretical and Methodological Guidelines for Its Study," *Latin American Research Review* 16, no. 2, pp. 3–32.

Oxhorn, Philip, 1998a. "Is the Century of Corporatism Over? Neoliberalism and the Rise of Neopluralism," in Philip Oxhorn and Graciela Ducatenzeiler, eds., *What Kind of Democracy? What Kind of Market? Latin America in the Age of Neoliberalism.* University Park: Pennsylvania State University Press, pp. 195–217.

———, 1998b. "The Social Foundations of Latin America's Recurrent Populism: Problems of Class Formation and Collective Action," *Journal of Historical Sociology* 11, pp. 212–246.

———, 1995a. "From Controlled Inclusion to Coerced Marginalization: The Struggle for Civil Society in Latin America," in John Hall, ed., *Civil Society: Theory, History and Comparison.* Cambridge: Polity, pp. 250–277.

———, 1995b. *Organizing Civil Society: The Popular Sectors and the Struggle for Democracy in Chile.* University Park: Pennsylvania State University Press.

———, 1992. *Class Formation or Class Deformation? The Popular Sectors and the Concept of Class in Latin America.* Montreal: Working Papers in Political Science, Department of Political Science, McGill University, nos. 92–93, November.

Oxhorn, Philip, and Graciela Ducatenzeiler, 1994. "Social Policies as Political Strategies: Processes of Inclusion and Exclusion," paper presented at the Latin American Studies Association International Congress, Atlanta, Georgia, March.

———, eds., 1998. *What Kind of Market? What Kind of Democracy? Latin America in the Age of Neoliberalism.* University Park: Pennsylvania State University Press.

Palermo, Vicente, 1995. "¡Síganme! La política de las reformas estructurales: El caso argentino, 1989–1993," Ph.D. dissertation, Universidad Cumplutense, Madrid.

Payne, Leigh A., 1994. *Brazilian Industrialists and Democratic Change.* Baltimore: Johns Hopkins University Press.

Petrecolla, Alberto, Alberto Proto, and Pablo Gerchunoff, 1993. "Privatization in Argentina," in Werner Baer and Michael E. Conroy, eds., "Latin America: Privatization, Property Rights, and Deregulation—1," special issue of *Quarterly Review of Economics and Finance* 33, pp. 67–93.

Pfeffermann, Guy P., and Andrea Madarassy, 1992. "Trends in Private Investment in Developing Countries 1993: Statistics for 1970–91," Discussion Paper 16. Washington, D.C.: International Finance Corporation.

Pinheiro, Armando Castelar, and L. C. de Oliveira Filho, 1991. "Privatização no Brasil: Passado, planos e perspectivas," mimeo, IPEA, Rio de Janeiro, August.

Pinheiro, Armando Castelar, and Ben Ross Schneider, 1993. "The Fiscal Impact of Privatization in Latin America," paper presented at the Latin America 2000 Conference, University of Texas at Austin, November.

Pinto, Aníbal, 1970. "Desarrollo económico y relaciones sociales," in Aníbal Pinto et al., *Chile, hoy.* Mexico: Siglo Veintiuno Editores, pp. 5–52.

Pion-Berlin, David, 1992. "Crafting Allegiance: Civilian Control and the Armed Forces in Uruguay, Argentina, and Chile," Discussion Paper no. 28, Center for International Studies, University of Southern California.

Portes, Alejandro, 1989. "Latin American Urbanization in Years of Crisis," *Latin American Research Review* 24, no. 3, pp. 7–44.

―――, 1985. "Latin American Class Structures: Their Composition and Change During the Last Decades," *Latin American Research Review* 20, no. 3, pp. 7–39.

Power, Timothy J., 1991. "Politicized Democracy: Competition, Institutions and 'Civic Fatigue' in Brazil," *Journal of Interamerican Studies and World Affairs* 33, no. 3, pp. 75–112.

Presidency of the Republic of Brazil, 1995. *White Paper: Reform of the State Apparatus*. Brasilia: Ministry of Federal Administration and State Reform.

Programa de Economía del Trabajo (PET), various years. *Economía y Trabajo en Chile*. Santiago: Informe Anual, PET.

Przeworski, Adam, 1985. *Capitalism and Social Democracy*. Cambridge: Cambridge University Press.

Przeworski, Adam, Michael Alvarez, José Antonio Cheibub, and Fernando Limongi, 1996. "What Makes Democracies Endure?" *Journal of Democracy* 7, no. 2, January, pp. 38–55.

Przeworski, Adam, et al., 1995. *Sustainable Democracy*. Cambridge: Cambridge University Press.

Przeworski, Adam, and Fernando Limongi, 1993. "Political Regimes and Economic Growth," *Journal of Economic Perspectives* 7, no. 3, pp. 51–69.

Putnam, Robert, 1993. *Making Democracy Work: Civic Traditions in Modern Italy*. Princeton: Princeton University Press.

Ramamurti, Ravi, 1992. "Impact of Privatization on the Latin American Debt Problem," *Journal of Interamerican Studies and World Affairs* 34, no. 2, Summer, pp. 94–125.

―――, 1987. *State-Owned Enterprises in High Technology Industries: Studies in India and Brazil*. New York: Praeger.

Ramirez de la O, Rogelio, 1993. "Economic Report on Mexico—September 1993." Mexico City: Ecanal, October.

Razeto, Luis, 1993. "Ideas Para un Proyecto de Desarrollo de un Sector de Economía Popular de Solidaridad y Trabajo Para Superar la Pobreza," in *Economía y Trabajo en Chile, Informe Anual*. Santiago: PET.

Remmer, Karen, 1996. "The Sustainability of Political Democracy: Lessons from South America," *Comparative Political Studies* 29, no. 3, December, pp. 611–634.

―――, 1991. "The Political Impact of Economic Crisis in Latin America in the 1980s," *American Political Science Review* 85, no. 3, September, pp. 777–799.

―――, 1990. "Democracy and Economic Crisis: The Latin American Experience," *World Politics* 17, April, pp. 315–335.

Republica Argentina, Ministerio de Economic y Obras Servicios Publicos, Secretaria de Programacion Economica, 1996. *Preview Economic Report for 1995*. Buenos Aires.

―――, 1995. *Economic Report for 1994*. Buenos Aires.

Ribeiro, Carlos A. C., 1992. "Efficiência técnica de empresas públicos e privadas no Brasil: 1978–1988," Ph.D. thesis, Department of Economics, University of São Paulo, Brazil.

Rodrik, Dani, 1994. "The Rush to Free Trade in the Developing World: Why So Late? Why Now? Will It Last?" in Stephan Haggard and Stephen B. Webb, eds., *Voting for Reform: Democracy, Political Liberalization, and Economic Adjustment.* New York: Oxford University Press, pp. 61–88.

Rostow, Walt W., 1960. *Stages of Economic Growth.* Cambridge: Cambridge University Press.

Rueschemeyer, Dietrch, Evelyne Stephens, and John Stephens, 1992. *Capitalist Development and Democracy.* Chicago: University of Chicago Press.

Ruiz-Tagle, Jaime, 1993. "Reducción de la pobreza y distribución de los ingresos en Chile," *Mensaje* 42, December, pp. 640–643.

Sachs, Jeffrey, Aaron Tornell, and Andres Velasco, 1995. *The Collapse of the Mexican Peso: What Have We Learned?* Cambridge: National Bureau of Economic Research, June.

Sachs, Jeffrey, and Álvaro Zini, 1995. "Brazilian Inflation and the 'Plano Real,'" paper presented at the nineteenth International Congress of the American Studies Association, Washington, D.C., September.

Salazar, Gabriel, 1990. *Violencia Política Popular en las "Grandes Alamedas."* Santiago: Ediciones Sur.

Schamis, Hector E., 1995. "On the Relationship Between Political and Economic Reform: The Chilean Experience," in Leslie Elliott Armijo, ed., *Conversations on Democratization and Economic Reform.* Los Angeles: Center for International Studies, School of International Relations, University of Southern California, pp. 164–178.

Schmitter, Philippe, and Terry Lynn Karl, 1991. "What Democracy Is . . . And Is Not," *Journal of Democracy* 2, Summer, pp. 75–89.

Schneider, Ben Ross, 1995. "Democratic Consolidations: Some Broad Comparisons and Sweeping Arguments," *Latin American Research Review* 30, no. 2, pp. 215–234.

———, 1992a. "A Privatização no Governo Collor, Triunfo do Liberalismo o Colapso do Estado Desenvolvimentista?" *Revista de Economia Política* 12, no. 1, January–March, pp. 5–18.

———, 1992b. "Privatization in the Collor Government: Triumph of Liberalism or Collapse of the Developmental State?" in Douglas A. Chalmers, Maria Carmo Campello de Souza, and Atilio A. Boron, eds., *The Right and Democracy in Latin America.* New York: Praeger, pp. 225–238.

———, 1991. "Brazil Under Collor: Anatomy of a Crisis," *World Policy Journal* 8, no. 2, Spring, pp. 321–347.

———, 1990. "The Politics of Privatization in Brazil and Mexico: Variations on a Statist Theme," in Ezra N. Suleiman and John Waterbury, eds., *The Political Economy of Public Sector Reform and Privatization.* Boulder: Westview, pp. 319–345.

Schumpeter, Joseph, 1950. *Capitalism, Socialism and Democracy.* New York: Harper and Row.

Schvarzer, Jorge, 1998. "Economic Reform in Argentina: Which Social Forces for What Aims?" in Phillip Oxhorn and Graciela Ducatenzeiler, eds., *What Kind of Democracy? What Kind of Market? Latin America in the Age of Neoliberalism.* University Park: Pennsylvania State University Press, pp. 61–88.

SECC (Secretaría de Comunicación y Cultura del Ministerio), 1996. "Juntas de Vecinos: Claves de la Participación," *Zona Pública,* no. 11. Santiago: Secretaría de Comunicación y Cultura, Ministerio, Secretaría General de Gobierno.

Short, R. P., 1984. "The Role of Public Enterprise: An International Statistical Comparison," in Robert Floyd, Clive S. Gray, and R. P. Short, eds., *Public*

Enterprise in Mixed Economies. Washington, D.C.: International Monetary Fund, pp. 110–181.

Silva, Eduardo, 1992–1993. "Capitalist Regime Loyalties and Redemocratization in Chile," *Journal of Interamerican Studies and World Affairs* 34, no. 4, Winter, pp. 77–103.

Skidmore, Thomas E., 1989. "Brazil's Slow Road to Democratization: 1974–1985," in Alfred Stepan, ed., *Democratizing Brazil: Problems of Transition and Consolidation.* Princeton: Princeton University Press, pp. 5–42.

———, 1988. *The Politics of Military Rule in Brazil 1964–85.* New York: Oxford University Press.

Smith, William, 1991. "State, Market, and Neoliberalism in Post-Transition Argentina: The Menem Experiment," *Journal of Interamerican Studies and World Affairs* 33, no. 4, Winter, pp. 45–82.

Smith, William, Carlos Acuña, and Eduardo Gamarra, eds., 1994. *Latin American Political Economy in the Age of Neoliberal Reform: Theoretical and Comparative Perspectives for the 1990s.* Miami: University of Miami North-South Center.

Stallings, Barbara, 1992. "International Influence on Economic Policy: Debt, Stabilization, and Structural Reform," in Stephan Haggard and Robert R. Kaufman, eds., *The Politics of Economic Adjustment.* Princeton: Princeton University Press, pp. 41–88.

Starr, Pamela K., 1997. "Government Coalitions and the Viability of Currency Boards: Argentina Under the Cavallo Plan," *Journal of Interamerican Studies and World Affairs* 39, no. 2, Summer, pp. 83–133.

Stokes, Susan, 1996. "Introduction: Public Opinion and Market Reforms: The Limits of Economic Voting," *Comparative Political Studies* 29, October, pp. 499–519.

Tavares de Almeida, Maria Herminia, 1995. "Pragmatism by Necessity: The Brazilian Path of Economic Reform," paper presented at the IIS-CLAS Democratization Seminar, Stanford University, Stanford, California, February 1.

Taylor, Charles L., and Michael C. Hudson, 1972. *World Handbook of Political and Social Indicators,* 2d ed. New Haven: Yale University Press.

Torre, Juan Carlos, 1994. "The Politics of Transformation in Historical Perspective," paper presented at the workshop "Social Change in Latin America: Toward the Year 2000," University of Maryland at College Park, April 8–9.

———, 1993. "The Politics of Economic Crisis in Latin America," *Journal of Democracy* 4, no. 1, January, pp. 104–116.

Touraine, Alain, 1995. *¿Qué es la democracia?* Mexico: Fondo de Cultura Económica.

———, 1989. *La parole et le sang. Politique et societe en Amerique Latine.* Paris: Editiones Odille Jacob.

———, 1987. *Actores Sociales y Sistemas Políticos en América Latina.* Santiago: PREALC/OIT.

Trebat, Thomas J., 1983. *Brazil's State-Owned Enterprises: A Case Study of the State as Entrepreneur.* Cambridge: Cambridge University Press.

Usher, Dan, 1981. *The Economic Prerequisite to Democracy.* New York: Columbia University Press.

Valenzuela, Arturo, 1978. *The Breakdown of Democratic Regimes: Chile.* Baltimore: Johns Hopkins University Press.

Valenzuela, Eduardo, 1993. "Sistema Político y Actores Sociales en Chile," *Proposiciones* (Santiago) 22, pp. 112–136.

Valenzuela J., Samuel, 1985. *Democratización vía reforma: La expansión del sufragio en Chile.* Buenos Aires: Ediciones del IDES.

Vergara, Pilar, 1994. "Market Economy, Social Welfare, and Democratic Consolidation in Chile," in William C. Smith, Carlos H. Acuña, and Eduardo Gamarra, eds., *Democracy, Markets, and Structural Reform in Latin America.* New Brunswick: Transaction Publishers and the North-South Center, pp. 237–261.

Viner, Jacob, 1958. *The Long View and the Short: Studies in Economic Theory and Policy.* Glencoe: Free Press.

Waisman, Carlos H., 1992. "Capitalism, the Market, and Democracy," *American Behavioral Scientists* 35, nos. 4–5, pp. 500–516; reprinted in Larry Diamond and Gary Marks, eds., 1992, *Democracy in Comparative Perspective: Essays in Honor of Seymour Martin Lipset.* Newbury Park: Sage, pp. 140–155.

———, 1987. *Reversal of Development in Argentina.* Princeton: Princeton University Press.

Walton, John, 1985. "Popular Protest and the International Economy: The I.M.F. Riots," paper presented at the conference "The Impact of the Current Economic Crisis of the Social and Political Structure of the Newly Industrialized Nations," São Paulo, Brazil, February 24–March 1.

Ward, Peter M., 1993. "Social Welfare Policy and Political Opening in Mexico," *Journal of Latin American Studies* 25, October, pp. 613–628.

Weber, Max, 1944. *Economía y Sociedad, Tipo de Dominación.* Mexico City: Fondo de Cultura Económica.

Weffort, Francisco C., 1991. "America Astray," Helen Kellogg Institute for International Studies, University of Notre Dame, Working Paper no. 162.

Weyland, Kurt, forthcoming. "The Fragmentation of Business in Brazil," in Francisco Durand and Eduardo Silva, eds., *Business Peak Associations in Latin America.* Boulder: Westview.

———, 1997. "Growth With Equity in Chile's New Democracy," *Latin American Research Review* 32, no. 1, 37–67.

———, 1996. "Risk Taking in Latin American Economic Restructuring: Lessons from Prospect Theory," *International Studies Quarterly,* no. 40, pp. 185–208.

———, 1995. "How Much Political Power Do Economic Forces Have? Conflicts over Social Insurance Reform in Contemporary Brazil," paper presented at the nineteenth International Congress of the Latin American Studies Association, Washington, D.C., September.

———, 1992. "The Dispersion of Business Influence in Brazil's New Democracy," paper presented at the American Political Science Association, Chicago, September 3–6.

Williamson, John. 1990a. "The Progress of Policy Reform in Latin America," in John Williamson, ed., *Latin American Adjustment: How Much Has Happened?* Washington, D.C.: Institute for International Economics, pp. 353–420.

———, 1990b. "What Washington Means by Policy Reform," in John Williamson, ed., *Latin American Adjustment: How Much Has Happened?* Washington, D.C.: Institute for International Economics, pp. 8–17.

———, ed., 1990c. *Latin American Adjustment: How Much Has Happened?* Washington, D.C.: Institute for International Economics.

World Bank, various years. *World Development Report.* Washington, D.C.: World Bank.

————, various years. *World Tables.* Washington, D.C.: World Bank.

————, 1995a. *Social Indicators of Development.* Baltimore: Johns Hopkins University Press.

————, 1995b. *Trends in Developing Economies.* Washington, D.C.: World Bank.

————, 1993. *Trends in Developing Economies,* Extracts, vol. 3, *Emerging Markets.* Washington, D.C.: World Bank.

————, 1992. *The Political Economy of Poverty, Equity, and Growth in Brazil and Mexico.* New York: Oxford University Press.

————, 1990. *World Development Report.* New York: Oxford University Press.

Zapata, F., 1998. "Trade Unions and the Corporatist System in Mexico," in Philip Oxhorn and Graciela Ducatenzeiler, eds., *What Kind of Democracy? What Kind of Market? Latin America in the Age of Neoliberalism.* University Park: Pennsylvania State University Press, pp. 151–167.

Zea, Leopoldo, 1980. *Pensamiento Positivista Latinoamericano.* Caracas: Biblioteca Ayacucho.

About the Contributors

Leslie Elliott Armijo, editor of *Financial Globalization and Democracy in Emerging Markets* (Basingstoke, UK: Macmillan; New York: St. Martin's, forthcoming), is the author of various articles on the interaction of democracy and economic reform and the politics of inflation, privatization, and financial reform. Her next book is *Democracy and Inflation: The Politics of Finance in Brazil and India*.

Manuel Barrera has been a professor and researcher for a number of years at the Universidad de Chile and the Universidad Católica de Chile. He was also founder and director of the Centro de Estudios Sociales. A specialist in labor studies and the politics of the popular sectors, his numerous publications include *Sindicatos bajo regímenes militares: Argentina, Brasil, Chile* (United Nations Research Institute for Social Development, 1990).

Graciela Ducatenzeiler is professor of political science and director of the Latin America Research Group at the Université de Montréal. Her various publications have focused on organized labor, politics, and populism in Latin America, with an emphasis on Argentina. These include *Syndicats et politique en Argentine* (Presses de l' Université de Montréal, 1980). She is coeditor, with Philip Oxhorn, of *What Kind of Market? What Kind of Democracy? Latin America in the Age of Neoliberalism* (Pennsylvania State University Press, 1998).

Philippe Faucher is a professor of political science at the Université de Montréal. He is author of *Le Bresil des militaires* (Presses de l'Universite de Montréal, 1981) and coeditor, with Thomas Bruneau, of *Authoritarian*

Capitalism: Brazil's Contemporary Economic and Political Development (Westview Press, 1981). His current research focuses on state reform and democracy, trade and technology policies, and industrial strategies.

Manuel Antonio Garretón is a professor of sociology at the University of Chile. He has published and lectured extensively on democratization, social movements, culture, and education in Latin America and Chile. His publications include *The Chilean Political Process* (Unwin and Hyman, 1989), *La faz sumergida del Iceberg: Estudio sobre la transformación cultural* (CESOC-LOM, 1994), and *Hacia una nueva era política: Estudio sobre las democratizaciones* (Fondo de Cultura Económica, 1995).

Peter Kingstone is assistant professor of political science at the University of Vermont. He is the author of *Crafting Coalitions for Reform* (Pennsylvania State University Press, forthcoming) and coeditor of *Democratic Brazil* (University of Pittsburgh Press, forthcoming).

Philip Oxhorn is associate professor of political science at McGill University. He is author of *Organizing Civil Society: The Popular Sectors and the Struggle for Democracy in Chile* (Pennsylvania State University Press, 1995) and coeditor, with Graciela Ducatenzeiler, of *What Kind of Market? What Kind of Democracy? Latin America in the Age of Neoliberalism* (Pennsylvania State University Press, 1998). He has published widely on the topics of civil society, social movements, and democratization.

Pamela K. Starr is a professor of international studies at the Institúto Tecnológico Autónomo de México. Her publications have focused on the comparative political economy of exchange rates, capital flows, and broader monetary policy in Latin America.

Carlos H. Waisman is professor of sociology and department chair at the University of California, San Diego. His extensive list of publications on issues of comparative political sociology includes *Reversal of Development in Argentina: Postwar Counterrevolutionary Policies and Their Structural Consequences* (Princeton University Press, 1987) and is coeditor, with Arend Lijphart, of *Institutional Design in New Democracies: The Cases of Eastern Europe and Latin America* (Westview Press, 1996).

Index

Aerolíneas Argentinas, 176
Aerolíneas Mexicanas, 176
Aeroméxico, 176
Air India, 193
Alberdi, Juan, 18
Alcalis, 178
Alfonsín, Raul, 163, 175, 180–182
Allende, Salvador, 87
Alsogaray, Alvaro, 183
Altimir, Oscar, 22
Alvarez, Michael, 21
Apathy, 84, 90
Argentina: austerity program, 211–212, 224–225, 231–233; autarkic capitalism, 48; authoritarian rule, 31; business-military relations, 29; collective expression in, 37; corruption, 34, 225, 226; currency board, 136, 251; democracy as precursor to economic liberalization, 4; economic statistics, 162–163; elections, 225, 228–229, 232–233; electoral politics effect on exchange rate policy, 223–233, 234–235; exchange rates, 203–204, 206–207, 212; foreign investment, 207–208; Frente Grande, 226; Frepaso, 232; government by technocrats, 18; impact of politics on economic liberalization, 7, 199, 242; income equality, 25, 39n7; inflation, 167, 207, 215, 223–224, 228,
231–232; interest rates, 212, 230; labor movements, 18, 33–34, 66, 183, 227; monetary policies, 8, 206–208, 210–214; nineteenth-century liberalism, 39n4; Partida Justicialista (Peronist), 135, 182, 226, 232; Peronism, 33, 181, 202n21; poverty levels, 25, 64, 227; presidential reelection amendment, 225, 228; privatization, 161, 175–176, 180–183, 196, 198; Radical Party, 181, 225, 232; regional polarization, 55; social expenditures, 78n2; social explosions, 55; state dependence on business, 32–33; structural adjustment, 62, 64, 135; taxation, 228, 229; tequila crisis, 149; U.S. relations, 183; World Bank loans, 183
Argentine Industrial Congress, 227
Arida, Persio, 147
Armed forces, 53, 244
Armijo, Leslie Elliott, 7–8, 115–116, 161
Art of association, 44
Autarkic capitalism, 48–49
Authoritarianism: controlled inclusion and, 31; economic liberalization under, 3, 35, 246; enclaves in democracies of, 67, 181; middle class support for, 40n17; myth of advantage

273

About the Book

The result of an ongoing collaborative effort, this book analyzes the constraints faced by Latin American countries as they seek both to consolidate fragile democratic regimes and restore economic dynamism in the context of a new, outward-oriented development model.

The authors focus on the relationship between the two goals, highlighting the interplay of societal and state-level actors and analyzing the possible tradeoffs involved as different countries pursue their own unique paths toward further development and democratization. The theoretical arguments offered are supported by detailed case studies from Argentina, Brazil, Chile, Colombia, and Mexico.

Philip Oxhorn is associate professor of political science at McGill University. He is the author of *Organizing Civil Society: The Popular Sectors and the Struggle for Democracy in Chile*. **Pamela K. Starr** is professor of international studies at the Institúto Technológico Autónomo de México. Her research focuses on Latin America's political economy.